BEFORE CULTURES

BEFORE CULTURES

The Ethnographic Imagination
in American Literature,
1865–1920

BRAD EVANS

The University of Chicago Press
Chicago & London

B R A D   E V A N S
is associate professor of English at Rutgers University.

The University of Chicago Press, Chicago 60637
The University of Chicago Press, Ltd., London
© 2005 by The University of Chicago
All rights reserved. Published 2005
Printed in the United States of America
14 13 12 11 10 09 08 07 06 05   1 2 3 4 5
ISBN: 0-226-22263-2 (cloth)
ISBN: 0-226-22264-0 (paper)

Library of Congress Cataloging-in-Publication Data

Evans, Brad.
    Before cultures : the ethnographic imagination in American
    literature, 1865–1920 / Brad Evans.
        p.   cm.
    Includes bibliographical references and index.
    ISBN 0-226-22263-2 (cloth : alk. paper) — ISBN 0-226-22264-0
    (pbk : alk. paper)
        1. American literature—19th century—History and criticism.
    2. Ethnology in literature. 3. Literature and anthropology—United
    States—History—19th century. 4. Literature and anthropology—
    United States—History—20th century. 5. American literature—
    20th century—History and criticism. 6. Ethnic groups in literature.
    7. Ethnicity in literature. I. Title.

    PS217 .E75E94 2005
    810.9'3552—dc22   2005008993

    ⊗ The paper used in this publication meets the minimum
requirements of the American National Standard for Information
Sciences—Permanence of Paper for Printed Library Materials,
ANSI Z39.48-1992.

CONTENTS

ILLUSTRATIONS

ACKNOWLEDGMENTS

One of my goals while writing this book was to avoid the pitfalls of interdisciplinary dilettantism. Any success in that direction is due in large measure to the enthusiastic reception—not to mention redirection—of my work by mentors, colleagues, and friends who have, themselves, managed to move fluidly between various disciplinary constituencies. Foremost among these is George Stocking, whose self-described "participant observation" as a historian among the anthropologists has been a guiding model. Being able to describe myself, in turn, as one of Stocking's students has opened innumerable doors for collaboration with others working on the history of anthropology from a variety of disciplinary perspectives. In this regard, I would like to thank, in particular, Ira Jacknis, Barbara Babcock, Ira Bashkow, Curtis Hinsley, Jim Boon, and Matti Bunzl for their conversation and correspondence. I owe a particular debt of thanks to Richard Handler, whose extensive and diligent engagement with the manuscript at its penultimate stage not only helped to solidify but also to extend many of its major arguments.

The University of Chicago was the perfect place to begin this move between the disciplines, and I am very grateful for the fact that conversations begun there are continuing today. I'd like to thank Shamoon Zamir, Chris Looby, and especially Ken Warren for their encouragement and ongoing insight into different aspects of this project. Bill Brown has earned my deepest gratitude over the years. First and last, he has motivated, prodded, inspired, and improved this project. It is also a great pleasure to acknowledge (at long last) friends from Chicago—Julie Dugger, Sabine Haenni, and Leigh Anne Duck—who have not only been lucid but admirably enduring sounding boards and readers all along the way.

Rutgers University has provided a supportive and invigorating environment in which to complete this project. A big place, it ensured that the conversations were many and diverse. My thanks to Louise Barnett, John Belton, Abena Busia, Dennis Cate, Chris Chism, Ann Coiro, Alice Crozier, Marianne Dekoven, Elin Diamond, Richard Dienst, Brent Edwards, Sandy Flitterman-Lewis, Billy Galperin, Marcia Ian, Colin Jager, Myra Jehlen, Stacy Klein, Richard Koszarski, Daphne Lamothe, T. J. Jackson Lears, John

McClure, Meredith McGill, Richard Miller, Mary Shaw, Shuang Shen, Mary Sheridan-Rabinow, Carol Smith, and Cheryl Wall. I would also like to thank the students of my graduate classes, and particularly members of the "Local Color" seminar, for helping me work the kinks out of various arguments. I am pleased to have colleagues as generous as Michael Warner and, especially, Marc Manganaro, both of whom read the manuscript in great detail and offered invaluable advice about it at early and late stages of its development. The enthusiasm of Ann Fabian, a recent addition to the list of those reading parts of the manuscript, provided a very much appreciated boost at a crucial moment.

I would also like to thank Bryan Wolf, Susan Hegeman, Michael Moon, and Wai Chee Dimock for their enthusiastic support. It has been my great fortune to have Alan Thomas as an editor and the University of Chicago Press as a publisher. My thanks to all there who have helped get this book to print. Beth Perry has been an extremely valued help in preparing the final manuscript for publication.

I am grateful to the American Studies, History, and Anthropology Departments at William and Mary College for inviting me to present parts of chapter 6 to their graduate conference in 2004. An earlier version of chapter 1 appeared previously as "Cushing's Zuni Sketchbooks: Literature, Anthropology, and American Notions of Culture" in *American Quarterly* 49 (1997): 717–45. An excerpt of chapter 4 appeared as "Howellsian Chic: The Local Color of Cosmopolitanism," in *ELH* 71 (2004): 775–812. My thanks to each of these journals for permission to reprint.

My final thanks goes to my family, both immediate and extended, who have given me a first-hand education in the anthropological sense of culture. I hope that some day Simon and Théo will come to understand the daily fuss about this book. And always, my thanks to Sophie, my best reader.

INTRODUCTION

The Failed Genealogies of Culture

Writing in the 1940s, W. E. B. Du Bois looked back to the late nineteenth century for the "significantly and fatally new" character of attention paid to "the differences between men; differences in their appearance, in their physique, in their thoughts and customs; differences so great and so impelling that always from the beginning of time, they thrust themselves forward upon the consciousness of all living things."[1] The differences may have thrust themselves forward from the beginning of time, but what made them significantly and fatally new in the world of Du Bois's youth was their failure to be contained, much less accurately described, by the hierarchies of order established in the previous century.

For Du Bois, this failure concerned in the first place the concept of race. Race had been conceived of as a static category, one that not only delimited particular populations but also denoted an unchanging and untraversable space between them. It was this space that had legitimated the trade in African slaves, as well as the European and American economic systems that flourished around slavery. As Du Bois understood, however, this conceptualization of race conflicted fundamentally with new methodologies emerging in the social sciences, which insisted that the study of man could only be based on the history of his change and growth, on the progressive development of his moral and physical characteristics. Since the old conceptualization of race as a marker of permanent difference had placed "the Negro" outside of history, it also placed him outside the domain of social scientific knowledge. The new methodologies should have evacuated race of any substantive meaning, or at least prevented its ongoing use on behalf of segregation, for as Du Bois remarked elsewhere, the Negro race in America had traversed the imagined temporalities of difference. The Negro had given to the nation its most vital story and song, provided three hundred years of "sweat and brawn to beat back the wilderness," embodied the spirit needed to confront the nation's gravest deficiencies in justice and mercy, and woven his own social being from the same "warp and woof of this nation" as everyone else.[2]

What then separated "the Negro" from "Anglo-Saxon America" without the institution of slavery? What differentiated the Indian "savage" from white "civilization" in the absence of a Western frontier? What defined "national character" if the nation included territories overseas, sectional differences between the States, differences in custom and language between regions, and unassimilated immigrant nations within the nation? These are questions fundamentally about categories of difference, categories that had been put into doubt by realignments within American society specific to the end of the century. One might similarly have asked what happened to "religion" in an age of Darwinism, or to "language" in an age of philology? How did one recognize "cultivation" in a Gilded Age of rapid accumulations of vast wealth, of Japanese screens and Negro minstrelsy in salons and drawing rooms, of regional dialect as a constitutive component of novels published in New York and Boston, of freak shows and ethnological exhibits of human beings, of streetcars and telegraphs and trains encouraging travel both out of but also into the cities? What happened to difference when it emerged not as a problem in the form of encounters "over there," but, with greater frequency and even more significance as the century drew to a close, as encounters "at home"—encounters that became integral to modern-day life?

The argument of this book is that the "significantly and fatally new" attention to differences described by Du Bois, both in the social sciences and in the arts, was catalyzed by a fascination with and concern over the limits of categorical knowledge suggested by these kinds of questions. Not only were many of the structuring hierarchies made obsolete by changes in American society, but there was also a growing recognition that they failed to correlate with the movement of a wide variety of things—languages, folk tales, customs, commodities, people, ideas, images, and, as we will see, literature itself—between populations and across geographically dispersed regions. The words needed to make sense of the asynchronous dissemination of such things were either inadequate or unavailable.

"Race" was one of the categories around which these things had been organized. Heading into the twentieth century, race still carried weight as the name given to the conflation of national and biological inheritances. One could speak of the races of man—"the Egyptian and Indian, the Greek and Roman, the Teuton and Mongolian, the Negro"—and mean something like what we might today call historical cultures, mean something more than a biological essence (*Souls,* 364).[3] But as Du Bois pointed out, the problem of race as it began to emerge at this time became increasingly the problem of the color line, and therein lay the violence of its unreason. Racial difference, evacuated of social and "cultural" content, became merely a difference of skin color. Race no longer need correlate with the stories people told, the things they did, the languages they spoke, or the literature they read; instead, it correlated with a biological essence. The wording of the Supreme Court case of *Plessy v. Ferguson* in 1896, which legislated the "separate but equal" clause, made this clear. One drop of blood would determine for legislative purposes not so much "cultural" difference as racial separation, a difference not of substance but of sign.[4]

Another such word was "culture," or rather "cultures," where the pluralization would have made all the difference in its use to describe a way of life, or a system of meaning shared among a people. "Cultures" in its anthropological sense, however, was not a word that entered the lexicon with force until sometime after 1910, more than a century after Johann Gottfried Herder began the move toward grounding social difference in the spirit of folk peoples, and another thirty years after E. B. Tylor and Franz Boas began, in their different ways, to make "culture" the object of anthropological attention. Du Bois, for one, never made the pluralized, anthropological version of culture his word. Throughout the course of an almost eighty-year intellectual career, in myriad tomes of written work, Du Bois almost never used the word culture as a pluralized noun in its anthropological sense to describe or define difference. He consistently avoided the term—and this despite his working relationship with Boas dating from the first years of the twentieth century, and despite the place he has since come to hold at the fore of African American cultural history.

Explaining how something like this anthropological category of "cultures" could have been imagined and depicted without being named or conceptualized is a central challenge to any appraisal of the character of attention to difference during this period. This book attempts to do so by offering a prehistory of the culture concept at several sites marked by their failure to deliver the concept as we know it. Such a prehistory of the culture concept, arguably the most significant category by which difference came to be understood in both the social sciences and humanities throughout the twentieth century, has a particular interest for what it shares with the flurry of intellectual activity now directed toward reconceptualizing those categories anew. One might easily argue that the character of difference has once again become "significantly and fatally new," as we move with energy not only "beyond culture" but "beyond the cultural turn," "beyond race," "beyond ethnicity," "beyond the nation," "beyond belief," "beyond secularism," "beyond Freud," "beyond postcolonial theory," and even "beyond Geertz."[5] As such,

Raymond Williams's contention that culture "is one of the two or three most complicated words in the English language" bears repeating once again, not only as a prelude for an attempt to expose yet another instance of its confounding difficulty but also as a reminder of the disciplinary and artistic richness that such slippage in the architecture of difference has produced, in the late nineteenth century as today.[6] Attentive as we have been over the last decade to get "beyond culture" in accounts of travel, contact and flow in yet another diasporic, transcultural moment, it ought to be of great use to remind ourselves of the ways in which the ideological and aesthetic strains of the moment "before cultures" anticipated our own.

*   *   *

Everything seems to have been in place for the emergence of the culture concept in the late 1880s or 1890s—so much so, in fact, that it is now exceedingly difficult to think about the period's aesthetic and social scientific fascinations without turning to the concept in its anthropological sense. Old order hierarchies, most notably master/slave and savage/civilized, were drawn into question by the end of both slavery and the Indian wars. Imperialism brought the United States and Western Europe into extended contact with *other ways of life*. Urban *mass culture* shaped itself around images of the other and by bringing exotic things and peoples back to urban centers as *cultural commodities*. How do we explain such *cultural* events and formations without the conceptual apparatus of *culture*? Both international exhibitions and stage acts showcased exoticism. Local-color fiction became the period's dominant literary modality, with its attention to difference coming in the form of writing in dialect, reproduction of folk stories and songs, and fascination with rural and immigrant peoples. Folklore underwent a theoretical revision and revitalization, becoming a science granting access to historical genealogies of diffusion and exchange. Photography and film emerged as new technologies for the reproduction of social difference as spectacle. There was, in short, an ethnological and aesthetic preoccupation with all manner of *cultural* things and *cultural* interactions to such an extent that we can barely describe it without the word *culture* or one of its variants. Without the anthropological concept of culture, without that word in the plural, we find ourselves without a comfortable vocabulary for describing the period's engagement with difference. So how did the cultural thinkers of the time do it?

It is in the late 1880s that Boas is said to have made his first definitive move toward the culture concept, marked most famously by his challenge to the evolutionary display of artifacts in the American Museum of Natural

History.[7] Otis T. Mason, then curator at the museum, had been comparing cultural items from different areas and different peoples side by side, by classing, say, musical instruments or weapons together by type. But Boas argued that the social significance of any object so compared would most likely be lost—that a rattle may be a primitive musical instrument in one area, but a complex religious symbol somewhere else. He argued that to best understand the rattle, it should be studied in context, as part of a psychologically complex structure of social interaction and meaning. One would show the rattle in use, surrounded not by other rattles but by the material and social context available from the location of its collection. And he appears to have carried the day: within several years of their controversy, Mason was making extensive use of dioramas, showcasing material culture in lifelike, tribe-specific contexts. When Boas worked out his contribution to the ethnographic exhibit at the Chicago World's Fair in 1893, he received permission to put on a Kwakiutl culture show, with fourteen individuals from the Northwest Coast performing ceremonials in a scene precisely reconstructed from an authentic village, Skidegate, which had been taken apart and transported east, totem polls, doorposts, and all.[8]

And yet this is a historical period largely passed over by Raymond Williams in *Culture and Society* (1958)—a period he describes as one in which "we shall not find . . . anything very new."[9] Terming the period the "interregnum" (post-Victorian and pre–World War I), Williams imagines it as a quiet time in the history of the concept, one of a "working out . . . of unfinished lines; a tentative redirection" (*CS,* 162). Alfred L. Kroeber and Clyde Kluckhohn's seminal volume on the culture concept, *Culture* (1952), differs from Williams's work in its emphasis on anthropological over humanistic definitions but nonetheless concurs that there was a "cultural lag" of nearly fifty years between Tylor's use of the term and its penetration into general British and American usage.[10] More recent historians of the culture concept have agreed with near unanimity. The concept is understood to have been "domesticated" sometime after 1910, and not so much as the result of innovators like Tylor or Boas, or of eccentric types like Frank Hamilton Cushing, arguably the first American anthropologist to have used the term in the plural in the late nineteenth century, but by the second generation of Boas's graduate students and modernist authors. The emphasis, in other words, has fallen instead both on anthropologists like Edward Sapir, Ruth Benedict, Margaret Mead, and Melville Herskovits and on poets and novelists like T. S. Eliot and James Joyce.[11]

It would be possible to go back, as Williams does, to Herder's work on folklore in late-eighteenth-century Germany in order to imagine the gradual emergence of the concept. And, of course, doing so makes good sense in the case of Boas, who came out of the German intellectual tradition initiated by Herder.[12] Boas studied in Germany under Rudolf Virchow and Adolf Bastian, the two leading figures in German anthropology in the second half of the nineteenth century; they, in turn, ran clearly in a line with the earlier work of the brothers von Humboldt in physical and linguistic studies; and they in turn with the brothers Grimm and Herder. As such, the culture concept could be imagined as something that Boas brought over with him when he emigrated from Germany; and then, to push that line of thought just a bit further, American anthropology could be understood in terms of the distinction described famously by Norbert Elias between German *Kultur* and French *civilisation,* folk-spirit and aesthetic cultivation, the social sciences and the arts, the plural and the singular.[13]

But that does not quite explain the problem of the culture concept's delayed period of incubation. Nor does it explain the contemporary theoretical paradox of "culture" in the United States. As Michel-Rolph Trouillot has put it, culture has become an anti-essentialist term with an essentialist bent, a term "deployed in academe to curb racialist denotations [but] . . . often used today in and out of academe with racialist connotations."[14]

The lag between the conceptualization of culture in the late nineteenth century and its deployment in early twentieth needs to be read in relation to two developments particular to the United States in its post-Reconstruction period. The first and most obvious development concerned race, and particularly the gradual evacuation of custom and manners from racial legislation. The anthropological concept of culture became useful when race no longer described type but denoted biology. Many have argued that culture was simply a substitute for race, that what occurred in the late nineteenth and early twentieth centuries was a "race into culture."[15] But the use of culture in place of race was not a simple substitution of learned behavior for biology, of nurture over nature. Rather, it came about precisely when race was evacuated of cultural meaning. Again, up to the 1890s, one could speak of race as a synonym for the nation, just as one could speak in Lamarckian terms of the "inheritance of social characteristics," there being a basic conflation of terms. But in the Reconstruction period, and I would argue precisely because of the nominal pressure put on the ordering hierarchies by the dissolution of the master-slave relation, race and social organization became divergent, at least before the law.[16] It was in this context that both Du Bois and Boas conceded race as a biological category, even as they argued for its ultimate irrelevance in either determining intellectual and social potential or describing the stylistic particularities of given communities.[17] Like the nativist limitations on immigration that began to be passed at the same time, segregation had the effect of making color irrelevant to conduct, and vice versa; with race imagined to be something new, culture emerged newly as well.

The second development was mass culture, which collapsed the distinction between what would come to be known as "cultures" and humanistic "culture" into products of the culture industry. If there had been a romantic move, following Herder, to collate custom and national character, so, in the late nineteenth century, did ethnographic alterity become intricately tied to the production of "high culture"; one sees Frank Hamilton Cushing alongside Henry James in the *Century Illustrated Monthly, Japonisme* in the work of American local colorists writing about "Bayou Folk," Tahitian women inspiring Gauguin inspiring, in turn, magazine covers for *Scribner's Monthly.* As I argue in the first chapter, the circulation of something like "cultures" became a sign of "Culture" in the late nineteenth century; the contact with or appreciation of this kind of multiplicity was a mark of being "cultured." But at the same time, and this is where the categorical distinctions began to fail, circulation also elicited a sense of discontinuity. When objects became marked and marketed as something like *cultural* things, attention was diverted from their connections to a particular people or place to the way they moved around, and moved around quickly. The objects, after all, were actively "disseminated" (both Homi Bhabha's word and Boas's), made to cross the conceptual categories of the old social hierarchies in ways that highlighted their disarticulation.[18] Such dissemination was, of course, nothing new. But the peculiar contradictions brought on when dissemination was, in effect, mass produced by the culture industry drew attention to disarticulation and discontinuity in new ways. The delay in the smooth development of the culture concept from the time of Herder (Williams's "interregnum" as well as Kroeber and Kluckhohn's "cultural lag") was tied up with a growing social scientific recognition of and aesthetic excitement over this discontinuity, wherein race, language and material culture seemed to continually cross paths—all over the map—without precisely matching up.

*   *   *

Du Bois's sense, then, of what was "significantly and fatally new" evoked a fundamental and highly productive tension between people's puzzlement over the failure of older conceptual categories to correlate with the experiences of modern life, and their growing fascination with a kind of social cohesion that would only later come to be called culture. This tension defines the parameters of what I will be calling "the ethnographic imagination," the experimentation, sometimes serious but often in the form of aesthetic dalliance, with new ways of perceiving, representing, and producing structures of affiliation and difference. The ethnographic imagination developed within the context of institutional shifts in fields such as philology, geography, folklore, anthropology, and literature. Its amplification at the end of the century in the United States was tied to social changes stemming from the Civil War, the closing of the frontier, extreme jumps in immigration, and overseas expansion; and its urgency in international contexts correlated more broadly to the increasingly rapid circulation of peoples, ideas and things around the globe. It is, in particular, a product of the entanglement of art and anthropology at the end of the century, of the correspondence between cultural objectification and the delayed emergence of a relativistic notion of culture.

In order to be clear about the periodization, let me offer three different examples that mark the ethnographic imagination. With a whimsical note at the end of "Rip Van Winkle," first published in 1819, Washington Irving clued his readers to a source in German folklore for his tale of Rip's twenty-year sleep in the Kaatskill mountains of the Hudson River Valley: "The foregoing tale one would suspect had been suggested to Mr. Knickerbocker by a little German superstition about the emperor Frederick *der Rothbart* and the Kypphauser Mountain; the subjoined note, however, which he had appended to the tale, shews that it is an absolute fact, narrated with his usual fidelity."[19] But it was not until 1883, over six decades later, that this source seemed sufficiently important for John B. Thompson, a major theologian of the period and a former pastor at Catskill, New York, to publish a detailed account of Irving's German source in *Harper's New Monthly Magazine.*[20] If intrigued by Irving's attention to German myth, critical attention up to that time had been more concerned about plagiarism than folkloric roots. Most parties seemed to agree, moreover, that this plagiarism was more nettlesome than damning of Irving's diversionary literary flavorings. Irving's borrowing defined the charm and wit of his self-proclaimed "sauntering gaze" and "vagrant inclinations"—those things that carried him to the fore as America's first professional author and by which "Rip Van Winkle" came to be recognized as one of America's first autochthonous legends.[21]

While acknowledging that the "charm of this legend is largely due to [Irving's] heritage and environment," Thompson's piece for *Harper's* stood at the fore of those that first fleshed out Irving's extended encounter with the originary folk tale. Thompson traced the legend back to the most popular collection of German folklore available at the time of *The Sketch Book*'s publication in 1819, Otmar's *Volkssagen* (1800), and in particular to the story of Peter Klaus, a country goatherd who, like Rip, drinks enchanted wine and sleeps for twenty years. But Thompson also acknowledged the connections between Irving's story and a remarkable array of other legends about long sleep, weaving something of a pre-Frazerian golden-bough of folkloric allusion and diffusion that ranged from Walter Scott's interest in border songs and ballads to "fables of heathen gods transferred to historic men when Christianity began to explode the popular beliefs and destroy the Asa-worship."[22]

Ultimately, Thompson's study crystallized around the same argument that was then underwriting the institutionalization of the study of folklore: that the diffusion of folkloric material, studied in the manner of philology, the search for historical traces embedded in contemporary tales, made it richer in local and national interest than the more traditional biographical and historical studies—and this because of the nature of its accretions from varied sources, each containing their own clues to the varied nature and transformative outcomes of contacts between peoples, language stocks, and nations.[23] Thompson's piece manifested an interest not only in literary sources but also in the transference of specific legends and beliefs from one society and generation to the next. It signaled a readiness, all the more novel because it was published in one of the nation's top literary monthlies, to understand folk literature in terms of the study of the dissemination of local populations and texts, and by consequence the desire to channel "all the mythologies—Aryan, Semitic, Turanian" into a unified, ethnologically informed account.[24]

A project moving in much the opposite direction was begun in 1884 by the well-known American archaeologist and ethnologist of the Pueblo Indians, Adolph Bandelier. While Thompson searched the ethnological record for sources to literary texts, Bandelier turned to romance as a way of "clothing [the] sober facts" of his ethnological research in a garb more comfortable to popular literary audiences.[25] His historical novel, *The Delight Makers* (1890), attempted to "make the 'Truth about the Pueblo Indians' more accessible and perhaps more acceptable to the public in general" by casting the fruits of his research on the Pueblo tribes as a conventional romance (*DM,* xxiii).[26] Putting decades of fieldwork in the American Southwest to use, Bandelier spiced up his narrative with details about clan rivalries, secret rituals, sexual practices, and prehistoric warfare. Notable within this mélange is Bandelier's manner of imagining the Pueblo tribes as historically complex social units—ones illustrative, if in uncomfortable ways by today's standards, of the shared folk psychology of "the American Indian." He explained, for example, "that great and often disagreeable quality of the American Indian, reticence," in terms of the matrilineal clan structure of the Pueblo tribes by which "[e]ach clan managed its own affairs, of which no one outside of its members needed to know anything" (*DM,* 13, 14). Similarly, though disparaging of the "slavish obedience to signs and tokens of a natural order to which a supernatural origin is assigned," he recognized in this practice a "succession of religious acts called forth by utterances of what he [the Indian] supposes to be higher powers surrounding him, and accompanying him on every step from the cradle to the grave" (*DM*, 208).

This account of the Pueblos was then combined with a serious literary project—a combination that embodied the idea that ethnology might infuse the literary imagination just as that imagination brought ethnology to life. Unlike the nostalgic, Cooperesque narrative of Indian extinction, *The Delight Makers* imagined a vital and continuous tradition of Native American social organization—one that, despite Bandelier's aspersions, could stand or fall on its own merits. Even though moving in the opposite direction from Thompson's study of "Rip Van Winkle," Bandelier's novel repeated the formula that transposed artistic and ethnological projects in the interest of generating color and excitement around difference.

A very different voice from both Thompson and Bandelier's announced its presence on the national literary scene when Hamlin Garland published *Crumbling Idols* in 1894, and yet we can again recognize in it an ethnological turn in this young writer's brash argument about American literature. Garland's ideas about aesthetics mirrored the developing methodologies of a Boasian anthropological science. Fashioning himself as a mouthpiece for the "local color" movement that had been growing since the late 1870s, Garland made a case against "the academic devotees and their disciples" (like Thompson) who would look to explain "the past by the study of laws operative in the present, and by the survivals of ancient conditions obscurely placed in modern things" (like Bandelier).[27] In other words, Garland was objecting precisely to the folkloristic line, which he seems to have equated with pedantic antiquarianism, not with what was modern in literature. And yet one need not look to Garland's involvement with the Department of the Interior during the Roosevelt administration, for which he led the effort to establish legal, Anglo-American names for the members of Native American tribes throughout the United States, nor to his tome illustrated by Frederic Remington, *The Book of the American Indian* (1923), to sense the centrality of an ethnologically informed conception of society to his cultural project.[28] Many of Garland's ideas for literature—his call for "indigenous" writing, for work that expresses the "quality of texture and back-ground that . . . could not have been written in any other place," for the literary treatment of subjects like "the mingling of races . . . the nomadic life of the farmhands, the growth of the cities, the passing of Spanish civilization"—reveal an ethnological attention very similar to Thompson's and Bandelier's. Like them, his artistic impulses crystallized around notions of society attuned to localized populations, a deep knowledge of everyday life, and the vitality of folk(loric) environments.

Taken together, these three projects can best be characterized by the energy with which they worked through new ways of perceiving and portraying social coherence—of thought, of action, of symbolism—despite the absence of a concept of culture. The projects suggest, by way of their contrasts, the provocative tensions of the ethnographic imagination. They highlight at least three interrelated, but distinct, disciplinary developments: the opening of folklore and literature to a deeper layer of social scientific and historical significance; a vitalization of the anthropological project by its infusion of narrative into artifactual things; and a belletristic attention to cultural specificity and its purported discontinuity with modern life. At the same time, these different versions of thinking through coherence, which only later came to be understood as being *cultural* coherence, were also never far removed from a growing awareness of ruptures between languages, peoples, and things as they were disseminated across the nation and the globe. Thompson's sense for the Hudson River folklore's origin in Germany; Bandelier's strange juxtaposition of prehistoric Indian custom and a modern romance genre; Garland's Indian renaming project: social scientific work on literary objects and in literary genres anticipated an anthropological notion of culture, but at the same time mitigated against it. Indeed, the "interregnum" or "cultural lag" in the move toward the anthropological concept can be read in terms of the pressures and productive tensions surrounding these projects, in terms of the increased attention to both coherence and incoherence in them.

*   *   *

The impetus for this project stems from the need for a better historical understanding of this transitional moment "before cultures," and, as such, this book is largely interested in matters of intellectual history. One of its discoveries, however, concerns a prototypical moment in the history of material culture. What follows is not only an inquiry into the intellectual history of the conceptualization of difference in literature and anthropology but also an inquiry into the ways that literary and anthropological texts came to stand, in themselves, as objects of ethnography. This move was particularly evident in local-color fiction, which predominates the literary examples in this book. Local color was written around the subject of a particular place, usually in dialect, with a narrator who was an outsider directing an ethnographic gaze on a peripheral community. Much like the "lore" of the folk communities such literature called to light, works of local color were positioned as cultural artifacts. Not only were they imagined to be the parts that would "get the whole of American life" represented in the museum world of literary magazines, but they were positioned in the market as imaginary fragments of cultures, objects around which cultural communities could be imagined.[29] Jacob Riis's *How the Other Half Lives* (1890) was published with a cover in blue denim, like that worn by the dwellers of his ghetto scenes. Lafcadio Hearn's *Youma* (1890) was in the paisley fabric of a Caribbean slave. Hamlin Garland, local color's most vocal proponent, imagined literature as an almost mechanical reproduction of locality. Local color could not be put in to a piece of fiction: "It must go in, it *will* go in, because the writer naturally carries it with him."[30] Just as in naturalism the human was recast as a brute, so was literature transformed into the brute output of a given social matrix.[31] In style and form, it was imagined by some to be isomorphic to the place and people it described.

This redescription of the literary text as an ethnographic object—and the move, in particular, to see in literature's materiality a sign of the social cohesion of a group—raises a fascinating epistemological problem about representation that is still very much with us. It likely goes to explain the success new historicist criticism has had with the period. Arguments such as Walter Benn Michaels's that "the only relation literature as such has to culture as such is that it is part of it" would have had a certain familiarity for the "old historicists" of the late 1800s.[32] As I discuss in more detail in chapter 3, the methodology might be said to have been formalized by Hippolyte Taine, the French philosopher and literary historian, who began to talk of literature in this way in formal terms in the 1860s. In the introduction to his *Histoire de la littérature anglaise* (1863), Taine argued famously that literature was the direct product of its race, moment, and milieu—the effect of a society's "internal mainsprings, the external pressure, and the acquired momentum."[33] Literature was subject to the same elemental causes as are other aspects of society: "Vice and virtue are products, like vitriol and sugar; and every complex phenomenon has its springs from other more simple phenomena on which it hangs" (8). The idea was, of course, an old one; Taine cited Herder, Goethe, and St. Beuve, noting that the historical turn dated back one hundred years in Germany and sixty in France. But for Taine, it went beyond the Herderian line to the extent that for all of Herder's interest in climate, landscape, race, customs, and politics, he rarely analyzed environmental factors as being determinative of the actual literature.[34] Folk literature shaped a national character for Herder, whereas for Taine folk character shaped a national literature.

The effect of Taine's argument was to make literature into ethnological material—not just something about national or folk character, but something representative of it. Taine described literature as a "fossil shell," an object you could pick up, turn over, look under and around, by way of getting to know not just the character of the individual who wrote it but also the nature of the society behind the individual. One read it, rather circularly, to elucidate the nature of English literature in terms of English national character, and, in turn, to elaborate English character by its literature. It was not of interest for what it said about a culture, but for what it could not help but say, suspended as it was in a web of meanings unique to a particular place, time, and people. And this, of course is the methodology of contemporary culturalist readings, significantly energized by the anthropologist Clifford Geertz, that have become dominant in the study of literature, history, and sociology since the 1980s.[35]

But at the same time, this fin de siècle objectification of literature as an ethnographic thing, an artifact, should also remind us of the limits to conceptualizing the relationship between literature and culture as such. Few authors besides Hamlin Garland—who claimed to have marked out in chalk everything Taine said on the periods of English literary history on the walls of his bedroom—appear to have taken Taine fully at his word.[36] Henry James, for one, Tainified Taine when he reviewed *Histoire* in 1872— a year before E. B. Tylor's *Primitive Culture,* with which Taine's work had certain methodological affinities. He praised Taine's history as "a great literary achievement," one that was "a more significant testimony to the French genius than to the English, and bears more directly upon the author's native literature than on our own."[37] And yet he resisted Taine's "premature philosophy," his "dogmas, moulds, and formulas" (470). The problem James had with Taine's philosophy stemmed precisely from its lack of appreciation for the "variety and complexity" of elements contributing to literature; James doubted that the science proposed by Taine had made "a complete analysis . . . at last decently possible, and with it a complete explanation" (470). Taine "plays fast and loose with his theory," wrote James, "and is mainly successful in so far as he is inconsequent to it" (470). As suggested by James more famously in "The Art of Fiction," literature could not be thought of in terms of a "mould," the fabrication of which might be taught to an author in increments: "Humanity is immense, and reality has a myriad forms; the most one can affirm is that some of the flowers of fiction have the odour of it . . . as for telling you in advance how your nosegay should be composed, that is another affair."[38] The description of the nosegay may well be limited by the range of significant and meaningful relations made available to an author, but, if he or she were good for anything, it should be for manipulating the flow of those relations into novel arrangements.

James's was an admittedly literary approach to the problem, but his concerns were not unique to literary critics. His argument worked on the level of authorial production, of imagining the extent to which authors were constrained, or not, by what we would now call their cultures, by the semiotic systems of meaning on which they could draw. Boas, for one, addressed something similar in 1902 when considering the popularity of anthropological inquiries into tribal "esoteric doctrine," such as that coming out of secret societies and clandestine rituals. Against conventional wisdom, Boas argued that esoteric doctrine "developed among a select social group from the current beliefs of the tribe," and as such was "the expression of thought of the exceptional mind . . . not the expression of thought of the masses."[39] Boas framed the project of anthropology—in unspoken contradistinction to the Jamesian proclivity for high culture—in terms of understanding not the exceptions but the masses. The point, however, ought not be the difference in their ends, but the similarity of their initial concerns about how to relate authorship to representation.

Another tact, the literalization of literature as a material object, encouraged an even more radical complication of the relationship between literature and the particular web of meanings out of which it was originally produced. For, in contradistinction to Taine's objective in reconfiguring literature as a fossil shell, the objectification of literature suggested not only its materiality but also its circulation and detachability. Indeed, one of the discoveries stemming from the study of diffusion at the end of the century was just this recognition that the circulation of objects failed to correlate with the circulation of peoples or languages—that, for example, folktales might be disseminated, like the spices that came from the East, well before and beyond extended contact between peoples. Literary and other cultural objects did not match up with other categorical boundaries, but rather moved quickly across them. As suggested in more detail in chapter 2, this discovery is usually associated with the British folklorist Theodor Benfey, but no less than Otis T. Mason was struggling with its implications in 1891: "In startling fashion, the same language, arts, social structures, beliefs, tales, and mottoes appear in regions far apart. Were they separately created? Did a certain people, like the modern Gypsies, travel about and carry these with them? Did the sayings and doings travel themselves across vast distances by a species of commerce?"[40]

The failure of *cultural* objects to be delimited by something like their *cultures* is often pronounced in the literary examples that preoccupy this book. Part of the reason stems from the way the realist movement in literature worked on an ideational level to encourage and presume the identification of audience and actors. Even readers of unusual local-color stories by Hamlin Garland or ghost stories by Henry James were asked to get "caught up" in the narrative, to make it part of their own reality despite its foreignness to them. Seemingly extraneous objects thus readily found their way into the realists' everyday. But the stakes were equally high, and often more visible, in supposedly unauthored objects like folklore. Joel Chandler Harris, for one, went so far as to call the "Uncle Remus" folktales he collected from ex-slaves in Georgia "a part of the domestic history of every Southern family"—a claim seemingly not incongruous, for him, with another made just pages later that the tales were likely of African origin.[41] Who was to say they could not be both? Uncle Remus's stories traveled rapidly and with relatively few impediments across the boundaries of race, language, and geography.

The period's preoccupation with the detachability of objects, and particularly of literary objects, from the "culture" of any particular place or time warrants attention from within the cultural historicist context of contemporary criticism. While authors obviously write from within a given system of meaning, their publications move quite freely out in the world. When literature is read, it once again must be made sense of, semiotically, by drawing on the possible meanings available; but those possible meanings are not necessarily the same as the author's. Although somewhat obvious, this point bears repeating. Figured not as a synecdochical "part of" a culture, but as what I will be calling "circulating culture," literature and objects of art, by the ease of their movement across any number of imagined categorical boundaries, post the limits of the "integrity" and "wholeness" of anything we might want to call a culture. They become vehicles for the articulation and disarticulation of different systems of meaning across discontinuous geographies and temporalities. Moreover, in their potential for longevity, their timelessness as imagined either artistically or by contrast to other more disposable commodities, literature and art objects move out of cultural time. To read Henry James, as to read Shakespeare or Herodotus, is to telescope time; it can be an exercise in reading the history of a past time, but it can also be one of reading the present, or even of reading for a sense of temporal discontinuity. As Wai Chee Dimock has recently argued, that which distinguishes literature is that it is both "ours and not ours, both in and not in our hands."[42]

For an earlier analogy from which to gauge the significance of this detachability, we might turn once again to Boas and what he did with diffusion. Contrary to many historical accounts, I would argue that Boas's institutional significance within the increasingly racist context of the post–*Plessy v. Ferguson* United States—as opposed to the significance of his methodological preference for the study of particular social systems—came not from his elaboration of "cultures" as the plural of Tylor's "that complex whole" but from his insistence in the face of the violent reduction of race to the color line that the rate of dissemination of cultural elements varied.[43] A kind of pluralization, after all, had been available since Herder and was similarly accomplished by the older category of "races." Boas's work on diffusion, by contrast, provided an empirical demonstration of discontinuities in the circulation of "races" (as carried by bodies moving from one place to another), "languages," and "culture" (by which Boas, at this time, most often meant material culture).[44] Whereas these elements were routinely conflated in romantic nationalist and evolutionary accounts of the relationship between society and the arts, Boas and his students insisted, over and over again in increasingly diverse contexts, that they were independent of one another.[45] If these categories failed to correlate—if cultural objects could be shown to travel across areas widely apart regardless of race and language—then romantic racialist and evolutionary theories could be empirically disproved. Not only was such correlation shown to be lacking, but it also came to be understood that the categories intersected and diverged at irregular angles and inconsistent speeds.

How might a similar attention redirect the current antinomies structuring the fields of literary criticism and anthropology? What might it say, for example, with regard to the move to increase cultural representation in the academy by adding "ethnic literature" to the canon? Or to the fact that, despite the ongoing postmodern critique, notions of authenticity and insider/outsider dichotomies are still so important to the production and representation of identities? For Boas, a lingering attention to the asynchronous diffusion of people and things across regions widely separated by geography and custom insisted on the failure of "race" and "nation" as adequate categories for anthropological description, leading in turn to his more frequent deployment of the culture concept in the later 1910s.[46] Today, to refocus attention on literature as circulating culture not only interrupts the boundedness of categories by which we imagine difference but also suggests the need for a more careful and fundamental analysis of the status of literature as an evidentiary object in cultural interpretation. For literature can be "part of" a culture, but how it gets perceived and represented as such may as easily stem from it "standing out" from the everyday of the semiotic system as from "fitting in" with it.[47]

*   *   *

A sense of the discontinuity between cultural objects like literature and anthropologically defined cultures can be productive theoretically. It would be a mistake, however, to exaggerate the discontinuity between anthropological and humanistic understandings of culture. When Taine enlists literature as an artifact of national character, when Garland finds work with the Department of the Interior, when Samuel Clemens joins Boas in the formation of the American Folklore Society, or when Frank Hamilton Cushing publishes alongside Henry James in the *Century Illustrated Monthly,* they make clear that the distinction in the preinstitutional period—before the academy establishes departments in either anthropology or English—was slim. As George Stocking has argued, E. B. Tylor's 1877 definition of culture as "that complex whole" was in many ways more humanistic than Matthew Arnold's for the way its evolutionary model leads to universalism, just as Arnold's deployment of culture as "sweetness and light" can be seen to have made way for a pluralism more prescient of the so-called anthropological turn than Tylor's.[48] Michael Elliott recently demonstrated the affinities between the anthropological narrative of collecting and the literary narrative of realism, just as James Clifford more famously linked the ethnographers' and surrealists' shared interest in the "continuous play of the familiar and the strange," which becomes itself characteristic of modernism more generally.[49] More recently, Marc Manganaro has argued that the very thing that makes the culture concept "institutionally productive or disciplinarily rich" has sprung from its "capacity for ambiguity, slippage, and transfer," from the perceived need between both critics and anthropologists to shore up the architecture of this embattled term.[50]

What can be said, by contrast, is that the postmodern critique of the culture concept has not affected the humanistic and anthropological fields equally. Anthropology has been if not more vulnerable then more defensive about the critique than have the humanities, leading to some anthropologists' ongoing suspicion that the field is being colonized by cultural studies, and to the frequent moves since the early 1990s to get "beyond culture" in order to "get on with doing anthropology."[51] But in many ways, this vulnerability seems to have inspired a much more probing engagement with reconceptualizing culture in anthropology than in the humanities—even if, as suggested by Robert Brightman, that engagement is often most aptly characterized by its mere "relexification."[52]

It strikes me as peculiar, in this regard, that cultural theorists working in the humanities, and particularly Americanists, have not been more eager to engage in a similar critique and reformulation.[53] Some of the more elegant defenses of the culture concept have originated from literary historians, but there has been less in the way of a felt need for its specific reformulation.[54] Indeed, the political application of postmodern theory in the humanities most often depends, explicitly or implicitly, upon a pluralized notion of cultures remarkably untroubled by the critique of culture undertaken over the last twenty years. The field of American studies, for one, seems ready to transform itself with what John Carlos Rowe calls a "comparative U.S. cultures curriculum," which demands more attention to the space of the Americas (plural) as "contact zone(s)," a "liminal region or border zone in which different cultures meet and negotiate—violently or otherwise—their neighborhood."[55] The question, of course, is what cultures? How does one conceptualize cultural units in such a zone of contact and, necessarily, exchange? Even if one were to avoid the deployment of culture in the plural, say in favor of such conceptual categories as "diaspora," "travel," "hybridity," and "cosmopolitanism," there would still be problems. The attention to "transculturation" highlighted by these sorts of categories has the subtle effect of rehabilitating cultures once again, for as Terry Eagleton puts it, strictly speaking "one can only hybridize a culture which is pure."[56]

Rowe's use of cultures to describe a new comparative model for American studies is predicated upon the need to reimagine the field in the face of what "promises to be a post-nationalist era" (5). Whether or not his belief in such a utopia proves to be the case, his deployment of cultures in this context is deeply ironic. And this is not because Rowe's methodology is based on the simplistic addition of heretofore marginalized or silenced "cultures" into the matrix of what gets taught as "the canon." He deploys a more complex understanding of the contested, loosely integrated, and highly porous nature of cultures. But lurking behind his deployment of the term lies a troubling anachronism, for it goes almost without saying that culture in the pluralized, anthropological sense would not have been used to describe difference in the period prior to 1910. To bring into play such an analytical lens, one needs to check for distortion. And perhaps the most obvious comes from recognizing that culture, once again, becomes the supplement for a vocabulary out of repair. If in the late nineteenth century culture began to be deployed in place of the biological essentialism of race, Rowe seems to deploy it now in place of the nation. Is this not Herderian romantic nationalism in reverse? If Herder argued for a unified German nation from the organic character of folk *Kultur*, are we now to argue for postnationality from the pluralized character of folk cultures?

*   *   *

What, then, can the relationship between cultural objectification and the emergence of the culture concept say to the ongoing critique of culture? To answer this question, we need first to note that the problem culture has faced in its postmodern critique has come not from its singularity but from its plurality. This critique calls into question the borders imaginatively inscribed around "cultures" as distinct worlds of meaning, which can lead back to an essentialist reification of culture's stability and homogeneity, of culture as a people not a practice. As Marshall Sahlins, among others, has pointed out, there is a certain irony to such critiques, coming as they do at the beginning of the liberatory deployment of the term by indigenous and minority peoples.[57] And one might also dispute that the description of cultures as bounded, nonporous, synchronous entities fairly characterizes anthropological definitions of the term, even as manifest in the most problematical modernist works by Mead, Benedict, Bronislaw Malinowski, and Edward Evans-Pritchard.[58] Nonetheless, as critical attention shifts to understanding global processes, and this spurred on as much by the end of the cold war as by the end of colonialism, the pluralized notion of cultures seems destined only to become more contested.

One of the more novel of many recent responses to this crisis of culture has come from the historian and political scientist, William Sewell. He argues for a return to the idea of culture as an analytical category in the singular, "culture" as the realm of meaning and practice integrated in but autonomous from other categories of social organization such as politics or economics. His desire to draw a line between the realm of anthropological meaning and these other categories of activity is misplaced, for as Richard Handler has argued "such activities have no 'concrete' existence prior to, or independent of, the semiotic processes in which they inhere."[59] And yet I am drawn to certain aspects of his project for the peculiar way it places literature in tension with anthropological cultures. Sewell recalls that, in anthropology, there has been not only culture in the pluralized sense of a "concrete and bounded body of beliefs and practices," but also culture in the singular as "an abstract analytical category"—a (Ruth) "Benedictine" definition of cultures as complex but stable wholes opposed to "Lévi-Straussian claims about the semiotic coherence of culture as a system of meanings."[60] He argues for the latter, wanting to limit the range of culture to a Lévi-Straussian, or more aptly Geertzian web of meaning; and he wants to wed this singular concept of culture to the critique of culture as a "sphere of practical activity shot through by willful action, power relations, struggle, contradiction, and change" initiated by James Clifford and George Marcus in *Writing Anthropology* (1986).[61] What I would take from Sewell's argument is the specific point that, within this theoretical matrix, a literary text is decidedly not the same thing as a culture, even if its production and reception is determined by cultural systems. Literature is, rather, a product emerging from an institutional sphere of activity given over to the production, circulation, communication, and use of meanings. It is not the system of meaning itself. And, as such, it too is not plural but singular.

This formulation is useful because it marks a categorical difference between detachable cultural items like literature and the semiotic system we call culture itself. What we need to continually disentangle is the object of the book—or, for that matter, the looted water jug, the confiscated war canoe, or the transposed African mask—from the semiotic systems by which they become visible.[62] This need does not arise because of some naive belief that material culture is concrete and culture abstract, or that by treating literature as a circulating object it becomes more tenable or sociologically concrete. Rather, if we attend to literature not merely as part of a culture but also as circulating culture—that is to say a thing produced from relations within a system of meaning, but also that weaves a web of signification around different geographical sites and times—then we may be able to produce a more careful analysis of literature doing things in a complex world. Fredrik Barth argues in similar terms for the character of new anthropological work "shifting [its] . . . gaze from generalizing about culture to giving a reasoned account of people . . . show[ing] how cultural images, knowledge, and representations are deployed, and sometimes created, by situated persons with purposes, acting in complex life situations."[63] While I am uncomfortable with the idea suggested by the title of the volume in which Barth's article appears, that one ever gets "beyond culture" by shifting from a cultural to a sociological gaze, this move does pull the epistemology of cultural and literary analysis into a sharper focus. In such a study one would need to specify evidentiary claims about what such a thing as a piece of literature might actually be in any given semiotic system, just as one would hesitate to follow Rowe in describing abstract entities called "cultures" that meet and negotiate, violently or otherwise, on neighborhood street corners. This mode of operation would not, to be sure, be a panacea to the problem of culture's ongoing critique, and, truth be told, I have no real desire to see that fascinating problem go away. But it does provide a platform from which to think through those aesthetically fascinating and theoretically productive moments when cultural objects and things we call cultures fail to match up, when literature is disseminated across unfamiliar webs of cultural meaning, when humanist culture and anthropological cultures remain related but also visibly distinct.

*　　*　　*

The chapters of this book follow anthropology into the space of American literary and aesthetic exchange. The closing decades of the nineteenth century are typically seen as ones where "armchair" anthropologists gave way to fieldworkers, and thus there might be a desire to imagine literature following the anthropologist out into borderlands and contact zones. However, as much as we think of the ethnographic encounter as one happening "out there," it was quintessentially one happening "here." Even as practiced by Boas, the work of anthropology happened not on the borders, but in the city—New York, to be exact, where one could find both the museum and the university. Relocating both anthropology and ethnographic fiction makes way for drawing fascinating parallels between ethnographic display and circus display, culture shows and freak shows, Kwakiutl Indians on the grounds of the World's Columbian Exposition and Sioux just off the grounds performing at Bill Cody's Wild West Show, Frank Hamilton Cushing at Zuni and Henry James in Venice.[64] The literature, specifically, of the ethnographic imagination has been described as "vacationistic prose," but what is being reimagined by this material is not a geographical locale but a cultural space—the space of the market, where "culture" is exchanged as a commodity.[65] Just as this work gets its airing in magazines and novels, it gets its anthropological and aesthetic charge from its circulation in mass culture.

The five chapters explore different aspects of this space by way of suggesting how cultural difference might have been imagined without recourse to a culture concept. There is a historical progression to the chapters, as well as a shifting attention to particular racial and ethnic groupings. The emphasis, however, falls on attending to the epistemological problem of how the idea of something like an anthropological "culture" might have been produced in the humanistic realm of folkloric and literary objects. The first chapter is largely about genre; the next three chapters explore the objectification and circulation of folklore and regional writing; the last chapter moves the entire argument forward into the twentieth century by showing how the persistence of very old ideas about race and history kept a new culture concept from emerging more rapidly. My goal, ultimately, is to make a case to both anthropologists and literary critics, and historians and theorists, that understanding the scale and infrastructure of the relationship between cultural objectification, especially in literature and the arts, and the emergence of the culture concept, especially in anthropology, is necessary to any historical elaboration of the perception and representation of multiplicity.

The first chapter, "Eccentricity: Cushing's Zuni Sketchbooks and American Notions of Culture," highlights the confusions that might arise when deploying the culture concept anachronistically. It suggests the extraordinary messiness of a distinction traditionally drawn in the history of the culture concept between German organic *Kultur* and French aesthetic *civilisation* when applied to the American literary market of the 1870s and 1880s, where such a distinction did not pertain. Cushing is often credited as being one of the first anthropologists to deploy culture in the plural. However, the autobiographical articles he published in the prestigious

Century Illustrated Monthly highlight not so much the autonomous character of something like "Zuni culture" as the contingent character of something like a "culture of consumers of the *Century*." Pictures of Cushing in Zuni regalia, placed as they were alongside writing by Henry James, were generative of a desire for the magazines themselves as objects of culture, and for culture in its variety of forms as a commodity.

The second chapter, "Circulating Culture: Reading the Harris-Powell Folklore Debate," takes as its key an acrimonious exchange between Joel Chandler Harris, the author-collector of the Uncle Remus folktales, and John Wesley Powell, arguably the most influential late-nineteenth-century American anthropologist. It comes as something of a surprise to see the extent to which folklore underwent a major reassessment and revitalization in the 1880s and 1890s. Emerging from work done in philology much earlier in the century, the folklore vogue was provoked by the recognition that folklore was discontinuous with any particular race or place—with the appearance, for example, of "The Wonderful Tar Baby" story in the American South, but also among Native Americans, in South America, Africa, Europe, and Southeast Asia. Studies coming out of the folklore vogue forced a rupture in the romantic nationalist conflation of race, language, and culture—a rupture that continues to speak loudly to the need to avoid conflating those categories today.

The third and fourth chapters, "The Object-Life of Books: Collecting Local Color" and "Howellsian Chic: The Local Color of Cosmopolitanism," carry on the issue of how literature both troubled and compelled the emergence of the culture concept. The third chapter explores the extent to which American regional writing emerged in the Herderian contexts also defining the folklore vogue, the extent to which regional fiction came to be seen as having an isomorphic relation to its folk environment. Following the lead of Hippolyte Taine, who was one of the first to transpose the German historical methodology into the study of literature, the chapter considers the categories that were actually used by regional writers to imagine and represent cultural difference. But it also sets the ground for arguing that many regionalist authors wrote vigorously against the move to think of literature as a representative artifact, or object of ethnography. Sarah Orne Jewett, in particular, is put forward in this context as an antiregionalist author of regional fiction, an author whose commitment to literary style anticipated the post-1910 anthropological concept of culture.

The fourth chapter pushes this reaction against the artifactualization of regional writing to its theoretical limits. It argues that the deployment of "local color" in realist fiction was indicative of the particular aesthetic pleasures derived, especially in the later 1890s, by putting regional objects into circulation. Far removed from Taine or Garland, from German-inspired models of literature as *Volksgeist,* this version of regionalism saw the deployment of cultural alterity as a way for American authors to flirt with the more decadent and experimental aesthetics of the fin de siècle. Bringing in an array of visual material from the poster craze of the 1890s, the chapter turns on its head the critique that has read American regionalism's anthropological dimension as a shy retreat from modernity, showing regionalism instead to have been playing upon a postimpressionist iconography. While on the surface leading literature away from the context of the ethnographic imagination, such a move had the effect of drawing attention to an emergent modernist style, a prototypical primitivism that drew its charge from the dislocation of ethnological objects.

The last chapter, "The Ends of Culture: W. E. B. Du Bois and the Legacy of Boasian Anthropology," considers Kroeber and Kluckhohn's cultural lag from one final perspective, that of Du Bois's resistance to the culture concept as it was developed in the early twentieth century by the second generation of Boas's graduate students. The chapter argues, in short, that Du Bois was no Boasian. However, it also argues that the Boas familiar to students of cultural history is, in many respects, a misrepresentation. A different Boasian legacy, having to do with his work with *Völkerpsychologie,* a field associated with the German Jewish Enlightenment, provides a better context for understanding the political nature of Du Bois's thoughts about the concept of culture. The chapter finishes with an extended reading of Du Bois's first novels, *The Quest of the Silver Fleece* (1911) and *Dark Princess* (1928), in which one finds a Du Bois who may have been a better student of the German historical method than even Boas. But one also begins to sense how the so-called emergence of the culture concept in the early twentieth century entailed something of a loss of the proto-postmodern fascinations of the period of the ethnographic imagination, and even a return to the romantic conflation of an earlier period.

CHAPTER ONE

ECCENTRICITY

Cushing's Zuni Sketchbooks and American Notions of Culture

＋·━◆━·＋

My dear Cushing:

I want to introduce the bearer, Mr. W. E. Curtis, Managing Editor of the *Chicago Inter-Ocean*, who will, in turn, introduce you to the ladies, and other gentlemen, in his party.

They all desire to become members of the Zuni Tribe, and, not being acquainted with any others, I am forced to call upon you to have them initiated. Please put them through in good shape, and draw upon me for the amount of the initiation fees.

Yours very truly,
W. F. White

In the summer of 1882,[1] a physically scarred white man pictured in the ceremonial garb of the Zuni Pueblo tribe, along with his Indian "brothers," made it onto the pages not only of *Popular Science Monthly*, but also of three of America's elite literary magazines: the *Atlantic Monthly, Harper's Monthly,* and the *Century Illustrated Monthly.*[2] On pages declared by their editors to be participating in the "wholesome movement . . . for the purification of American public life," Frank Hamilton Cushing held forth on his ritual initiation into the Priesthood of the Bow, the highest priestly society of the Zuni, and of the trials he endured to do so.[3] Alongside Henry James writing about Venice and the influence of *Punch* illustrator George Du Maurier on London society, one reads of the Zunis piercing the lobes of Cushing's ears while doing "a little shuffling dance . . . in time to a prayer chant to the sun" ("My Adventures," 511). Paired with the serialization of a new novel by the dean of American realism, William Dean Howells, one finds Cushing's description of a dog's horrible mutilation at the hands of two Zuni clowns during "the Dance of the Great Knife" (207). By thus situating Cushing's adventures, America's new class of genteel magazines created a stark juxtaposition, quickly becoming de rigueur, between "high Culture" and the first portents of an anthropological concept of culture.

Cushing has been remembered historically as not only the colorful figure who helped invent the ethnographic practice of participant-observation but also as one of the few American anthropologists, perhaps the only one, to have predated Franz Boas in using the term "culture" in its plural, relativized form.[4] As such, he can be used to mark the early end of Alfred Kroeber and Clyde Kluckhohn's "cultural lag"—that stalled period before the paradigmatic shift from social-evolutionary to cultural anthropology, from a universalistic understanding of tribes like the Zuni as ancient ancestors of modern western civilization to a relativistic understanding of them as having a local and particular historical trajectory and complex social organization. If it was Boas who established the institutional structures needed to finally shift anthropology toward a cultural paradigm in the 1910s and 1920s (by 1926, every major anthropology department in the United States was headed by one of Boas's former students), it was probably Cushing who first coupled a notion of "culture" with both the impulse to see life from the native's point of view and doubts about westward expansion, giving the word its relativist twist.[5]

But the articles by and about Cushing make it necessary to complicate any purely anthropological genealogy of the culture concept, for they force the anthropological history of the term back into contact with the contemporaneous solidification of culture in the sense made most famous by Matthew Arnold: "culture being a pursuit of our total perfection by means of getting to know . . . the best which has been thought and said in the world and, through this knowledge, turning a stream of fresh and free thought upon our stock notions."[6] As pointed out by Raymond Williams in his keyword definition of the term, the Arnoldian notion of culture, though long in the making, did not become common before the mid-nineteenth century. Returning the term to the context of the United States, we can add that the corresponding stratification of the concept—giving us what has typically been identified as "highbrow" and "lowbrow" culture, but which might better be understood as varying modalities of producing and consuming cultural commodities—did not occur until the heavy commercialization of the late nineteenth century, roughly at the time of Cushing's adventures in Zuni.[7]

All of these versions of culture were emerging not only at the same time but also in many of the same venues, such that we might say the interplay between them became largely codeterminative. Just as the literary magazines began to give space to something like Cushing's version of anthropological cultures, high Culture was being made conspicuous by its intimacy and comfort with the circulation of ethnographically coded peoples, tales, and objects. The anthropological, the Arnoldian, and the material commingled on the pages of the quality magazines not only in the juxtaposition of Cushing and James, but in that of Joel Chandler Harris's dialect tale "At Teague Poteet's" and the refined poetry of Edmund Clarence Stedman; C. E. S. Wood's narrative of an expedition "Among the Thlinkits in Alaska" and the revered American music critic, Richard Grant White, on "Opera in New York"; and in Charles G. Leland's exposé on "Visiting the Gypsies" and an article by John Burroughs remembering the great Henry David Thoreau.[8]

What Cushing's presence—and particularly his presence as "a savage"—in the periodicals thus forces is a refusal of the dichotomy established by Norbert Elias in his pathbreaking work, *The History of Manners* (1939), between German *Kultur* and French *civilisation,* the folk and the civilized, the vernacular and the courtly, the low and the high—and, in the contemporary academic context, the anthropological and the literary. In the American situation, this dichotomy was purposefully collapsed, producing juxtapositions like that of Cushing and James, which have been little attended to from either historical or theoretical perspectives.

The excitement generated around such juxtapositions clearly had to do with a more generalized turn-of-the-century fascination with the exotic and oriental; however, it also came from a particularly social-scientific task the magazines seem to have set themselves. Much of the work carried on in the periodicals—carried on in the absence of a named anthropological concept of culture—concerned exploiting pictures of difference and also trying out new categorical frames by which to understand it. There was a provocative element of experimentation in this framing that encouraged a desire for the magazines not only as vehicles for Arnoldian self-cultivation but also as objects representative of a particular, Cushingesque socio-anthropological group. Beyond all else, however, what was generated was a desire for both versions of culture as a commodity—a desire that explains the facility of Cushing's penetration both into the Zuni Pueblo and into the salons of American high society. Cushing's presence in the magazines can be used to piece together the logic of this desire, as well as the preliminary steps that would have been necessary for readers to conceptualize not only the Zuni and Cushing, but also themselves along cultural lines—to think of themselves as being cultivated, and also as being part of a culture. What we can uncover in rereading Cushing, in other words, is how, *avant la lettre,* readers of the magazines might have begun to formulate a notion of anthropological cultures that was both self-encompassing and worthy of possession.

ECCENTRICITY

"Borders" currently have a popular double life, being central both to critiques of the culture concept in anthropology and to a project of remapping United States cultural history in literary and cultural studies; the border paradigm can be misleading, however, when thinking about Cushing on the pages of the monthly magazines.

At least since James Clifford and George Marcus's *Writing Culture* (1986), it has repeatedly been made clear that to conceptualize difference in terms of culture requires the construction of borders, leading to the axiom that cultures are made, not given. And so, along with a debate about the extent to which boundaries actually were important to the classical anthropologists of the twentieth century, there has been a move to get beyond culture by focusing, instead, on the permeability and shiftiness of borders—on "travel," "hybridity," "diaspora," and "flow" as less essentializing ways of focusing ethnographic attention.[9] At the same time, and in large measure moving out from these interventions in anthropology, the border has become a key modality in U.S. cultural history for thinking through the racial, national, and colonial contours of interactions between diverse cultures in the Americas. Already in 1995, Donald Weber had drawn on Renato Rosaldo to recognize "border" as "a key word—perhaps the key word—in current American studies and in cultural studies" because it served "as compensation for political erasure on the part of marginalized groups in the academy."[10] This move, propelled in particular by new attention to globalization and a number of wonderful pieces of auto-ethnographic fiction, is already becoming well-trodden ground.[11] One thus sees scholars like John Carlos Rowe and José Saldívar leading a push for a "comparative" approach to U.S. cultural studies, which, with respect to literature, implicitly means reading for borders, where texts reflect and enact the conflict between cultures, nationalities, languages, races, and ethnicities in particular places and times.[12]

While this methodological and theoretical reorientation has given us a new sense of both fields, it can also be extraordinarily misleading when used to think of the historical situation of Cushing on the pages of the genteel monthly magazines. For one thing, it is simply anachronistic to think that the borders describing Cushing's situation in 1882 would then have been understood as being *cultural*. Because the idea of a border draws implicitly on conceptual categories, there could not have been a *cultural* border before the culture concept. There were, by contrast, recognized differences between stages of social-evolutionary development, language stocks, religions, races, and geographical locales. For each of these categories, however, it also should be remembered that the character of the border—its relative permeability or impermeability, for example—would have been imagined differently. For evolutionary anthropologists like Lewis Henry Morgan and John Wesley Powell, whites and Native Americans shared a common humanity but were separated by what was a nearly indelible border, marked in centuries of unilinear development. Powell once noted that although whites who came in contact with Native Americans tended "to overlook aboriginal vices and to exaggerate aboriginal virtues," it was not "to be forgotten that after all the Indian is a savage"—and presumably would continue to be so in future generations.[13] For religious missionaries, by contrast, the border between "pagan" and "Christian" must have been much more readily traversed.

Another kind of problem awaits readers of literary texts looking to deploy the border paradigm, namely, that stemming from the indeterminacy of the space Cushing and the Zunis inhabited once they had appeared on the pages of the magazine. Indeed, one might well ask how to figure the implicitly geographical metaphor of the border in this monthly magazine context, for the metaphor itself leads to the confusion of a place like Zuni with the space of the literary market. Rather than thinking of Cushing's experience as a "border" situation, we would do well to consider the extent to which his adventures with the Zuni mirrored what I will be describing as the "eccentricity" of his eastern, magazine reading, club-attending audience. Of interest is the alacrity with which Cushing was incorporated into the overriding logic of these magazines. Cushing's adventures in Zuni found a natural home on the pages of the journals, which leads me to suggest that the success of this phenomenon had already moved well beyond the initial "contact zone" at Zuni. Rather, the border as a place had been enveloped by and reproduced within genteel parlors and on the pages of the quality magazines, which, themselves, circulated with great ease from coast to coast, across any variety of imagined boundaries.[14]

Let me be clear on how my approach in the next pages differs from other historical and ethnographic accounts. Implicitly focusing on Cushing as a "border" figure, historians Curtis Hinsley and Jesse Green have demonstrated the anthropologist's impact on Zuni and the role played by various institutional forces shaping anthropological investigation of Native Americans at the end of the nineteenth century. Hinsley, in particular, has produced a series of superb examinations of Cushing's role with regard to the ideological framework of the Smithsonian's collecting practices.[15] What I want to suggest, by contrast, is that Cushing's appearance in the genteel monthlies also provides an impetus for taking the examination of him out of this frontier context in order to think more broadly about what must have changed in order for the new anthropological conception of culture to emerge popularly. Although Cushing's trip to the Southwest literally took him to a reservation border, Cushing himself was framed in *Harper's* and the *Century* neither as a frontier figure, nor as someone inhabiting shifty border zones. In their sketches of the young ethnographer, the magazines gave little hint of any transgressions of which Cushing might have been guilty; nor did they even offer many signs of the existence of two "cultures" sufficiently homogenized to enact an "encounter." In thinking about Cushing, then, I will not be concerned with rehearsing questions about how the Zuni actually reacted to Cushing or to Cushing's role in the institutional history of anthropology, topics which have already been covered in some depth.[16] Instead, what this chapter tries to work out is the process by which difference would have been understood by readers of and writers for the magazines in this period before cultural borders—for participants in the emergent culture industry who had no immediate recourse to anthropology's culture concept.

The imaginative borders between Cushing, his audience and the Zuni had already been brought into question by historical events in the late 1870s and 1880s. In 1893, ten years after Cushing's magazine appearances, Frederick Jackson Turner famously declared the "closing" of the American frontier. From materials contemporary to Cushing's journey to the Southwest, we might safely conclude that it had been closed some time before Turner's declaration. Cushing, a twenty-two-year-old prodigy of the secretary of the Smithsonian Institution, Spencer Baird, arrived in New Mexico in 1879, just two days after the last spur of the Topeka & Santa Fe Railroad had been laid—an act that effectively incorporated Zuni and the other New Mexican pueblos into the transcontinental rail system. The situation was analogous to that being duplicated on reservations throughout the country, the railroad encircling the West in preparation for the mechanically regular filling up of space with settlements. As one reviewer put it in an article on the "New Northwest" for the *Century*, the "companies know that settlers will follow the new road and occupy a broad band of country on either side of it. A given population will afford a given amount of freight and passenger business; thus the problem is as simple as a sum in arithmetic."[17]

In place of the frontier came the process of incorporation, which Alan Trachtenberg has made well known as "the emergence of a changed, more tightly structured society with new hierarchies of control, and also changed conceptions of that society, of America itself."[18] While control, as of railroad timetables and land settlement, is certainly one aspect of this incorporation, another, less often remarked, is the extent to which bourgeois boundaries, in the name of containment, had to be extended and enlarged. Certain locales and certain subjects—like Indians, Darwinism, and the Orient—were compartmentalized, there freed to burgeon like eccentric tumors on the incorporating machine. To the extent that this process of incorporation took as part of its project the inclusion of areas and peoples formerly separated by a variety of now defunct borders (the Zuni by the desert, the Mexican by the Rio Grande, the black by slavery), it entailed more than just homogenization and imperialist mapping. It also meant expanding the figurative borders by which society defined its identity, opening up the imaginative geography of the national self in order to accommodate the Other found to be in there already. To close the frontier meant giving up a border; at least in some instances, giving up a border would also have meant having to inhabit a position—either pleasurably or with trepidation—of what I am calling eccentricity.

As already suggested, the genteel monthly magazines abounded with apparent contradictions in content, packed with articles like Cushing's that seem to put to the test notions of hierarchy and control. Yet eccentricity also prevailed on more personal levels, as is suggested by the letter quoted in the epigraph that Cushing received in Zuni in April, 1883. It would seem to be one thing for the progressive Chicago newspaper, the *Inter-Ocean,* to have been active in supporting Cushing's work, as they were on several occasions. But it was quite another to have members of their community "initiated" into the tribe—even facetiously. The living room of Cushing's austere editor at the *Century,* Richard Watson Gilder, in the heart of literary Boston, had been similarly "initiated" into the eccentric. George Washington Cable, who at the time was one of the *Century*'s most respected contributors of Southern local color, noted that he had heard there the rising young American soprano, Clara Louise Kellogg, perform "Negro" songs, accompanying herself on the banjo. On other occasions, he reported, the Polish American actress Helen Modjaska was encouraged to recite, sometimes in Polish.[19] In the same volume of the *Century* in which Cushing made his first appearance, Kellogg appeared in an exotic costume not so dissimilar from Cushing's, the "American prima donna" (as she calls herself) playing the role of the Ethiopian slave girl, Aida, in Verdi's 1868 opera (see fig. 1.1).[20] The mere presence of "primitives" in American high society was obviously not new, as most baldly documented by the importance of slavery in the domestic life of the Southern plantation. What was new was the status attributed to them as the bearers of "high" cultural value. The extent of this

1.1 *Clara Louisa Kellogg, in* Aida, pictured in the same volume of the *Century Illustrated Monthly* (vol. 24, 200) as Cushing. The costume of the "American prima donna" rivals that of the ethnographer, giving just one example of the extent to which the eccentric went on stage in Eastern cultural life. University of Chicago Library.

valuation is staggering, making it reasonable to suggest that the spatializing concepts of "border" and "frontier" are not fully adequate models for determining the logic by which Cushing, the Zuni, and their primitive counterparts became attractive to a genteel, magazine reading audience.[21]

Richard Brodhead has effectively argued that the newfound popularity of regionalist, "vacationistic" writing—of which Cushing's articles must be seen a part, but which, more famously, gave rise to local-color fiction by the likes of Sarah Orne Jewett, Mary Wilkins Freeman, Hamlin Garland, Joel Chandler Harris, Mary Noailles Murfree, and Kate Chopin—should be linked to a Veblenesque audience of high culture connoisseurs. In apparent reference to articles like Cushing's, he notes the centrality of travel writing, ethnography, and regional fiction in the quality magazines: "The great staple of these journals, the virtually mandatory item in their program of offerings, is the short piece of touristic or vacationistic prose, the piece that undertakes to locate some little-known place far away and make it visitable in print." Brodhead argues that, with such pieces, an American elite that fashioned itself "through its care for high art" further defined itself "by its other distinctive leisure practices . . . particularly its arts of leisure travel."[22] And here, he may very well have had Cushing's visitors from the *Chicago Inter-Ocean* in mind. But one of the things Brodhead leaves open in his account is the way in which these articles marked not only a kind of detached and voyeuristic observational practice—"vacationistic prose"—but also an incorporation of that otherness into the very construction of what it meant to be an "American elite." It was not enough to go look at the Zuni, or Jewett's folk at Dunnet Landing on the coast of Maine. There seems to have been a push to inhabit, indeed, to acquire, that space—to live in their homes, eat their food, wear their clothes—and then take it all back home, in the form of a photograph collection, a native headdress, a Southern banjo, a magazine article. A literature of tourism and ethnography may have been fashioned by an American leisure class, but that class was similarly fashioned by the objects of their observation—objects that also made their way back home with the traveler to constitute the eccentric content and tenor of their class.

In his piece on "Venice" appearing in the same edition of the *Century* as Cushing's first two articles, Henry James aptly noted a version of this acquisition: "There is nothing more to be said about it [Venice]. Every one has been there, and every one has brought back a collection of photographs."[23] If we take James as an example of the elite tourism Brodhead is talking about, we might suggest that visiting Venice for James ideally involved not just seeing but inhabiting the place. James warned in the article that one must stay long in Venice, not just a week but several seasons, to appreciate it fully. This, of course, was the same argument Cushing had made to justify his extended stay at Zuni.[24] And rather like Cushing after his trip to Zuni, one can easily imagine James coming home from his trip costumed in Italian garb. The imaginative context for modern life was thus not so much incorporated as expanded, the so-called borders between different ways of life reframed in terms of an aesthetically and scientifically heterogeneous space.

We should keep in mind that the articles appearing about Cushing staged eccentricity in a very public fashion. They produced in his image a de-centering of white, eastern, upper-class formality, expressly fissuring suppositions of purity and propriety. In an article for the *Century* detailing a trip back East that Cushing made in 1882, Sylvester Baxter repeatedly colored his account with anecdotes concerning Cushing's struggle to be both Zuni and civilized. He stressed Cushing's reluctance to exchange his "picturesque Zuni costume . . . for the dress of civilization" and the "cutting of his hair, which was eighteen inches long, and which was making him unpleasantly conspicuous."[25] And though Baxter tempered Cushing's negotiation of both Zuni and eastern expectations, the magazine itself took full advantage of them. On the hair issue, for example, Baxter wrote that Cushing got it cut but that he also had it "made up [presumably into a wig] so that he could wear it beneath his head-band when back at Zuni" ("Aboriginal Pilgrimage," 529). The magazine made no such concession. They featured Cushing in four illustrations, each time in Zuni costume and with long hair (fig. 1.2). The suggestion here seems have been that Cushing's notoriety functioned in relation to his ability to stretch the bounds of eastern propriety. The more he stretched, the more he fit into the *Century*'s publishing scheme.

More broadly, from 1870 to 1890, the gravity of the relationship between whites and Indians changed dramatically, making way both for the rapid expansion of museum holdings and exhibits and for the institutionalization of anthropology as a science (alternatively read as the massive decimation of Indian material wealth and the advent of scientists as spies for colonial governments). Again, both of these activities might be read as the production of bourgeois identity via the occupation of eccentric things, which, it should be stressed, was not the same thing as their mere "appropriation." During his stay at Zuni, Cushing helped Smithsonian collecting expeditions acquire over 12,600 Zuni artifacts, a shocking number when considering that the pueblo's population numbered less than 2,000 residents. In 1881 alone, over 21,000 pounds of materials were amassed. In its first twenty-five years of existence, from 1879 to 1904, the Smithsonian's Bureau of Ethnology collected at least 41,500 objects, which was still only one-third of the museum's ethnological holdings. The collections of exotic materials in

1.2 *Frank H. Cushing,* accompanying Sylvester Baxter's "The Aboriginal Pilgrimage," *Century Illustrated* 24 (1882): 528. Cushing is pictured here in his most classic pose, wearing much the same Zuni costume later painted by Thomas Eakins. University of Chicago Library.

eastern museums literally exploded during the period, far outstripping anyone's ability to formulate the materials into coherent displays.[26] Even as
new buildings began to be constructed in Washington in an attempt to house
the Smithsonian's collection, new agents of collection, primarily museum
anthropologists, were posing severe challenges to the possibility of containment. But that assumes, of course, that containment was a goal; given the
numbers and the clues about how these objects were being read in the magazines, it is far from clear that containment was ever in the works.

In addition to new avenues of genteel literary and scientific development, the revised dynamics also opened up a new industry based on a popular staging of the incorporation of Indians into the "American West."
Representations of Native Americans, to be sure, had been widely popular
before the 1880s, among the most famous versions being James Fenimore
Cooper's Leather-Stocking Tales (1823–41) and George Catlin's nostalgic oil
paintings and journals (1840s to 1867). By the 1880s, however, the tenor of
the representations had changed rather dramatically. Opening May 17, 1883,
to an estimated audience of 8,000 people, Buffalo Bill's Wild West Show
marked the transformation of the Indian from vanishing threat to rising star.
William Cody's recruitment of nearly sixty Pawnee and Sioux Indians to perform in his show, both as the "bad guys" in the ambush of the Deadwood
Stagecoach and talented athletes in foot races and bronco riding, went far in
shaping the popular white image of the Indian at the end of the century. For
the 1885 tour, Cody promoted Sitting Bull's rise to popular stardom, paying
the Sioux chief $50 per week, two weeks pay in advance, a $125 bonus, plus
rights to hawk photographs and autographs of himself on the side, to play the
role of himself: Custer's slayer. Despite the apparently ignominious situation
of the proud Sioux chief being booed by American audiences (he was
applauded in Canada), his presence in Buffalo Bill's spectacle marked a different role for American Indians—one that clearly resonated with the popularity of Cushing's articles and other Indian paraphernalia being "seriously"
collected in America's new museums.[27] While staging already popular
stereotypes, Cody's production recast the dynamics of white-Indian relations
by recruiting and paying "real-life Indians" to play themselves, thereby further pushing outward on the boundaries of "civil" society.

Cody's "real-life" show highlights the way that incorporation entailed a
certain amount of theatrical doubling, with Indians and white men playing
each other—but also playing themselves—in an eccentric burlesque (or
opera, in the case of the magazines) of expansion. In the process, borders
were also restaged in both popular and genteel arenas: the Wild West show,
the parlors of genteel households, the pages of refined magazines. This staging and restaging led to a productive imbalance between the idea of an

incorporated national space and the colorful Otherness discovered to be in there already. Masked within the magazine's rhetoric of purification and uplift was a vertiginous new zone of eccentricity—distinctly not a "contact zone" in any geographical or border sense—that was exemplified by the likes of Cushing, his Zuni friends, and the Chicago socialites who become part of their tribe.[28]

THE ZUNI SKETCHBOOKS

The problem to understand, then, is on what grounds the move might have been made from this zone of eccentricity to that of a perceived cultural cohesion. For this, one might turn to Cushing's articles, which theatricalized the process of identification both at Zuni and in the magazines. As told by Cushing in his autobiographical account for the *Century,* his adventures at Zuni consisted of a series of picturings: picturing the Zuni, picturing himself, and, ultimately, picturing his American audience. Central to this tale were his Zuni sketchbooks—obtrusive items he reported having carried with him everywhere he went in Zuni and around which he structured the plot of "My Adventures." In the article, the Zunis' resistance to being pictured in these sketchbooks is used to set up a dramatic tension, needing resolution and thus moving forward the plot, between Cushing's desire to observe and record Zuni life and his unease at being similarly scrutinized by them. "My Adventures in Zuni" can be read as a staging of Cushing's progressive capitulation to being pictured—of his need to "go on to the stage," in the words of Sylvester Baxter, and be seen in order to see ethnographically.[29] Indeed, by the end of the series, Cushing has "become" Zuni, thus offering to his genteel audience a celebration, not a resistance, of such publicity.

The dramatic tension of "My Adventures in Zuni" builds from the moment Cushing first describes bursting upon the scene in the pueblo. Alone, with no introduction and not speaking the Zuni language, the young anthropologist clambers up the adobe homes to witness a ceremonial dance, only to become the spectacle himself:

> The regular *thud, thud* of the rattles and drum, the cadence of rude music which sounded more like the soughing of a storm wind amid the forests of a mountain than the accompaniment of a dance, urged me forward, until I was suddenly confronted by forty or fifty of the men, who came rushing toward me with excited discussion and gesticulation. One of them approached and spoke something in

Spanish, motioning me away; but I did not understand him, so I grasped his hand and breathed on it as I had seen the herder do. Lucky thought! The old man was pleased; smiled, breathed in turn on my hand, and then hastily addressed the others, who, after watching me with approving curiosity, gathered around to shake hands and exchange breaths, until I might have regarded myself as the President, had not an uproar in the court attracted them all away. . . .

At last, gaining my wished-for position on the edge of the terrace, I came face to face with nearly the whole population of Zuni. (*Century* 25, 192–94)

This strange scene of shared spectatorship—not of secretly peaking in on the Zunis, but of coming directly into contact with them, "face to face"—repeats itself every few pages in the first of the three articles, continually focusing attention on the uncomfortable strangeness of Cushing's situation.

Cushing's biography has by this time been sufficiently rehearsed to obviate the need of it here; suffice it to say that he had been assigned the task of penetrating the sociological organization of a typical pueblo tribe and producing an in-depth study of it—a detailed project the likes of which had not before been undertaken.[30] He ended up staying there from 1879 to 1884, interrupted only by a seven-month trip East with six Pueblo Indian companions in 1882—a trip that occasioned the publicity surrounding him at that time. Returning to Zuni in October of 1882, he took with him not only a new wife, Emily Magill Cushing, daughter of a successful Boston financier, but also his brother and sister-in-law, the artist W. L. Metcalf, and an African American cook "trained in an old Virginia family." His return to Zuni thus brought with it the "refining touch of a woman's hand," along with the trappings of genteel, late-nineteenth-century colonial life: "civilized furniture," "excellent oil-paintings," and "Japanese screens."[31] Eccentricity had incorporated the reservation.

The first two years had been far less comfortable, and it was predominantly in his discomfort that Cushing found his popular magazine audience; he did not make it back into the quality magazines after 1883. His *Century* articles replay the process of initiation, with no hint of the changes to come. Rather, one gets the colorful story of Cushing going native. Frustrated after a couple weeks in Zuni at his inability to discover the inner workings of the tribe, Cushing describes taking the extraordinary step of moving his belongings into the Zuni governor's home, having decided to stay and live there the duration of his visit. He suggests that such a tactic was not only surprising to the Zuni, who nonetheless seemed to accept it, but that it was evidently shocking to the other members of Cushing's Smithsonian party, who, in apparent disapprobation, moved on to another pueblo without either saying goodbye or leaving him adequate provisions.

Although Cushing's project for the Smithsonian was to provide a detailed ethnographic analysis of the tribe, he remains the center of attention in the *Century* articles. The ongoing tensions over the sketchbooks keep the attention of the Zuni—as well as that of his magazine audience—on him. "I made fair progress in the good graces of this odd group," writes Cushing of the Zunis with whom he shares his living quarters,

> but still by them, as by the rest of the tribe, I was regarded as a sort of black sheep on account of my sketching and note-taking, and suspicions seemed to increase in proportion to the evident liking they began to have for me. Day after day, night after night, they followed me about the pueblo, or gathered in my room. I soon realized that they were systematically watching me. They were, however, pleasant about it, and constantly taught me Mexican and Indian words, so that I soon became able to carry on a conversation with them. My apparent estrangement from the other members of our party aroused in some of them sympathy, in others only additional suspicions. It thus happened that the Indians began to watch me still more strictly, not only by day, but throughout whole nights. (*Century* 25, 203–4)

The Zunis' "systematic" but "pleasant" gaze mimics the would-be gaze of the anthropologist, the benevolently unobtrusive observation that Cushing had been sent to accomplish. In this sense, the sketchbook comes to stand in as a metonym for ethnographic observation, in effect signifying the anthropologist's battle to infiltrate, observe, and describe the native's world; or, to give this act a name, to objectify Zuni life, to make objects on the pages of his sketchbook represent what he saw around him.

Yet as he proceeds, Cushing repeatedly writes of becoming similarly objectified by the Zunis. In fact, in so much as the article proceeds dramatically, it does so as a series of episodes during which he is increasingly required to "stand out" in order to "fit in" with the tribe. Cushing writes of the tension over the sketchbooks building to the point where a secret ceremony, the "Dance of the Great Knife," is arranged by the Zunis with the express purpose of bullying him into putting them away. He relates that having "succeeded in sketching three or four of the costumes," an intermission in the dance occurred, at which time two Zunis, their "bodies nude save for short breech-clouts," broke out in an "excited harangue" which at first made everyone laugh but "was soon received with absolute silence, even by the children."

> Soon they began to point wildly at me with their clubs. Unable as I was to understand all they had been saying, I at first regarded it all as a joke, like those of the Keó-yi-mo-shi [sacred clowns], until one shouted out to the other, "Kill him! kill him!" and the women and children excitedly rising rushed for the doorways or gathered closer to one another. Instantly, the larger one approached the ladder near the top of which I sat, brandishing his war-club at me. Savagely striking the rounds and poles, he began to ascend. A few Indians had collected behind me, and a host of them stood all around in front. Therefore, I realized that in case of violence, escape would be impossible.
>
> I forced a laugh, quickly drew my hunting-knife from the bottom of the pouch, waved it two or three times in the air so that it flashed in the sunlight, and laid it conspicuously in front of me. Still smiling, I carefully placed my book—open—by the side of the pouch and laid a stone on it to show that I intended to resume the sketching. Then I half rose, clinging to the ladder-pole with one hand, and holding the other in readiness to clutch the knife. The one below suddenly grabbed the skirt of the other and shouted, "hold on, he is a kí-he! [friend] We have been mistaken. This is no Navajo." Jumping down to the ground, the one thus addressed glanced up at me for an instant, waved his war club in the air, breathed from it, and echoed the words of his companion, while the spectators wildly shouted applause. . . .
>
> The Keó-yi-mo-shi freed from their restraint, rushed about with incessant jabber, and turned their warty eyes constantly in my direction. As I replaced my knife and resumed the sketching, the eyes of nearly the whole assemblage were turned toward me, and the applause, mingled with loud remarks, was redoubled. Some of the old men even came up and patted me on the head, or breathed on my hands and from their own.
>
> (*Century* 25, 206–7)

It was surely with more accuracy than he realized that a commentator at Fort Wingate suggested to Sylvester Baxter that for Cushing to get the information he wanted he had to "take his own part in the performance": "It is no streak of eccentricity that prompts him to dress that way; no desire to make himself conspicuous. . . . Cushing, to make a success of his investigations, can not stand contemplating his subjects from the outside, like a spectator at a play."[32] Cushing's performance here, played out on the page not only as performance but also as a vital and potentially violent confrontation, finally gains him the right to observe the Zuni at will.[33]

I want to focus on the theatricality with which Cushing describes the scene for the magazine, the way he claims to have forced a laugh, flashed the knife in the sunlight, and carefully placed his sketchbook, "open," on the ground before him. He stresses his own theatricality here. But when Cushing goes on the stage, it is to play the role of himself, as if to suggest that an act of theatrical doubling is necessary to make himself visibly different from the Zuni. On the literal level, we might assume that Cushing acted to identify himself as a white man, someone carrying a knife, controlling the pueblo's destiny—"no Navajo." But then, who knows what really happened, or whether it happened at all. Rather, in the context of the periodicals and the zone of eccentricity they were cultivating, we need to imagine the scene differently. With his description, Cushing would have us believe that the result is not simply one of power, but one of performance. He gains his position as picturer of the Zuni because he allows himself to be pictured, because he "plays along" with their jest. He encourages us to believe that it is because of his brave clowning that the Zuni accept him, recognizing him as "a kí-he," a friend fit to become initiated into the secret societies of their tribe. He willingly joins them on stage, is pictured in order to picture them, is objectified so as to collect cultural objects.

What becomes so fascinating about this scene of reciprocal picturing is that the magazine engaged in a none-too-subtle reenactment of Cushing's performance for its readers: the magazine posed itself—on both literal and metaphoric levels—as Cushing's Zuni sketchbook. Accompanying Cushing's text was the image of *The Dance of the Great Knife*, drawn from a perspective that reproduced Cushing's as he sat observing the ritual (see fig. 1.3). The picture seems like it should be the one Cushing describes completing just before the Keó-yi-mo-shi make their way across the square toward him. It is, moreover, punctuated by the arresting stare of a Zuni figure ascending the ladder in the lower-left corner—a stare aimed directly at the reader-ethnographer. This singular Zuni face and its mocking grin interrupts our gaze, insisting upon the fact that we, too, have been pictured by the Zuni.[34] A strong visual complement to Cushing's engaging first-person prose, the picture would seem to invite readers to participate in the ethnographer's performance and allow themselves to be seen. Indeed, I would suggest that if Cushing's colloquial storytelling invites such an identifying move, the image insists upon it. The magazine works to reconfigure its audience's

1.3 *The Dance of the Great Knife,* illustrated by Willard Metcalf for Cushing's autobiographical series in the *Century Illustrated* 25 (1882): 205. Metcalf, a few years younger than Cushing, lived for a time with the anthropologist in Zuni before going on to art school in Paris. University of Chicago Library.

image of itself, inviting readers to picture themselves as objects of attention. It positions its readers as Cushing-like performers, implicitly putting a material frame around their bodies as they pursue an ideal of refined cultivation.

Taken in the larger context of Cushing's popularity in the genteel magazines, what we might call the "tension of the sketchbooks" provided a metonymic signifier not just of his project at Zuni but also of the affect of the *Century*'s project of picturing Cushing on their pages. The next section will work to elucidate this affect more fully, but we can already make a number of assertions about it by extrapolating from Cushing's articles. First, the sketchbooks stood in for the process of incorporating Zuni life within the expanded U.S. ethnographic borders, representing the tension that such incorporations created for their audience. Second, they highlighted a performative aspect of cultural identification, not just the "act" of sketching but the series of acts that Cushing performed in order to be allowed to do so. And finally, they suggested multiple layers of objectification: first, on the level of Cushing in Zuni being both observer and observed; second, on the level of Cushing in the magazines, being sketched on their pages, objectified by a genteel audience; and finally by the mimetic picturing and objectification of the audience itself. The sketchbooks thus represented a mélange of picturers and picturings—a mélange that can be usefully understood by turning to the context of historically shifting notions of culture.

MAGAZINE CULTURES

Having settled the question of the sketchbooks in the first of his three installments, Cushing repeats the practice of building on the tension between observation and participation in the following pieces. "My Adventures in Zuni, II" centers on the variety of poses Cushing needs to assume in order to be adopted into the tribe and given his Zuni name, Té-na-ts-li, the name of a sacred plant "the flowers of which were the most beautiful in the world, and of many colors, and the roots and juices of which were a panacea for all injuries to the flesh of man" (*Century* 25, 511).[35] For the most part, this consists of the gradual adoption of the Zuni's "full costume": thin black trousers, blue woolen leggings, a coarse woolen blanket shirt, a heavy gray serape, two strings of black stone beads for a necklace, a black silk headband, and earrings (510–11). "My Adventures, III" brings the tension to a head when Cushing is forced to evade marriage with a Zuni maiden—a marriage desired by his hosts to solidify his adoption into the tribe. The issue was clearly a sensitive one for Cushing, who surely hoped that his appearance in the magazine would, as he puts it in the article, "disarm charges and criticisms" that had been leveled against him (*Century* 26, 41). In the article, Cushing describes dodging, successfully, numerous attempts at matchmaking; as noted before, the final resolution of the problem did not come until after his trip East, at which time he was married to Emily Magill—a resolution for which the dramatic structure of the articles has no place. What the articles have place for are disconcerting pictures of both the Zuni and Cushing, pictures that allow the magazines to play the role of the ethnographer in a sketching project.

One popular model for accounting for the tensions signified by a work like Cushing's has been to locate a central contradiction and ambivalence between discourses of U.S. expansion and antimodernist nostalgia.[36] Articles by and about Cushing have thus been plotted as both "microcosmic" signifiers of the transference of aesthetic stewardship from Indians to white men and as the demarcation of an antimodern "Other place" and "Other people" where whites can go to restore themselves. However, at the end of his sharpest essay on the subject, Curtis Hinsley suggests that this Other place is not just one of recuperation from the commercialized world but also "a reassurance of good intentions and better selves."[37] It is a point that merits pause because it would seem to move us away from the binary of expansion and nostalgia. How, working from within the logic of the *Century*, could picturing Cushing have provided "reassurance of . . . better selves"? How, in other words, would this series of picturings—the ethnographer gone savage, the genteel magazine audience become the object of a savage gaze—have served the ends of cultivation?

The easy answer to this question is that the savage was pictured under the stewardship of the government, thus indicating not just savagery controlled but also controlled benevolently. However, this answer does little to get us into the logic of the magazine and its commercial relationship with its audience. The market forces propelling the *Century* into mass circulation reproduced on the level of the consumer enactments of eccentricity and control, desire and containment, theatrical "initiations" into the primitive and differentiations from it. The magazine invited its readers into close contact with the heathen natives, encouraging mimetic reenactments of Cushing's adventures at Zuni. But, at the same time, it attempted to harness the force of those enactments commercially, bringing them back into the propagation of sales.

Two ways to think about the use of the magazines as evidence about the cultural life of their audience present themselves. One is to consider the content of the magazines as representative of the cultural values of their audience, what we might simply call a "give the public what they want" perspective. The other, which seems more in tune with the ambitions of the *Century,* is to consider the magazine's content as representative of the values its editors think their audience should aspire to—a "you become.what you read" perspective. The editorial policy of the *Century,* which especially at its beginning had a decidedly Christian evangelical flavor to it, was consistently imagined from this second perspective. Typical of editorial pronouncements was one in which the editors "rejoice that we and our companions have had the privilege of establishing an agency so powerful in the molding of public opinion, and the elevation of public sentiment."[38] Repeated throughout the volumes of the *Century* was this idea that the magazine did not simply offer quality material, but that it served an educational role in the broader cultivation of American society.

With such a definition of purpose, we seem clearly back into the Arnoldian definition of culture as the pursuit of spiritual perfection. But the anthropological notion of culture pursued by Cushing was far different. As remarked by Norbert Elias, the idea of movement was key to the Arnoldian definition—the civilizing process being one "constantly in motion, constantly moving 'forward.'" The notion was distinct from that of German *Kultur,* which Elias described along Herderian lines as referring "to human products which are there like 'flowers of the field,' to works of art, books, religious or philosophical systems, in which the individuality of a people expresses itself."[39] When Cushing edged toward cultural pluralism in describing the Zuni to his superiors at the Smithsonian, he clearly had this materialist German sense of "flowers in the field" in mind:

> To repeat: that the arts of this Civilization, industrial as aesthetic, are regulated by rules or formulae handed down in unvarying language from generation to generation. That the religious, social, and political organizations and institutions are no less rigidly ruled by instructions contained in myriad prayers, "ancient talks," and songs, dating back at least as far as the prehistoric period.[40]

The German notion as outlined by Elias pertained directly to the material aspects of Cushing's Smithsonian collecting—of museum anthropology. Pueblo culture located in pottery, artifacts, rituals and songs—items collected, sketched, and possessed. On the most obvious level, the distinction here was the procrustean one between the material and the ideal. But contained therein were a number of permutations worth noting, particularly with regard to temporality. Unlike the universal forward movement denoted by the Arnoldian notion, Cushing's denoted a blend of historicity and stasis: the Arnoldian notion looked forward to antic- ipated progress, but Cushing's looked back to the ancient past in the present.

The German connection could not have been more real for Cushing. Struggling to find an American audience outside the monthly magazines, he turned for a time to Europe—and Germany in particular—to find it. As his friend John Bourke confided to him in a letter, "you should strive for a *European* reputation. America offers no suitable field for you. Very few of our people care for the Indians, and nearly all of them manifest a suspicion of a man who presumes to consider their manners, customs and ideas wor- thy of note and preservation" (*CAZ*, 326). With the archaeologist Adolph Bandelier, Cushing began to sell Zuni materials to the Royal Museum in Berlin. Bandelier, moreover, corresponded with him about producing a pueblo "Atlas," imagined as a lavishly illustrated souvenir book, for a German audience (*CAZ*, 318). While this search for a new audience did not explicitly link Cushing's "Pueblo culture" and German *Kultur*, it suggested lines along which such ties were likely imagined.

Brought together on the pages of the genteel monthly magazines, these two notions of Arnoldian and Herderian cultures created a new hybridized entity. Conveniently, "the best which has been thought and said in the world" became, in the magazines, that which sold well—a move that com- bined Arnoldian idealization and material *Kultur* in the form of a commod- ity. "Influence" for the magazine clearly depended on circulation statistics, on how many people were reading the magazine, and it was in this context that the *Century*'s editor, R. W. Gilder, exuberantly wrote:

> "Our Readers!"—The most anonymous and impersonal of editors could not write that immemorial phrase, under such fortunate cir- cumstances as the present, without some sort of sentimental feel- ing concerning it; without just a touch of honorable pride; without, indeed, a serious sense of responsibility. For, think what that means, with the "rule of five" (as it may be called), which quintu- ples the original purchaser and reader of each individual copy of a monthly periodical, and which makes actual readers of the *Century* to number between six and seven hundred thousand persons,—*an innumerable company scattered throughout the length and breadth of the civilized world!*[41]

Gilder's satisfaction at the circulation statistics posted by the journal reflected not just pleasure at good sales but also confirmation of the maga- zine's cultivating influence—an influence directly equated to the journal's circulation and, thus, economic success. *Century* contributor Cosmo Monkhouse summed up this philosophy of capitalist aesthetics even more succinctly in the same volume when he argued that the "flourishing" of contemporary art was due to its "root" ability to fulfill desires:

> The root is in all cases a popular need, and it is not only true that art will not flourish without this need, but also that it will not flourish unless it grows out of that need and satisfies it. If our art is poor, it is our own fault, and not the artist's, and if some men feel that they are above the spiritual and intellectual level of modern art, let them paint better pictures, or write better books, so as to make the world desire nobler pictures.[42]

Gilder and Monkhouse were playing to the same tune. In educating artists, Monkhouse also meant to educate his readers in a certain type of commodity-based reading. Readers were to consume as their desire directed them, judging their art and shaping their morality by a sense of their "need"; and, of course, that need could, and should, be "influenced" and shaped by a publication like *Century*. With his "innumerable company scattered throughout the world," Gilder ingeniously (if unconsciously) created an organic culture machine that produced and consumed its own desire. The *Century*'s sense of "responsibility," then, appeared to be a responsibility to shape, among other things, cultivated consumers.[43]

In thus producing its audience, the magazine made Arnold's concept of culture pay its own way. But it also posited itself as an object around which its readers could know themselves, an object that both pictured and epitomized them. Its message was that a gap existed between public sentiment and the imagined perfection of that sentiment, between the level of cultivation represented by the magazine and that of its audience. We should recognize not only the existence of this gap but the interest that the magazine had in "cultivating" it. In positioning itself as a tool for and symbol of cultivation, the *Century* insisted on the notion that its audience was in need of the prompting, and thus in need of the magazine. This gap, moreover, plotted neatly into a commercial strategy for producing desire—desire, in this sense, being the assertion of a disjunction between the ethnographic idea of "who we are" and the Arnoldian one of "who we want to be." The magazine's market value was directly related to its ability to produce this disjunction and then stand in as the commodity to satisfy it.

The key to all of this for understanding the formulation of an anthropological culture concept comes from this gap, which depended upon the ability of the magazine to objectify its readers, real and imagined, for the readers themselves. As argued before, the magazine strove to do so through the multilayered process of picturing. Positioning itself as the medium, and secure mediator, of eccentric adventures, the *Century* performed the role of the sketchbook when it reproduced Cushing. To take the example of another picture of Cushing, an image of the Zuni and the ethnographer at the Paint-and-Clay Club that accompanied Baxter's article about the trip East, the sketchbook again signaled an auto-ethnographic moment (fig. 1.4). Baxter wrote of the evening that the "Indians . . . captivated the artists' eyes, and sketchbooks and pencils were in use all evening" ("Father," 530). But just as the members of the club were "captivated" by the Indians, so were they made captive by the *Century*'s artistic frame. They had been sketched by the magazine's observers, objectified for the magazine audience, transformed into an audience publicly viewing itself. Like Cushing's sketchbooks, the magazine images encouraged eccentric picturings, not just of the Zuni but

1.4 *The "Song": Zunis at Paint-and-Clay Club,* with Cushing in the center, accompanying Sylvester Baxter's *The Aboriginal Pilgrimage, Century Illustrated* 24 (1882): 531. Baxter wrote of the evening that the "Indians . . . captivated the artists' eyes, and sketchbooks and pencils were in use all evening." But just as the members of the club are 'captivated' by the Indians, so they are made captive by the *Century*'s artistic frame. University of Chicago Library.

of those white men watching and picturing the Zuni. This scene, then, enacted once again the collecting of material objects, sketches; but this time the acquisition spread over to the magazine itself. In purchasing the magazine, the readers reproduced the action of sketching the Zuni, playing in the scene along with Cushing and his cultivated audience, becoming members of the austere club. This image, like others in the magazine collection, not only objectified the members of its audience but also objectified them as consumers and connoisseurs of the magazine, which was itself now recognizable as something like an artifact of their way of life.[44]

Ultimately, we want to be able to move back out to the level of the conceptual frame for these picturings, where we can see in the confluence of Cushing and the *Century* three different prototypes of a culture-concept in play. First, the *Century* editorial staff, especially as personified by Richard Gilder, explicitly worked to cultivate an Arnoldian notion of the term, launching on its editorial pages a movement for the spiritual perfection of its readers as a response to the machinery of modern materialist life. Second, the magazine anticipated and evoked something like culture in its anthropological sense, encouraging its readers to step up on the stage of the magazine's pages and become visible to themselves as consumers of the magazine—as, in effect, a readership. Cushing's sympathetic sketching of the Zuni alongside the *Century*'s sketching of its audience, like similar juxtapositions of *Kultur* and *civilisation* throughout the magazines of the period, forced the issue of a more public and reflexive reckoning of one's own way of life as precisely that, one way among many. Third, what emerged from this mélange was a logic of cultural objectification, along with a new kind of commodity. The *Century*'s work with the Cushing sketchbooks echoed the move in museum anthropology that was pushing forward a sense of culture as the material productions of both primitive and cultivated peoples, deeply embedded things like pottery and songs that could be sketched, collected, and displayed as representative objects. One could get culture as a commodity, the perfected collectible, the material object that promised to bring its purchaser one step closer to cultivation even while imposing the impossibility of such a rapprochement. Picturing Cushing thus modeled, materialized, and objectified Arnoldian culture, putting an ethnographic costume on perfection so that it, like an artifact, could be bought and sold.

It seems fitting that the most famous high culture substantiation of the project of picturing Cushing was performed by the period's preeminent realist portraitist, Thomas Eakins, in a painting completed in 1895, near the end of Cushing's short life (he died in 1900, see fig. 1.5). For the portrait, Cushing had constructed a Zuni ritual environment in Eakins's

1.5 *Frank Hamilton Cushing,* by Thomas Eakins. The portrait of Cushing has finally merged him with the Zuni folk object; but at the same time, he becomes an object of "high culture." From the collection of the Gilcrease Museum, Tulsa, Ok.

Philadelphia studio—again, eccentricity—and reinhabited the Zuni clothing he had been forced to put aside nearly ten years earlier after having been recalled from the field by his superiors at the Smithsonian.[45] The painting is notable for being saturated with a burnt sienna color that permeates background and foreground, Cushing's haggard face and the floor upon which he stands, his costumed body and the ritual objects beside which he is posed. The effect does not so much bleed Cushing's figure into the background as bring the objects adorning the studio space into his plane: artifacts attain an uneasy equivalence with Cushing himself, the totemic shield hanging from the wall, on which is pictured the winged figure of the Zuni god of war, achieving a certain vitality alongside Cushing's worn, scarred face. An equivalence develops between the ethnological objects and the painted body, suggesting the creep of materials from Zuni collections to the body of civilization. It is not a particularly pleasant looking painting, and is visually dull even by Eakins's standards. And yet, the effect is fascinating. The picture of Cushing has finally merged him with the Zuni folk object; but at the same time, he becomes an object of high culture. Still more than a decade before both the formal emergence of an anthropological culture concept and of the aesthetics that came to be known as modernism, Eakins's portrait of Cushing suggests that the distinctions between objects of ethnography and objects of art had already become complexly interconnected.

CHAPTER TWO

CIRCULATING CULTURE

Reading the Harris-Powell Folklore Debate

——✠——

Ancient mythology has been carefully studied by modern thinkers for purposes of trope and simile in the embellishment of literature, and especially of poetry. . . . Now, science has entered this field of study to compare one mythology with another, and preeminently to compare mythology with science itself, for the purpose of discovering stages of human opinion.

—John Wesley Powell, introduction to *Zuni Folk Tales* by Frank Hamilton Cushing (1901)

And so by fateful chance the Negro folk-song—the rhythmic cry of the slave— stands to-day not simply as the sole American music, but as the most beautiful expression of human experience born this side of the seas. It has been neglected, it has been, and is, half despised, and above all it has been persistently mistaken and misunderstood; but notwithstanding, it still remains as the singular spiritual heritage of the nation and the greatest gift of the Negro people.

—W. E. B. Du Bois, *The Souls of Black Folk* (1903)

A significant change in the scientific context for the study of folklore complemented the rise of interest in popular magazine articles like Cushing's. The period saw the publication of Joel Chandler Harris's *Uncle Remus* tales, the most popular volumes of folklore in the country's history, as well as the first volume of the most influential scholarly work on folklore to date, Sir James George Frazer's *The Golden Bough* (1893); it saw an intense interest in dialect fiction that led not only to *Huckleberry Finn* (1884) but also to the wide range of "local color" writers looking to record the everyday life and folkways of country people; it saw the founding of a national academic organization, the American Folklore Society, of which both Samuel Clemens and the anthropologist Franz Boas were a part, and the development of a forum for discussion with that society's *Journal of American Folk-Lore;* and it saw the frequent publication of folklore and debates about it in the nation's leading periodicals. Simon Bronner has described the intensity of attention to folklore during this period as a "vogue" that rose and then disappeared again in the early twentieth century. Bringing statistical evidence to bear, he notes that fourteen articles on folklore were indexed in *Pooles* from 1887 to 1892, seventy-seven from 1892 to 1896, and only seven from 1902 to 1905. The *Reader's Guide* indexed 177 articles on folklore from 1890 to 1909; from 1910 to 1924, it listed only fifty-eight.[1] There was, in other words, an intense and newfound interest in the collection of folklore at the end of the Gilded Age that disappeared in the early twentieth century, only to reemerge in different forms in the 1920s in such places as Harlem and Boasian-trained departments of anthropology.[2] Ironically, this folklore vogue coincided with the "cultural lag" described by Alfred Kroeber and Clyde Kluckhohn, with the "quiet time" in Raymond Williams's genealogy of the gradual development of culture concepts.

The folklore vogue was propelled by controversy, which surely contributed to both the cultural lag and the eventual shape of the culture concept in the 1910s and 1920s. Beginning in the late eighteenth century with Johann Gottfried Herder, and carried on in the early nineteenth most famously by the Grimm brothers, folklorists had turned their attention to folklore as a secondary artifact of national character—not, that is to say, for its content but for the way it could be used, almost despite itself, as evidence in a comparative study of *Volksgeist*, or folk spirit. In the English context, one sees this most obviously with Sir Walter Scott, whose collections of border minstrels had also become an integral part of American musical culture and continued to be deeply appreciated in the United States into the 1870s.[3] However, by the 1880s, when the field became organized institutionally, attention had decisively turned to a study of origins, and to one problem in particular: the occurrence of similar tales among different peoples in places widely apart. In 1890, William Wells Newell, the first editor of the *Journal of American Folk-Lore,* wrote that it had been a "rude shock" for folklorists to discover that, against the romantic nationalist conceptualization of folklore as a sign of national character, folklore was radically discontinuous with the categories taken to constitute the nation—and specifically with race and language. Folklore traveled widely across those categories, and at much greater rates, leaving Newell to conclude that "differences of race and language are not necessarily an indication of differences in tradition."[4] Folklore became controversial, in other words, precisely because of its detachability, its objectification as what I have termed "circulating culture."

In this chapter, I will focus on a case that highlights the folklore vogue in remarkably telling ways. One finds in the American context a peculiarly acrimonious debate between John Wesley Powell, arguably the most institutionally significant late-nineteenth-century American anthropologist, and Joel Chandler Harris, a Southern journalist and amateur folklorist who went on to become the country's most well-read raconteur of African American folktales. Their falling out was over the origins of the Uncle Remus tales. One year after Powell had been selected to head the Smithsonian's Bureau of American Ethnology (BAE), the nation's first federally funded research institute devoted to anthropology, Harris maligned both him and the institution in the introduction to the first of his many collections of Remus tales, *Uncle Remus, His Songs and Sayings* (1880). Harris wrote that,

> Professor J. W. Powell of the Smithsonian Institution, who is engaged in an investigation of the mythology of the North American Indians, informs me that some of Uncle Remus's stories appear in a number of different languages, and in various modified forms, among the Indians; and he is of the opinion that they are borrowed by the negroes from the red-men. But this, to say the least, is extremely doubtful, since another investigator (Mr. Herbert H. Smith, author of "Brazil and the Amazons") has met with some of these stories among tribes of South American Indians, and one in particular he has traced to India, and as far east as Siam.[5]

In the second volume, *Nights with Uncle Remus* (1883), Harris went further in deriding Powell and separating African American from Native American folklore. Again citing Powell and the Smithsonian by name, Harris argued against the theory that "the Southern negroes obtained their myths and legends from the Indians" by claiming that "it is impossible to adduce in support of such a theory a scintilla of evidence that cannot be used in support of just the opposite theory, namely, that the Indians borrowed their stories from the negroes."[6] The Indians took the "Tar Baby" story; they took "the story of how the Rabbit makes a riding-horse of the Fox or the Wolf"; they took the story of "how the Terrapin outran the Deer"; they took these and many others, and any "student of folk-lore who will take into consideration the widely differing peculiarities and characteristics of the negroes and the Indians, will have no difficulty . . . in distinguishing between the myths or legends of the two races" (xxviii, xxxi). What could Powell have been thinking?

This dispute is incredibly rich for being formulated around the fundamental questions of race and national character then animating post-Reconstruction U.S. politics. We should hear in Harris's complaint competing answers to the problem of the origins of folklore. Powell's Bureau was overwhelmingly evolutionary in orientation, and his suggestion that the tales had a Native American origin lent itself to an evolutionary explanation. This version of events assumed that all peoples, confronting similar situations in similar stages of evolutionary development, would respond in kind. Because Powell felt that the Indian tribes were more primitive, and thus closer to the natural sources for folklore, and that the Africans were, by nature, an imitative race, he could assume that the tales originated with the Indians. For Harris, by contrast, the question was not one of evolution but of dissemination. Folklore had a single point of origin, from which it moved out across the boundaries of race and nation. And so the question became one of tracing folklore back to the site from which it had originally been dispersed, much as philologists had traced language back to its Indo-European roots. Although Harris's intent became more difficult to track in later volumes, where he was more explicitly nostalgic for the period of slavery, he was in these first two volumes clearly interested in looking to Africa for source material, and thus to acknowledging both the existence and survival of African cultural material.

What we should also hear is the legacy of the romantic nationalist reading of folklore filtered through the United States' deplorable racial history. Harris was reacting to the prominence given by Powell's Bureau of American Ethnology, and in turn by the national government, to the collection of Native American materials. The founding of the Bureau set up the country's stewardship not only of Indian peoples, which came with the end of the Indian wars and the reservation movement, but also of their material and mythological past. Its museum work institutionalized what, before, had only been a figurative transfer of Native American ways of life to the new life of the nation.[7] Harris's deployment of African American folklore countered this move—begging, of course, the question of whether either Native American or African American folklore was by rights part of a European American tradition—in order to offer an alternate mythology for the nation. For Harris, the tales were "part of the domestic history of every Southern family," and, as such, implied a national mythology running back not to the Bureau's Indians but to his family's ex-slaves. Their debate thus echoed the ongoing sectional conflict between North and South, only transferring it into a racialized folkloric register.

The question of the origins of Uncle Remus's tales became a significant preoccupation of early American folklorists, one cited more frequently than any other in the early volumes of the *Journal of American Folk-Lore* (*JAF*). In this chapter I want to make four points in attending to the debate surrounding them. The first is to draw attention to the epistemological shift that reframed folklore as a certain kind of public, circulating text-object. If folklore provoked controversy during the period of its vogue, it was largely because of this reframing; that folklore no longer provokes us in the same way may be because we have lost sight of it as an object. The second is about diffusion. A dawning appreciation of the detachability of folklore from race and language posed the basic challenge to romantic nationalist and social-evolutionary categories by which difference had come to be understood. It was, moreover, this discontinuity that provided a crucial mechanism by which the concept of culture could emerge as a separate entity in the work of Boas and others at the *JAF*. The third point concerns the need to revisit "objectification" and "dissemination" in cultural theory. As I suggested in the introduction, the object-status of folklore and literature led not only to the construction of integrated and stable identities but also to the opposite. One of the complaints about collections like Harris's has been that they objectified a more vibrant, oral, storytelling culture; however, the nineteenth-century history of folklore collecting showed a surprisingly liberatory potential of folklore coming, precisely, from thinking of it as a particular kind of circulating text-object that was discontinuous with any specific folk group. Finally, I want to take up the Harris-Powell debate from this differently historicized and theorized position in order to highlight the remarkable pattern of obfuscation that led, and continues to lead, to readings that enmesh "The Tar Baby Story," among others, in a proprietary struggle. This final point concerns the paradoxical and retrogressive folk politics, still present today, of claiming folkloric objects for one's own despite the recognition that what most marks them as folk objects may well be the ease and rapidity of their dissemination.

THE "RUDE SHOCK" OF SAMENESS: PHILOLOGY AND THE FOLKLORIC OBJECT

To understand the folklore vogue, we need to be able to dislodge it from a number of contemporary contexts. There is no question that, today, folklore has a reputation for being uncontroversial, as witnessed by the decision at the end of the "culture wars" to appoint folklorists William Ferris and William Ivey to "save," respectively, the embattled National Endowment for the Humanities (NEH) and the National Endowment for the Arts (NEA). So uncontroversial was his nomination in 1997 that Ferris, a scholar of Southern culture, black music, and folklore, became the first chairman of the NEH to reach office without a Senate confirmation hearing. In the glow of multiculturalism, folklore has settled back into a comfortable and close relationship to cultures; it seems unthreatening because it is rooted and somewhat bucolic, apparently unaffected by postmodernity and the scandals of its aesthetic productions.

In the late nineteenth century, by contrast, folklore's intellectual, aesthetic, and ideological value was much less settled. Broadly speaking, the interest in folklore at the turn of the century was of a kind with the period's popular fascination with and aestheticization of strange and exotic peoples—a fascination most easily recognizable in magazines like those publishing Cushing and in places like the Midway Plaissance of the 1893 World's Columbian Exposition in Chicago, where a main draw was the live display of "savages" and "barbarians" from the four corners of the earth. But what propelled folklore's rise to prominence, and especially what preoccupied its more scientifically oriented collectors, was not simply its reproduction of an alterity ready made for consumption, but a series of sharply contested disagreements about what folklore was and how it created meaning. There was no consensus about whether folklore represented simple entertainment or material of historical and philological importance, a sign of racial inferiority or proof of a unique way of life; nor whether folklore spoke in evolutionary time or documented more recent times of migration and diffusion; nor about its aesthetic and moral value, the relative value of it when it came from different racial sources, or the directionality of the influence of each particular racial tradition on the other. The folklore debate was located directly at the center of a morass of competing and confused opinions about what such things as race, religion, language, history, citizenship, and culture might actually have meant in an increasingly modern, commercial, and urban world.

Behind this morass was that singular problem of sameness, a problem folklorists of the proceeding generation had little expected. Peoples separated not only by vast geographical spaces but also by enormous differences in custom, it was discovered, told the same stories and sang the same songs. Coming about on the heels of imperial moves in India and Africa and the consolidation of the American territory was the realization that people of different races, nations, and languages, spread across vast geographic areas, shared a variety of fairy tales, stories, songs, and sayings.[8] When Newell referred to this discovery as a "rude shock," he echoed the findings of previous commentators, among them T. Frederick Crane, who had noted in the first volume of the *JAF* that folklore and popular literature "diffused and interchanged with extraordinary rapidity and ease."[9] Newell noted findings that the Basques of Spain assimilated lore of modern Europe, that the Bretons adopted that of their French neighbors, that the Scottish Highlanders incorporated tales from the hated English, and that ballads of the Middle Ages were "common property . . . from Italy to Norway, from Spain to Greece" ("Diffusion," 26). It was this preoccupation with similarity that jumped off the pages of the most influential work of comparative folklore in the late nineteenth century, Frazer's massive *The Golden Bough* (1890); but it was also similarity, not difference, that preoccupied early debates among American folklorists at the academic level between two modes of understanding folklore, either as evidence of social evolution or proof of the historical diffusion of cultural traits from a common source.

Even before the problem of sameness emerged with force, folklore had been developing into an increasingly serious subject for collectors, who realized that historical and scientific stakes could be attached to it. It is important to understand *how* those stakes became visible. It largely happened around an epistemological recategorization of folklore as a kind of public object, an artifact circulating beyond the control of any individual author or performer and also across the hierarchical categories marking social difference. Dislodged from its associations with oral traditions and peasant populations, folklore became the period's most obvious and controversial example of circulating culture.

The typical article on folklore from the 1850s had been analogous in tone to Washington Irving's treatment of the Hudson River valley in *The Sketch Book of Geoffrey Crayon.* It was whimsical and gay, dilettantish and antiquarian, geared more for genteel entertainment than for history or philosophy. A *Putnam's Magazine* article from 1855, "Negro Minstrelsy—Ancient and Modern," which, refreshingly, decried the bowdlerization of the minstrels, nonetheless captured the tone of the early work in its introduction. "It is now some eighteen or twenty years," the article began,

> since an enterprising Yankee . . . produced upon the boards of one of our metropolitan theaters, a musical sketch entitled "Jim Crow." Beyond the simple fact of its production by the estimable gentleman above referred to, the origin of this ancient and peculiar melody is beyond the reach of the modern antiquarian lore. Whether it was first sung upon the banks of the Alatamaha, the Alabama, or the Mississippi; or, whether it is pre-American, and a relic of heathen rites in Congo, or in that mysterious heart of Africa, which foot of civilized man has never trod, is a problem

whose solution must be left to the zeal and research of some future
Ethiopian Oldbuck.[10]

What might strike us as questions with potential scientific merit come off
here in the register of a wit, a wordsmith producing a quick-paced sketch
full of gentle humor for the entertainment of an audience literate in but not
exclusively given over to science.

One senses a distinct change in articles from the 1880s and 1890s—
indeed, it is fair to say that the "Ethiopian Oldbuck," Oldbuck coming from the
character of Jonathan Oldbuck, a whimsical virtuoso in Sir Walter Scott's
Antiquary, had arrived in numbers.[11] Only by 1880, Oldbuck was no mere
"antiquarian"; he was a folklorist. Take, for example, an 1881 review of Harris's
Uncle Remus in *The Dial* that began with a direct reference to a Herderian tradition, citing Max Müller, a German-born philologist teaching in Britain:

> It seems only the other day that Max Müller in the second volume
> of his "Chips" (1869) called attention to the importance of the com-
> parative study of Folk-lore. Already the literature of the subject
> makes a respectable library, and in the volume before us we have a
> contribution from a new and almost unworked field. The half-dozen
> examples of negro tales published a few years ago in "Harper's
> Monthly" and the "Riverside Magazine" served only to whet the
> appetites of lovers of legend; and we trust that Mr. Harris has not
> now exhausted his repertory in this entertaining collection."[12]

The reference to Müller's work on comparative philology, *Chips from a
German Workshop,* clearly set the tone of this review, written by W. F. Allen,
who was well known by then for having been the main editor of a seminal
1867 collection of folklore, *Slave Songs of the United States.* The article went
on to address Harris's work from three different perspectives: first, it took
on the question of diffusion, whether the folklore was of North American
Indian or African origin; second it noted the writer's strict attention to
dialect variations between Georgia, the sea-island region, and the "'Jim
Crow' negro talk of the border slave-states"; and, finally, it suggested their
bearing upon the political question of reconstruction and the future of the
South. These elements combined to give the songs a weight they did not
have in earlier articles: the songs were not just for entertainment, but
revealed, in Allen's own words, "[t]he sentiments and habits of the negroes
themselves" ("Southern," 184). The material was still "entertaining," but, cat-
egorically, it was of a kind with the collection of Native American artifacts
by the Bureau of American Ethnology.

In the 1855 article, not only were the categories by which the minstrels were understood predominantly aesthetic, but they were also imagined to be the products of individual talents. They were praised for their "severe beauty, perfect dramatic structure, and succinct impressive narration," commended for being "original . . . peculiar, genuine and unadulterated," and promoted as worthy for "several volumes, handsomely bound in Turkey morocco, and superbly embellished" ("Negro Minstrelsy," 74, 76, 79). The author suggested that the collector would be able to find an original song of some merit on every plantation in the South; given his estimate of 35,000 plantations, one would, indeed, expect quite a large number of "handsomely bound" volumes.

In 1896, by contrast, W. S. Scarborough, an African American philologist and professor at Wilberforce College, argued in the *Arena* that "Folk-lore in its broadest sense is a record of a people's history."[13] Although he gave the material an evolutionary spin, he imagined it carrying value not so much as entertainment but as an artifactual clue into the development of African American culture, its migration pattern and retention of African cultural sensibilities. Similarly, in a 1901 article in *The Independent,* Annie Weston Whitney argued that black folklore was not only of philological importance, but that it had a value for the black population that could be felt "historically, socially and politically."[14] Whereas the earlier articles situated folklore in theater performances or parlor rooms, the later ones reimagined the cultural terrain by placing an emphasis on particularly recognizable folkloric places, such as in the steamship engine room or in black churches. And whereas the earlier works placed an emphasis on the contribution of the minstrels to American music more generally, the later ones began to imagine them as records of the historical past of a particular people. Those unique elements of performance that would have linked folklore to individual artists fell away; in its place was a free-floating object with largely unmediated connections to the conditions of life of a people.

The roots of this development were philological, following a line in the understanding of the diffusion of language that had emerged earlier in the century. Michel Foucault famously characterized this change as a rupture between an eighteenth-century discourse of representation and a nineteenth-century discourse of history.[15] In philology, the breakthrough came largely out of the study of Sanskrit and the conviction that it was the source for the Indo-European family of languages. Language, newly recognized as being historical and transmutable, became the object of comparative study across geographical areas; from it, philologists began to piece together a history of migration and contact, survival and transformation, between different social groups. By contrast, seventeenth-century grammarians, mostly

French, had used language to construct a more or less direct correspondence between thought and the world: words were imagined to be signs for the thoughts and ideas of private individuals. And so Thomas Hobbes, writing in *Elements of Philosophy* (1656), thought of language only secondarily in terms of communication with other people: it was, in the first instance, a mnemonic tool for recalling previous thought. Language, as such, was private; only belatedly did it turn outward to the social world of other people.[16] A comparative analysis of different languages, a methodology upon which modern philology depended, would have made little sense in this earlier period, for any such analysis would ultimately have broken back down to the lessons of an individual's encounter with signs.

Philologists began in the early 1800s to turn from this general study of signs to a comparison of the syntax of related language families. Breakthroughs in the study of Sanskrit revealed the hidden roots of the Indo-European family of languages, connecting them to an ancient and geographically distant past previously unimagined. Colonialism brought a related attention to both the variety and incommensurability of languages, a subject taken up by Wilhelm von Humboldt, one of the direct influences on the later work of Franz Boas.[17] Humboldt developed philology's ethnographical line by arguing that "[l]anguage is the external representation of the genius of peoples," which was, of course, consonant with a German romantic fascination with folk thought as the organic root of national spirit. What philology added, however, was a sophisticated method for reading that character not only in terms of psychological characteristics but also from the historical record provided in language about the manner and outcomes of conflicts between language groups.[18] Language was understood to be formed from unconscious accretions, additions and mutations from foreign sources—influences that did not come under the purview of the story a people told about itself, and, indeed, that told a story well beyond the grasp of native speakers of the language untrained in philology. Languages were thus reconceptualized as public objects, things evolving not from private thoughts but from a course of historical interaction and migration well beyond the control of individual speakers. Rather than represent a private individual's timeless encounter with his own mind, language represented a people's historical encounter with other peoples the world over.

To the extent that folklore was wrapped up in the problem of origins, it was seen to function as a public object in precisely the same way as language. It ceased, in words Foucault used to describe language, "to be transparent to its representations, because it is thickening and taking on a peculiar heaviness."[19] The emphasis here, it should be noted, was different from that initially interesting Herder, with whom the attention to folklore as an ethnographic object is generally taken to have started. According to Herder, folklore worked at a very elemental level to provide a common stock of feelings and sensations that, almost like morphemes in a language, could be built upon to produce more complex associations. Of fables, for example, he wrote that they were "in keeping with the nature of their [a nation's] thinking, their climate and their language": "Out of this, then, for the poet a sacred *mythology* comes into being that is national and ever was for them a magic spring to create fictions and to conjure up images with."[20] Both Herder and the brothers Grimm emphasized the geographical delimitation of language and folklore, with the transmission of folklore closely following the hereditary dispersion and migration of the people to whom it belongs. But as the colonial century progressed, it became clear that folklore functioned independently of language and, in fact, that it dispersed with much greater alacrity across not only geographical spaces but also social groups. Rather than a simple evidentiary marker of the *Volksgeist,* or folk spirit, folklore was a composite from which traces of the spirit could be induced, but only by way of historical investigation. As such, folklore became an object that was collected, broken down into its parts, indexed, cross-listed, and mapped for its psychological content and for its historical accretions.

The philological school of folklore was most prominently carried into the United States institutionally by Francis James Child and his student, George Lyman Kittredge, both literary scholars at Harvard. In their work, one can see the culmination of this movement to render folklore as an open-ended *thing* continually being shaped and translated in public. By 1904, when Kittredge was completing a final volume of *English and Scottish Popular Ballads* from Child's extensive collection, he could write in the introduction that it was generally accepted that "A ballad has no author. At all events, it appears to have none. . . . If it were possible to conceive a tale as *telling itself,* without the instrumentality of a conscious speaker, the ballad would be such a tale."[21]

But the point was carried popularly at a much earlier date. In an 1877 article on black folklore published in *Lippincott's,* William Owens insisted upon the "heaviness" of what might otherwise be considered simple, even childlike material. The article started with a broad and, by then, uncontroversial assertion of the continuity between a race and its folklore, noting that the study of the "peculiarities—or rather idiosyncrasies" of a group's folklore would "furnish a fair index of their mental and moral characteristics." However, in the next paragraph, he went on to make an extended claim either for the African origins of that "medley of songs, stories, sayings and superstitions" found in the black South, or for its diffused complexity:

> The folk-lore of Africo-Americans [was] . . . brought from various tribes along the West African coast, and so far condensed into one mass in their American homes that often part of a story or tradition belonging to one tribe is grafted . . . upon a part belonging to another people, while they are still further complicated by the frequent infusion into them of ideas evidently derived from communication with the white race.[22]

One sees here not simply the deployment of folklore to describe a historically complex social group, "Africo-Americans," but, even more profoundly, the conceptualization of folklore as a public object. Dislocated from any particular speaker, the "medley" was imagined as being shared by a group that had little subjective control over it, even given the index of their mental and moral characteristics. At the same time, the vocabulary of "grafted" and "infusion" suggested that these tales had to have a certain physical density; and, as objects with such a physical substratum, they could more easily be slotted as "specimens" of the historical contact between and transmutation of racial and national types.

The kinds of knowledge suggested here depended on the refiguration of folklore as a certain kind of text-object. Following what Steven Conn effectively describes as the "object-based epistemology" of late-nineteenth-century museums, we might see the collection of folklore as analogous to the object register of the collection.[23] This may be easier to imagine with regard to Native American than African American material, given the quantity of objects American ethnologists had already collected from them and the uncomfortable readiness with which curators placed them alongside exhibits of natural history. But the object-base was just as evident in the treatment of African American material. The model was explicitly laid out by Otis T. Mason in an address to the American Folklore Society in 1891, when he argued that, since folk thought could not be separated from folk practice, "[t]he best plan is to keep the library, the gallery, and the museum under one regime."[24] The argument carried over into both scientific and literary collections of folklore. In the first of his volumes in the "Library of Aboriginal American Literature," Daniel Brinton wrote that his purpose was to reproduce "rude specimens of literature" in order to make the "material" needed for study more widely available.[25] Harris, in the second of his Remus introductions, referred to himself as an "editor and compiler" (*NWUR*, xliii). George Bird Grinnell referred to his Pawnee tales as "material" that was "collected" for preservation on a trip made expressly for the purpose.[26]

Recognizing this object-based epistemology provides us with a context for explaining one of the most striking formal characteristics of folklore's collection in the 1890s, namely the lack of any clear organizing principle to hold the miscellaneous pieces of folklore together—except that of accumulation. Kittredge extended Child's collection of popular ballads with 307 new pieces, but the collection itself was given no internal structure. Jeremiah Curtin, who had trained with Kittredge at Harvard, produced a collection of American Indian creation myths in 1898 that gave twenty-two tales with no specific geographical, temporal, or tribal order.[27] Grinnell organized a number of volumes by tribe—*Pawnee Hero Stories and Folk Tales* (1889) and *Blackfoot Lodge Tales* (1892)—but, again, gave no internal organization. Lafcadio Hearn, best known for his Southern local-color writing and collection of Japanese folklore, published a delightful collection, *Gombo Zhèbes* (1885), of 352 Creole proverbs, numbered and arranged alphabetically. One might assume that the dictionary format was undertaken for ease of use in reference, but the slender and decorative book was clearly designed for people who would be inclined to pick it up as they would a meal of "gombo" on a "flying visit to New Orleans" (see fig. 2.1).[28]

Perhaps the most famous example came with Harris's *Uncle Remus*. His book literalized the strategy by separating the most famous tale, "The Wonderful Tar Baby Story," into two segments. Remus begins the story in chapter two, stopping at the point when Brer Rabbit had landed with all four paws in the tar. Chapter three, "Why Mr. Possum Loves Peace," makes no mention of the incident and has no thematic connection to it. In chapter four, after an unnarrated passage of time—"One evening when he [the little boy] had found the old man with little or nothing to do"—the story resumes (62). But by then, the tale had been fragmented into its disparate parts, showing the extent to which it carried on in a public that Remus could call upon but not control.

William Owens's article in *Lippincott's* was not only typical in this respect but also carried its significance forward by suggesting that the fragmented nature of the tales carried meaning in itself. After beginning with two pages of detailed introduction on issues ranging from diffusion to the native religion of west Africa, he proceeded to drop in six different folk tales, each one unrelated to the next, with never more than a sentence of introduction. First he gave the famous "Tar Baby" story, then followed quickly the foot-race between Buh Rabbit and Buh Frog, a series of episodes where Buh Wolf tries to catch Buh Rabbit, the story of the "Tiny Pig," one about a Rooster going back on his word, and a "last story . . . more purely African, at least in its *dramatis personae,*" about Buh Elephant and Buh Lion ("Folk-Lore," 754). Commentary between each story was kept to a bare minimum, usually less than two sentences on

Little Dictionary of Creole Proverbs.

———o———

[Most of the proverbs quoted in Martinique are current also in Guadaloupe, only 90 miles distant. All proverbs recognized in Louisiana are marked by an asterisk (*). The indications, MAURITIUS, GUYANA, MARTINIQUE, HAYTI, etc., do not necessarily imply origin; they refer only to the dialects in which the proverbs are written, and to the works from which they are selected.]

———o———

1. **Acoma tombé toutt mounn di: C'est bois pourri.** (Quand l'Acoma est tombé, tout le monde dit: C'est du bois pourri.)
   " When the Acoma has fallen everybody says: 'It's only rotten wood.' "[1]—[*Mart.*]

2. **A fòce macaque caressé yche li ka touffé li.** (À force de caresser son petit le macaque l'étouffe.)
   " The monkey smothers its young one by hugging it too much."—[*Mart.*]

3. **Aspère[2] iéve dans marmite avant causé.** (Attendez que le lièvre soit dans la marmite avant de parler.)
   " Wait till the hare's in the pot before you talk."—Don't count your chickens before they're hatched.—[*Mauritius.*]

4. **Avant bois[3] d'Inde té pòté graine, macaque té nouri yche yo.** (Avant que l'arbre d'Inde portât des graines, les macaques nourissaient leurs petits.)
   " Before the Indian tree(?) bore seed the monkeys were able to nourish their young."
   —[*Martinique.*]

5. **Avant zabocat macaque ka nouri yche li.** (Avant qu'il y eût des avocados, les macaques nourissaient leurs petits.)
   "The monkey could nourish it young, before there were any avocadoes."[4]—
   [*Martinique.*]

---

[1] The Acoma, says Turiault, is one of the grandest trees in the forests of the Antilles. The meaning of the proverb appears to be, that a powerful or wealthy person who meets with misfortune is at once treated with contempt by those who formerly sought his favor or affected to admire his qualities.

[2] Evidently a creolization of the Spanish *esperar.*

[3] The word bois (wood) is frequently used in Creole for the tree itself; and pié-bois ("foot of the wood") for the trunk or stump. "Yon gouòs pié-bois plis facile déraciné qu'mauvais l'habitude" (A big stump is easier to uproot than a bad habit), is a Martinique Creole dictum, evidently borrowed from the language of the white masters. I am sorry that I do not know which of the various trees to which the name bois d'Inde has been given by the Creoles, is referred to in the proverb—whether the mango, or China-berry. No tree is generally recognized by that name in Louisiana.

[4] The Avocado was the name given by the Spanish conquistadores to the Persea gratissima, whose fruit is the "alligator pear." But M. Turiault again traces the Spanish word back to the Carib word Aouacate.

2.1 Lafcadio Hearn's fine arts edition of collected creole proverbs, *Gombo Zhèbes* (1885), is remarkable for the stress its alphabetical arrangement put on accumulation, as opposed to content or context. Author's print.

either the likelihood of the tale's origins in Africa or its similarities to others in the European tradition. The "Tiny Pig," for example, was said to be very like "the Anglo-Saxon story of the 'Three Blue Pigs,'" which in turn was placed in the "class of stories approaching somewhat in character those related of our own Jack the Giant-killer, leaving out the giants" (753). But that was all; the next story, about the rooster, was simply introduced as one that "bears some features of American negro life, grafted probably upon African stock" (754).

Given the detailed organizational apparatus of his introduction, Owens's deployment of the folklore would seem to come to remarkably little effect. There was no apparent thematic or ethnographic connection between the tales; they were not used to produce the "index" of the morals or customs of Africo-Americans; they were not balanced by an equally grand conclusion at the end of the article. The emphasis, in other words, was on the value of the folklore as artifacts, even if they had not yet been definitively placed in their collection. These were only pieces of the puzzle, miscellany, and frag-ments—pieces, nonetheless, that suggested by their very fragmented nature the existence of a more complex interaction that had been shaped from a long history of accretion and transmutation across places, races, languages, and time.

REMUS AS PUBLIC OBJECT IN THE DEBATE OVER DIFFUSION AND EVOLUTION

The particular debate kicked up by Harris in his introduction to the Uncle Remus volumes proceeded precisely along these lines. The problem was not that of the nature of the relationship between folklore and any particu-lar racial or national people, but rather that of how folkloric objects came to be shared by peoples of vastly different geographical, linguistic, historical, religious, and racial backgrounds. As framed initially by Harris, but picked up on in many subsequent articles, the question was one of accounting for the appearance of the wonderful "Tar Baby" story in the American South, and in Canada, the West Indies, Brazil, the Bahaman Islands, South Africa, and even India.[29] Just after naming Powell, Harris countered with Mr. Herbert H. Smith, author of *Brazil and the Amazons* (Scribner's, 1879), who "has met with some of these stories . . . as far east as Siam" (40). Harris made a relativistic intervention here, though obliquely, by suggesting that the Negro was just as capable of folkloric invention as the Indian. But he also set the grounds for a more extensive debate, carried on by others writ-ing in the *Journal of American Folk-Lore.* Not only because of its boldness, but certainly aided by it, the issues Harris raised in his debate with Powell had incredible force in the folklore community, surfacing repeatedly as a point of reference for the argument emerging in the early years of the American Folklore Society between models of social evolution and historical diffusion.

Harris figured prominently in a chapter written for the inaugural issue of the *JAF* in 1888 by T. F. Crane, one of the new journal's four editors, who rehearsed the problem Harris had raised in his introduction to *Remus* over the African or Amazonian origins of the deer and the tortoise myth. Crane broadly outlined three theories concerning the problem of origins. The first was Grimm's theory that the popular tales (in his case of Germany) were part of the myth of particular races and were taken with them at their dispersion. The second was that of Theodor Benfey, a favorite of Continental scholars, who argued that the popular tales of Europe were imported into it from India and translations of Oriental storybooks. Whereas Grimm argued for dispersion through personal contact, Benfey preferred a model of dispersion through literary channels, with folklore traveling like a spice between peoples across the routes of trade. The third was the evolutionary model, attributed to the British folklorist Andrew Lang, which proceeded from the first two theories' inability to account for the similarity between stories coming from places where contact was not possible or likely, particularly with regard to the collection of folklore from "remote tribes of savages" (in Crane, "Diffusion," 11). Holding for the "identity everywhere of early fancy," Lang argued that folklore was "derived and inherited from the savage state of man, from the savage conditions of life, and the savage way of regarding the world." [30] The stories were not disseminated, but originated in many different places following the same natural responses of primitive man to his environment.

As for Crane, he tended to agree with Lang but mentioned several times the importance of keeping in mind the rapid diffusion of tales: "experience has proved that every kind of popular literature is diffused and interchanged with extraordinary rapidity and ease" ("Diffusion," 12). And he had previously weighed in with a vote for the African origin of the deer and tortoise myth in a *Popular Science* article dated April 1881. That said, Lang's model of evolutionary folklore was picked up in some form by nearly all of the major players in U.S. anthropology up to the 1890s. For a rather complex case, one might take the example of Daniel Brinton, an anthropologist at the University of Pennsylvania. His editing of a multivolume collection of literature by "aboriginal American authors," unduly overshadowed by the more institutionally savvy names in ethnology, coincided neatly with the move to conceptualize this work as a second-order, public artifact. But while his "anthology of America" offered the chance for the circulation of textual "specimens," Brinton's overarching sense of evolution permeated the work, as when he spoke of the verse of "the ruder races" being like that of the "earliest and simplest poetry."[31] More typical than Brinton was William McGee, one of the mainstays of Powell's BAE from 1893 to 1903, who wrote an *Atlantic Monthly* article praising the alacrity with which social scientists in the United States had adopted the "tenets of the new law"—adopted it even more quickly than those in Great Britain.[32]

Despite the predominance claimed by McGee for social evolutionary arguments, my real interest lies rather with the line established by Benfey. His argument analogizing the diffusion of folklore to that of print material was a significant irritant to the romantic conflation of folklore with race and national character.[33] As such, what it entertained was a model for thinking folklore alongside modernity. His hypothesis, originally developed with regard to Sanskrit, implied a way of imagining folklore as a postproduction *thing* moving through space, being modified or translated by different publics. The concept demanded a sense of the asynchronous and discontinuous movement of folklore, languages, and peoples around the routes of trade. Indeed, Benfey's account opened up folklore to external influences with a speed and alacrity that the "races" with whom they originated and the "languages" in which they were told could never be. For races and languages to amalgamate in such a way would take generations, but within the conceptual space of folklore it could happen almost overnight.

This move to dislodge the object of folklore from "its" folk had the effect of disrupting the romantic nationalist and evolutionary narratives attached to it; if the anthropological concept of culture of the twentieth century was in any way new—was anything more than the old Herderian idea about *Volksgeist*—I would suggest that it was largely because of the argument for discontinuity initiated here. As already suggested, the conflation of folklore and racial or national character dated at least from the late eighteenth century. Linda Dowling has noted that the "English Romantics and their successors had [so] thoroughly assimilated the assumption that a language expresses the essential and characteristic spirit of a people [that] the origins of the notion in Herder and Humboldt had become quite obscured."[34] Against this romantic-nationalist paradigm—a paradigm that also underwrote the social evolutionary linkage of race and folklore in the line taken by Powell and the BAE—most *JAF* folklorists insisted on the need for a more precise understanding of the distinction in kind between the categories of language, race, and national character. Nowhere does one see this more clearly than in the work of Boas, one of the *JAF*'s founding editors and, implicitly, a follower of Benfey's model of folkloric diffusion.

It is difficult for us to perceive Boas's engagement with diffusionist arguments because of the importance historians of the culture concept have placed on his particularist methodology, especially as it was manifested in the debate with Otis T. Mason about the arrangement of ethnological museums.[35] George Stocking first drew attention to these museum debate articles in a series of essays that have proven to have incredible interdisciplinary appeal.[36] What is troubling about the success of Stocking's intervention, however, is that dependence upon it has occluded the significance of a "comparativist" study of the diffusion of cultural elements to Boas's own line of critique of both evolutionary and romantic racialist positions. In this context, it is important to recall that the first of Boas's museum debate articles acknowledged the problem propelling the study of diffusion in its title, "The Occurrence of Similar Inventions in Areas Widely Apart." The article even began by enumerating the same three hypotheses put forward by Crane in the *JAF* to explain the phenomenon in the study of folklore: the migration of a certain race; the migration of ideas; or the evolutionary continuity of invention in response to similar effects of nature. It was only to the last one of these explanations that the articles forcefully objected. Boas's preference for the tribal display of objects should not obscure the significance, manifest in much of his early work, of the study of diffusion.

Indeed, while Boas may have preferred particularism, his main line against evolutionary theory, which at the time was not veiling its racist political bent, was the study of diffusion—a point that Stocking actually made in his initial recovery of Boas, even if it has not received its fair share of attention.[37] Boas studied diffusion with great regularity, publishing on it at least six times between 1891 and 1914, with most of these articles being reprinted in *Race, Language and Culture* (1940).[38] Particularly with regard to folklore, Boas repeatedly stressed the inability of the evolutionary model to explain the "liberal exchange" of songs and stories "all over the northern half of the continent, from the Atlantic to the Pacific Ocean, and also between northern Mexico, the Western Plateaus, and the Plains of the Mississippi." As he wrote in 1905,

> The amount of dissemination in the New World seems to be almost the same as that found in the Old World, where we can prove by literary documents that the tales have traveled so far that they occur now in Japan and in Spain, in India and in Siberia. Nothing travels so easily and seems to be absorbed so readily as a tale.[39]

Boas argued that even if one were to concede differences of mental characteristics between the races, which he was grudgingly willing to do, race as a category failed to either explain or differentiate the dissemination of mythological elements. There was nothing to suggest that members of the same race living in areas widely apart developed the same folklore, but countervailing evidence existed that suggested that members of different races living in even remote contiguity—attached, for example, only by a trade route—shared the same tales. If race and folklore were fundamentally discontinuous, then some other category of accounting for the particularity of different populations needed to emerge. That concept, especially post-1910, was a shared system of meaning that came to be called "culture."

Boas's argument, like those of others writing for the *JAF*, challenged the social-evolutionary theories that dominated the Smithsonian Institution and the Bureau of American Ethnology.[40] Perhaps more profoundly, however, they marked a trajectory away from Herderian notions of romantic nationalism. The seminal move of the late nineteenth century was not the theorization of culture along E. B. Tylor's line of calling it that "complex whole which includes knowledge, belief, art, morals, law, custom, and any other capabilities and habits acquired by man as a member of society."[41] Tylor's 1871 definition only demonstrated that there was a remarkable conceptual sameness to both evolutionary and romantic nationalist discourse in which the vogue for folklore took root—a sameness that conflated language, race, and culture. By contrast, the move to an object-based epistemology that attended to the postproduction dissemination and rearticulation of folklore "in areas widely apart" set the stage for the relativist, antiracist intervention of twentieth-century anthropology. In the 1910s and 1920s, Boas and his students turned frequently to complementing the fundamental point about discontinuity with the study of what Boas came to call "literary style."[42] In this mode, the Boasians would attend to what particular cultures did with diffused elements once they had them, the point being to show that different cultures produced different meanings around similar objects. But it was the first part of this two-step, the initial move to recognize folklore as circulating culture, a public and detachable text-object, that carried the antiracist, antievolutionary charge.

WORD SHADOWS: OBJECTS AND OBJECTIFICATION

To study the dissemination of folklore means to conceive of folklore as an object in circulation. In this sense, the late-nineteenth-century understanding of folklore differed from that developed in the 1920s and 1930s by Boas's students. Zora Neale Hurston provides a prominent example. For Hurston, folklore was primarily a cultural performance, an ongoing banter on the store porch in Eatonville, Florida. "Ah come to collect some old stories and tales and Ah know y'all know a plenty of 'em," Hurston wrote at the beginning of *Mules and Men* (1935), addressing herself to a group of old acquaintances: "'What you mean, Zora, them big old lies we tell when we're jus' sittin' around here on the store porch doin' nothin'?'" asked B. Mosley."[43] For Hurston, folklore was bound to a particular place and time, to one B. Mosley telling lies on a porch in Florida, and to a particular style of talking. It was of a particular locale, a place defined not only by the temporality of an oral exchange but also by the paradigmatic nature of anthropological fieldwork. As such, Hurston's conceptual framework differed significantly from that of late-nineteenth-century diffusionists, who conceptualized folklore as a post-performance object, a *thing* moving about in the world. Figured not as a performance but as an object, folklore for the diffusionist was about space, about the disembodiment of cultural objects as they moved with more or less alacrity from one locale to the next.

To think of folklore as an object leads, as those familiar with the political questions surrounding this material will immediately recognize, directly to the question of its dynamic or static nature, its tendency to make way either for a vibrant cultural movement or one that was "objectified." To put it simply, one would expect cultural objects to lead to cultural objectification, a bad thing. However, much of what made folklore provocative in the late nineteenth century was its status as an object—an object whose circulation demonstrated its discontinuity with the categories of race, language, and nation. Indeed, rather than neutralizing the cultural and aesthetic vibrancy of the form, this rendering of folklore as an object had the potential to signal the emotive space beyond its own limits, the excess of historical and ethnological meaning it carried.

Even in the most politically retrograde of the articles on black folklore in the United States, there ran a sense of the excess signification carried by folkloric objects—the sense that they represented a more spiritually and historically expansive meaning that was just beyond the grasp of the collector. We might describe this excess by co-opting the title of one of these offensive pieces from the *Atlantic Monthly* in 1891, "Word Shadows." The main content of this article was a list, without any clear organizational principle, of nearly one hundred turns of phrase, a "glossary of plantation patois" collected by the author during his life in the South. The words recorded were of a certain kind of prurient aesthetic interest for the author, a "grotesquerie" with "that piquant flavor that all the world favors." But it was so because even dialect, oral speech, came to take on the object status of folklore more generally, and thus cast shadows that went beyond the words on the page:

> If shadows of material objects are grotesque, even more so are the shadows cast by words from fairly educated lips into the minds of almost totally ignorant people. Display in utterance of these quaint word-shadows, if one may so call them, makes dialect.[44]

What provoked the anonymous author was clearly the idea that language itself was open to racial contamination.[45] His goal seems to have been to reinscribe lines of differentiation by describing the deformation of "white" speech by "black" speakers as "grotesque." His effort, however, was based on a paradox. For even as he worked to reinscribe the lines, he showed them to be porous, open to disruption by shadows.

If such lines were porous, they were rendered so by the object status of speech itself. Tellingly, the author metaphorized "plantation patois" as an objective medium of translation from one cultural group to the next. Words cast shadows, and dialect was not simply utterance but the display of utterance. But how do words cast shadows? How is utterance displayed? The author could simply have had in mind people talking; but his logic suggests a more profound irritation at the site of the connection between orality and the materiality of display. The phrases "word shadows" and "display in utterance" offered weighted and remarkably acute readings of how folk speech had moved beyond the realm of simple orality and into that of a more opaque, and potentially more troubling, artifactuality. All of the elements of materiality, history, and publicity were in play here. Words were no longer originating from individual thoughts but were being cast about between races and, in the process, were being deformed—a historical but also largely arbitrary process.

As many critics have argued, to the extent that folklore was used to assert difference between "primitive" minorities and "civilized" whites in American society, the folklore vogue of the late nineteenth century can be read as having underwritten an antiprogressive agenda, one that saw in short order the promise of the civil rights agenda of the Reconstruction era come to an end and racial segregation ratified as the law of the land.[46] And yet even in an article as offensive as "Word Shadows," there seems to have been a sense that there was a deeper way for those words to mean, a way that the white author could not follow. It is almost as if the dialect the author described was not about orality at all, nor even quite about marks made on paper, but about the indescribable shadows cast from and playing beyond marks on paper. Eric Sundquist, when he takes up "Word Shadows" in *To Wake the Nations* (1993), notes the way the description of "plantation patois" seems to get beyond itself, suggesting a cultural vibrancy that the author alluded to but could not understand.[47] As a display in utterance, speech became a "grotesquerie" in the way that the face uncannily did when transposed in a wax mask at a Smithsonian exhibition or at Madame Tussaud's. Its interest came not from the exactitude of its replication, but from its flaws—the limitations of artificial materiality that gave one the sense that it was, after all, only a replica of something much vaster and more complex.[48]

"Word Shadows" thus makes visible a point about the practice of folklore in the nineteenth century. But it also highlights a method for understanding folklore's production of meaning that was made current in the 1980s. Sundquist is still that methodology's most impressive spokesperson in that his work offers a virtuoso performance of cultural recovery of an Africanist cultural heritage in African American nineteenth-century cultural production. However, his own recourse to orality as the defining category by which to understand African American folk heritage oddly delimits the claims about this material that were made by nineteenth-century diffusionists—if not, too, the claims we might now want to make with regard to it. In effect, Sundquist's assumption is analogous to the literary critical "intentional fallacy" that the narrator of a text is its author. Only here, it amounts to what we might call a cultural fallacy: the assumption that a folktale is of a particular culture.

For Sundquist, folklore's African American cultural meaning needs always to be "heard" between the lines, requiring "an apprehension of what is implied or silent, of the 'talk' that is dangerous or subversive but is, nonetheless, a key element in the retrieval of history" (*To Wake,* 389). But because it is described in the register of an oral performance, the historical content Sundquist seeks to recover seems peculiarly limited to an in-group imagined to have been conscious of its dangerous and subversive qualities. Sundquist speaks of black folklore in terms of the way it was "animated by an essential aural aesthetic," which is to say by the felicity of its play with white speech and white speech codes (311). Folklore produced its meaning in the figurative context of someone "talking," say the author of "Word Shadows" or the people that author was listening to. This turn to orality defines "black culture" as the coded subversion of the literacy of a dominant "white culture": "African American authenticity," a highly problematic category to which Sundquist remains wedded, is to be found in "a deviation from, or subversion of, a dominating set of cultural standards" (294). As readers of that material, we then have to make a call, as Sundquist does repeatedly in his assessment of folklorists during the vogue years of the 1880s and 1890s, as to whether people were "signifying" or not, whether or not they were speaking in a "coded language" (311). We cannot avoid this Manichean insider-outsider choice, which at root determines cultural intention, for it decides what we think we should be hearing. If the tales are to count as being representative of black culture in the late 1800s, then the folkloric speakers must have been conscious of what they were saying and also of how they were saying it.

This conceptual framework differs fundamentally from that of the late-nineteenth-century diffusionists in that it is interested less in tale than story, less in plot than the point made by its telling, less in *langue* than *parole*. This move to the telling of the folkloric story, to its performance, was undertaken in the 1980s and 1990s in an attempt to avoid "objectifying" culture. What the move obscures, however, is the provocation in the diffusionists' framework for conceptualizing what folklore was and how it carried meaning: folklore's basic challenge to the categories of race and language. Moreover, it runs the risk of recapitulating the romantic fantasy that there is an essential continuity between folklore and particular races and nations.

Another example. One of the more appreciative analyses of black folklore from the late nineteenth century came in an early piece by Henry Louis Gates, dated by the beginning of the so-called culture wars. In it, Gates argues that it had been a mistake for twentieth-century African American artists to abandon the dialect tradition, which he takes as the form in which African American art resonated most profoundly with a collective black consciousness. He turns to speech as the essential trait defining "black structures of feeling," "a coded, danced speech which carried its own significations . . . its own hermetic, autonomous universe":

> the black artisan [is] bound to his or her language, a language inextricably interwoven with music. The medium of music itself carries its own value and its own tradition. . . . It would be as idle to attempt to utter poetry without syllables as it is for a black poet, functioning mythopoeically, to utter poetry without music.[49]

Gates's emphasis on orality is quite exciting, and in many respects does seem to characterize what is most vibrant about African American cultural life today. But the emphasis comes at a price, for it moves our attention away from the site of the work's dissemination—its circulation as a work of art through the hands of readers potentially far removed from the imaginary bounds of this hermetic subculture. The very metaphor of orality suggests proximity, a story or tale that was heard or seen, as with Hurston on the porch in Eatonville. By contrast, the point of looking at folklore as an object was distance. Folklorists wanted to gauge the effect upon folklore of its travel through diverse places, its contact with varied sources. And the fascinating effect of thinking of folklore in these terms, as an object, was that it demonstrated the historical plasticity of social groups and not the hermetic retention of cultural traditions. The diffusionists' interest in objectifying folklore was, in other words, fundamentally anti-essentialist, for it made collapsing races and nations with stories and songs impossible.

A sense for the discontinuity between folklore and race groups is rarely maintained in contemporary work on nineteenth-century folklore. The odd result is that Boas, the turn-of-the-century anthropologist, often championed a more recognizably postmodern theoretical position than many late-twentieth-century literary critics swayed by his anthropological concept of cultures.[50] To make this argument is not to contravene the many evocative readings that have recently been produced of the key tropes from the slave spirituals, nor is it to say that the cultural distinction of the sorrow songs and American Indian folklore recovered from the nineteenth century is not to be found in their metaphorical richness and expressive sonority. It is, however, to say that, as it was recorded in the 1880s and 1890s, this richness and sonority passed through an object-based register that had the effect, conceptually, of opening both folklore and cultures up to the influence of "outside" sources. In taking a similar line in his examination of slave spirituals, Ronald Radano comes to the conclusion that their heterogeneous social construction should "pose a serious challenge to the modern conception of black music as a transhistorical essence."[51] A challenge to the conceptualization of folklore as a "transhistorical essence" was precisely the one made by Boas, along with others studying diffusion in the *Journal of American Folk-Lore.* They were led by the comparative study of folklore to an understanding of the plasticity of the form: to the manner in which it moved across the so-called borders marked by race and language—and in terminology contemporary to our own moment, moved even between cultures.

THEORY TO PRACTICE: THE POLITICS
OF THE HARRIS-POWELL DEBATE

The character of folklore as a public, circulating object, related to and yet distinguished from races and language groups, made it a highly volatile cultural commodity in the unstable political context of the late nineteenth century. Its volatility explains its vogue: the interest surrounding it developed precisely because of its ambiguity as a marker of social distinction. One of the odd results of such ambiguity, however, was folklore's strict institutional reinscription. It is here, perhaps, that one can begin to best understand what was holding back the development of the anthropological culture concept through folklore on an institutional level. The "postmodern" implications of diffusion in the study of folklore were largely overwritten by the political exigencies of "postsectional" racial and political conflicts in the period after

Reconstruction. The result was a return to a proprietary understanding of folklore.[52]

Although the collection of both African American and American Indian folklore came to be understood in terms of this object-based epistemology, the two followed vastly different lines of institutional development. The literary magazines, while enthusiastically publishing "Negro" folklore, seem only to have been willing to accept travel narratives and adventure stories of life among Native American tribes—things like Cushing's adventures in Zuni, Joaquin Miller's poetry of the Sierras, or Charles Alexander Eastman's recollections of "Indian Boyhood." By contrast, the scientific organs avoided African American material in favor of Native American folklore. In its first twenty years, *The Annual Report of the Bureau of Ethnology* published nearly eighty scholarly studies on American Indian life and folklore, just short of twenty others on mostly archaeological work in Central and South America, but not a single article on any topic relating to either the country's black population or Africa.[53] The *Journal of American Folk-Lore* was only slightly more interested in African American material, its banner year coming with its third volume in 1890, when it ran five articles on African American folklore, eleven on American Indians, and nine on other fields ("German Legends in Pennsylvania" being a favorite). The standard ratio is roughly 10:10:1 in favor of Indian and Euro-American folklore over African American. Whereas surprisingly large quantities of black folklore came out in the magazines, Native American folklore belonged to the ethnologists in Washington.

In practice, the answer to the problem of origins gave way to a proprietary debate in which scientific questions were impossibly intertwined with sectional politics. Thus, to rediscover the "rude shock" that came when it was discovered that folklore circulated across geographical, racial, and national boundaries is also to insist, somewhat paradoxically, that folklore was taken hold of by a socially unsettled populace in order to reinscribe the differences between other peoples and themselves on other than cultural grounds.

Both Harris's and Powell's emergence in the fields of folklore and ethnology followed a post-Reconstruction trajectory. So, for example, it was not Harris's interest in diffusion but his nostalgia for the "old darkey" stories that the literary press exploited when it pursued a post-Reconstruction project of national reconciliation.[54] His closest political affiliations came from his association with Henry Grady, the outspoken proponent of "the New South," with whom Harris co-edited the Atlanta *Constitution.* Moreover, it is likely that the failure of Harris's Remus stories to find a permanent place in the cultural life of Powell's BAE was due in large measure to a lingering sectional conflict. The BAE had been founded directly on the heels of the Union Army's turn from fighting the South to fighting the Indians. It became a northern institution the moment that Powell, who had lost his arm in the Civil War and captured the nation's imagination with his exploration of the Colorado River, was named to head it.

Harris's discontent with the BAE in the 1880s surfaced in surprising places, but perhaps nowhere more directly than when he turned from the reproduction of black folklore to a novella about the white folk of middle Georgia, "At Teague Poteet's." The story was first published in the *Century* in 1883, shortly after the appearance of the first Remus volume, and was later collected in *Mingo* (1884). The crux of the novella was familiar to sectional reconciliation narratives: a Southern gentleman's daughter, named Sis Poteet, marries a northern businessman and moves off to the city, thus wedding the old South to the new. But Harris complicated the narrative by drawing in questions not only about what part of folk life was due to racial heritage and what part to evolution but also about the way that sectional differences dating back to the Civil War were recapitulated by display strategies used by ethnological museums and the BAE. Indeed, in certain respects, Harris's argument in this story forecasts that of Boas when he takes on Otis Mason on the subject of museum display several years later.

Although the main events occur over a short period in 1879, the novella starts many generations earlier with the arrival of a French ancestor, Gérard Petit, to South Carolina. The question that Harris begins with in bringing the great-great-grandfather Petit into the equation precisely restaged the diffusion-evolution debate. He writes that as Petit moves inland toward the Georgia mountains, "the *je, vous, nous* of France met in conflict the 'ah-yi,' the 'we uns' and the 'you uns' of the English-Pennsylvania-Georgians"—a conflict that, over the course of generations, had never been entirely resolved.[55] This presents a philological problem of language dispersion, and, as Harris is clear to point out, "je, vous, nous" gives way to "'you uns' and 'we uns'": the new language "belonged to the time, and the climate suited them," as it soon does to Gérard Petit, despite his resistance ("At Teague Poteet's," 40). Language proves discontinuous with race.

But there are other characteristics, of an apparently racial nature, that take longer to be assimilated. Teague Poteet, the father of the girl soon to wed in reconciliation, does not hold many customs in common with his ancestor, but we are told that he shares with him a sentiment of revolt that sends him away from the town of Gulletsville just as his ancestor had gone away from France. His daughter, too, holds onto something of the French charm: "In some mysterious way she inherited the beauty and grace and refinement of a Frenchwoman"; she grows to be "[u]nlike the typical American girl," whose "sweetly severe portraits" contrast with Sis' "natural brightness and vivacity" ("At Teague Poteet's," 53–54, 74). What then explains these characteristics? Rather than answer, Harris poses the problem as a diffusionist-evolutionist riddle: "[I]t is a question whether [Teague] inherited this trait from France or from the Euphrates,—from Gérard or from Adam" (44).

In the meantime, the Civil War engulfs Hog Mountain, where the Poteets have finally come to reside. Here again, Harris highlights conflicts between racial, linguistic, and national lines of genealogy. Poteet is something of a libertarian, and with his fellow neighbors on the hill, he repulses both the secessionists from the town below them and Sherman's advancing Union troops. They just want to be left alone. Same thing after the war: the government sends agents to shut down a moonshine operation that Poteet had set up to pay for Sis's education in town. Poteet and his neighbors on the mountain resist, showing the extent to which local custom is out of step with the political issues of the nation. They win, and the government assents to go away save one, the man Sis ends up marrying. Even the marriage, though, takes place outside the nationalist framework. The cementing act of the young man's love had been to alert Poteet to the agents' raid before it happened. The point for us to draw from the story is that, on almost every level, it describes the discontinuity between law and language, nation and custom. Different parts of the community are assimilated at different rates, making crosscurrents of influence impossible to track.

The story ends with a nameless old woman being put on exhibit as an ethnographic curiosity at the 1881 Atlanta Cotton Exposition (not the same one at which Booker T. Washington makes his famous "compromise" speech). She is part of what is clearly a comparative display, like those that Boas would be rejecting. The old woman had been drawn away from the hills of middle Georgia to "aid in illustrating the startling contrasts that the energy and progress of man have produced":

> They sot me over ag'in the biggest fuss they could pick out, an' gimme a pa'r er cotton kyards. . . . The folks, they 'ud come an' stan' an' star', an' then they 'ud go some'r's else; an' then new folks 'ud come, an' stan', an' star', an' go some'r's else. They wuz jewlarkers thar frum ever'where's, an' they lookt like they wuz too brazen to live skacely. Not that I keer'd. No, bless you!
> ("At Teague Poteet's" 165–66)

The old women may say she did not care, but Harris makes no mistake about the fact that he did not think it appropriate to use her for a timeline of civilization. Indeed, Harris's story imposes upon that scene a domestic context, preferring to exhibit her according to what Boas might have called "the tribal arrangement of collections."[56] From amidst the "brazen" stares comes Teague Poteet's daughter, Sis, the one who had moved away from the hills to marry a northern man and live in the city. Sis walks right up and kisses the old woman, a gesture of intimacy which, in reuniting the ethnographic object with her cultural group, causes the old woman to "sot right flat whar' I wuz, an' [have] a good cry" ("At Teague Poteet's," 167).

This public display of cultural affection, which is analogous in effect to Harris's hostility to Powell in the introductions to *Uncle Remus,* challenged the institutional importance of the Smithsonian as plotted against either the paucity of such cultural institutions in the South or the reconciliatory stance of the literary monthlies.[57] As suggested by Harris's increasingly caustic tone in the Uncle Remus volumes of the 1890s and early 1900s, his embrace of the New South seems to have been motivated by his resentment over the "bullying attitude of the politicians who set out during the reconstruction period to carry things their own way."[58] In the 1905 volume, *Told by Uncle Remus,* Harris had Remus complain of "the dubious ways of city life" in Atlanta; upon returning to the plantation, Remus is exasperated by the newest "little boy," who seems to pay dearly for his subjugation to the manners of "a different age—a different time."[59] Similarly, in a 1904 article, Harris admitted that he may be drawing "portraits of ideal negroes who exist only in the imagination." But "be it so," he continued: "I know that in some of its aspects [slavery] was far more beautiful and inspiring than any of the relations that we have between employers and the employed in this day and time."[60]

Given this context, Harris's attack on Powell can be read in terms of the incompatibility of their mappings not only of folkloric but also of U.S. nationalist origins. Their argument highlighted how the resources of the official folklorists of the U.S. government had been directed almost exclusively to work on the American Indian, and how that attention manifested a move, contested by Harris, to produce a national mythology of industrial progress. But even more fundamentally, their argument demonstrates how an entire range of political questions that might have emerged around the study of folklore in terms of a theory of diffusion were co-opted by the prevailing political situation. The scene of the kiss urged a recuperation of the domestic folk-time of slavery as the ideal of national culture, for a return to a time and place where the tales of black folk and Creole kisses could be at home in a white economic system. But it did not even come close to opening up a more radical challenge to the conceptual categories being used to usher in segregation and other discriminatory race-based policies. The challenge to romantic nationalism and social-evolutionary theories that had been promised by the debate over the origins of the Tar Baby tale—a debate in which the objectification of folklore had seemed to open up an entirely new way of figuring the free-flow of culture—became consumed in Harris's and the country's nostalgia.

CODA: HARRIS AND PROPRIETARY CULTURE

So where does this leave Harris and Uncle Remus today? How does his debate with Powell register against the desire some critics have had to recuperate his work on black folklore?[61] Harris, particularly in the later volumes, seems to have lost interest in the storm he had helped to stir up about the dissemination of folklore. He only became more reactionary, more of an apologist for slavery. And it does not help his current standing that the character of Remus only gained in importance as time went on. Harris, on the one hand, never produced the tales without Remus, never recorded them publicly without the apologist baggage carried in the frame narrative. He did, on the other hand, produce Remus and the apologist baggage without the tales. Any treatment of Harris, as collector, needs to recognize that he assimilated those tales to an apologist project from the beginning, and thus that his politics cannot be separated from his own telling of tales.

I think it is important, nonetheless, to pose our problem with Harris in the right way, which is to say in a way consistent with the kind of object we imagine folklore to be. The proprietary debate between Harris and Powell recapitulated the romantic nationalist conflation of folklore with race and language, and this despite what both men knew about folklore's dissemination. It incorrectly assumed cultures to be closed systems, and that we might actually know whether a particular tale is or is not representative (whereas we never can). To avoid doing the same, we should keep in mind the claim facilitated by studies of diffusion that race, language, and culture are discontinuous entities. While the telling of the stories may demonstrate the cultural particularity of a certain community, their own "literary style" in Boas's words, the tales themselves have by now been fragmented, disseminated, and assimilated in multifarious ways.[62] In our own political context, it can be incredibly useful to be able to distinguish between circulating culture and the semiotics of any particular cultural system.

In 1987, Julius Lester published a wonderful new volume of Brer Rabbit stories in which he took out both the character of Uncle Remus (except in the title of the collection) and much of the heavy dialect. I find this collection quite delightful, and yet think that Lester made a mistake when, in the introduction, he reinscribed the tales in a proprietary debate. Lester writes, in response to a question of "whether it is all right for a white person to tell black folktales," that they can, though "[u]ndoubtedly, a black person with roots in the Southern black tradition will bring an added dimension to the telling of these tales to which most whites will not have access."[63] This answer seems to assume that there is a privileged site of access, and so falls into what I earlier described as the cultural fallacy. Lester's response is consistent with the theoretical moves made by Sundquist and Gates. At stake is a question of access to cultural intention, to the excess of meaning, or "added dimension," that folklore carries in its telling. I would rather have had Lester argue that the idea that these are "black" folktales is fundamentally unsound—that what the continued popularity of the tales suggests is the basic discontinuity of race, language, and culture. There is no question that, given the complex racial history of the tales in the United States and abroad, certain people will have different ways of accessing the stories, and more or less rich ways of telling them. But the more interesting theoretical point is that, against the backdrop of their widespread diffusion across populations and over centuries, these tales offer a fundamentally material provocation of the racial lines that have defined social affiliation in the United States. At least since the 1870s, when Harris and other folklorists began to circulate them in print, Brer Rabbit stories have had little to do with either living in the South or having roots in a black tradition. The tales may be objects around which such a social affiliation might be produced, but they are, at the same time, intersecting that tradition at tangents, passing across and out of those geographically and racially defined spaces, and moving through altogether different categories of affiliation.

When reevaluating the folklore revival in political terms, the more provocative line comes with thinking of Brer Rabbit as circulating culture, not cultural property. When Newell, who had never formally trained as a folklorist, died in 1906, Boas published a memorial for him in the *Journal of American Folk-Lore* that praised his artistic temper and human sympathy. Boas wrote that these qualities "enabled him to see things that had been hidden from the eyes of anthropologists."[64] By "anthropologists," one can only imagine that Boas must have had Powell's old group from the BAE in mind, those for whom the evolutionary model continued to quarantine folklore from more provocative ground by collapsing it with the category of race. By contrast, if folklore was as provocative at this time as I have been suggesting, if it generated the level of anxiety about cultural display that it seems to have done, it must have been because it failed in unexpected ways to maintain the line between the races. The "Wonderful Tar Baby Story," circulating across the boundaries erected to constrain it, became that of a transracial and a transnational public. The story had been, in terms Antonio Gramsci would later use to describe folklore, "assimilated in bizarre new ways" by variously affiliated groups of people across a range of geographical, political, and customary spaces—assimilated in ways that even Harris could not have controlled.[65]

THE OBJECT-LIFE
OF BOOKS

Collecting Local Color

⤙ ⇌⟐⇌ ⤚

Doris went away slowly up the hillside, through the long autumn grass, into
the shadow of the fruit-trees. Dick could not follow her, but for some minutes
he stood still. What a picture for a man to paint! What a woman for a man to
love!

—Sarah Orne Jewett

In Sarah Orne Jewett's 1885 novel, *A Marsh Island*,[1] a bohemian artist
from New York, an urban and urbane collector of local color named
Dick Dale, spends the summer in the country making sketches of the
rural scenery and quite literally falling in love with the native inhabitants.
Toward the beginning of the novel, Dale finds the kind of regional treasure
he is looking for in the second floor bedroom of a country farmhouse, where
he hopes to spend the summer. Led to the room by a dark, back stairway,
Dale comes across an admirable little water-jug:

> There was a plump-looking bed, like a well-risen loaf, and a
> straight-backed chair or two, and a small three-cornered washstand,
> toward which his paint-streaked hands led him at once. He lifted
> the water-jug with admiration. It held very little, but it was of an
> adorable shape and quality of ancient English crockery, and he
> reminded himself that he might find a way through old Mrs. Owen's
> heart to her closets; for who knew what unappreciated treasures
> might be hidden away? (23)

Readers familiar with Jewett's attention in other works to the quaint artifacts of rural life may recognize in Dale's attraction to the water-jug that of the girls in *Deephaven* (1877), who have "great sympathy" with an old sea captain for his "fashion of keeping worthless treasures," or that of the narrator of *The Country of the Pointed Firs* (1896), who leaves Dunnet Landing at the end of the summer with "a quaint West Indian basket" and "coral pin," lasting mementos of her acquaintance with the village and Mrs. Todd.[2] Such treasures and mementos served Jewett as objects around which to narrate the ephemeral qualities that made life among the folk of rural Maine distinct, objects symbolic not only of a particular way of life recognizable as something like "a culture" but also of her characters' and her readers' connections to it.[3]

Holding a primary place among such mementos for the public at large were Jewett's own books—Jewett's books and other art objects in the regionalist mode of what was then called "local color." Not only were the things *in* Jewett's books of significance from an ethnographic perspective, but so too were her books, themselves, especially when they began to be framed *as* things.[4] Local color became popular in the post-Reconstruction era to an extent difficult to underestimate: had you opened any magazine, glanced through any journal, strolled through any gallery, what you would almost certainly have found were brief, impressionistic sketches offering glimpses of the peculiarity of life in other places, among peoples marked either by their accents, clothes, or customs as being "colorful."[5] This popularity was propelled by the same uncertainties about the classification of differences between peoples that animated the folklore vogue. As with folklore during the same period, local-color fiction was posited as an object around which ethnographic inquiries could be staged: it was no longer taken to simply be about local places and peoples, but was reimagined as being fundamentally representative of them.

The main argument of this chapter is that Jewett's books, and those of local-color writers and artists more generally, were slotted into the same epistemological framework as folklore. This move becomes visible to us when we note the new kind of thing some people were imagining literature to be: it was transposed as a material object, a "fossil shell," in the words of the influential French historian Hippolyte Taine, through which one could discern the history and character of the society from which it originated.[6] As noted by René Wellek, the field of comparative literature, pluralist in nature, emerged at this time precisely along these lines: "the treatment of the work of literature as a 'thing,' a projected object that thus can be handled as a totality, can be compared with other works, can be seen as a link in a series, and can be isolated from the mind of its creator or reader."[7] As I will explain in more detail in what follows, this object-oriented, comparativist approach had a genealogy in German historical and social scientific methodology coterminous with that of the emerging study of philology, folklore, and anthropology.

But before getting there, another problem needs to be untangled. Understandably, critics of nineteenth-century American regionalism in the last twenty years have frequently invoked an "anthropological dimension" when describing its participation in the scramble to document, understand, market, and consume the plurality of local regions—no longer, after the Civil War, to be thought of as "sections"—making up the nation.[8] As already suggested, this new dimension was typified by the appearance of both Frank Hamilton Cushing and Joel Chandler Harris on the pages of the national literary magazines; it was characterized, more broadly, by what the social historian Neil Harris has described as the "restless, sometimes desperate desire to learn the habits, the thoughts, the working patterns, and dreams of others in the community" that manifested itself in "the fiction, the newspapers, the amusements, and the education of a people."[9] But more often than not, critical deployment of the "anthropological" in the context of regional fiction has worked by way of a loose analogy, the point of which has been to bring regional fiction into line with the nationalist, racialist, and imperialist baggage attributed broadly to the field of anthropology.[10] In being "like" ethnographic writing, regionalism worked "to tell local cultures into a history of their suppression," imagined that native inhabitants "possessed primitive qualities that . . . left them in need of interpretation by outsiders," and surfaced as the "engine of power" by which "America's psychological space, like its open range and developing city space . . . [was] mapped and marketed" by capitalism.[11]

The problem with these accounts is that they have not lingered over what was perhaps the most striking aspect of the local-color craze, namely that it happened at a time when the primary structuring category of "cultures"—the category that has underpinned most moves to consider regionalism as even having an "anthropological dimension"—had not yet been formulated as such. The anthropological dimension of nineteenth-century regionalism, thus, developed without nominal recourse to an anthropological concept of culture, leaving one to puzzle over the manner in which difference might actually have been described ethnographically without it. We might be tempted to assume that local color was anticipating the culture concept, and with just a little hubris might even suggest that the anthropologists got it from writers and literary critics. The anthropologist Franz Boas, after all, invoked "literary style" when, in the 1910s, he began with greater regularity to formulate "culture" as the object of anthropology.[12] However, as critiques of the racialist and nativist tendencies of post-Reconstruction local color have gone to show, such was not exactly the case.[13] Rather, regional writers most frequently staged elaborate engagements with the older structuring categories of nation, race, and environment, in some instances (and often inadvertently) showing their limitations; not infrequently they also made visible some new categories as well, in particular that of the literary itself. Each of the three sections of this chapter explores instances of local-color fiction's intersection with different structuring categories first outlined by Taine, one of the first to use the new German historical method to study literature. The last section elucidates the ways in which Jewett's critique of the move to frame and collect her own writing as an object of ethnography evoked a realm of analysis that, had it come later on, might best have been described in terms of an anthropological concept of culture.

THE NATION: REGIONALISM AND COMPARATIVE LITERATURE

Although the politics have frequently and dramatically shifted, the critical impulse to collect local-color fiction has been most frequently driven by the sense that it represents in particularly acute terms the character of the American people. For Hamlin Garland, regional art reflected the "sincere wish to embody American life and characteristic American thought"; for Barrett Wendell in 1900 and Fred Lewis Pattee in 1915, it marked a common "literary method"; for Bliss Perry in 1912, it revealed deep commonalties under surface differences; for Arthur Hobson Quinn in 1936, it marked the strength of the union; and for Warner Berthoff in the 1959, it served to form "American masters."[14] The nationalist reading may have skipped a generation when, catalyzed by feminism, Jewett and America's female local colorists were reframed as representatives of a matriarchal subculture, a community of women.[15] But that move, which placed a gendered regionalism outside the realist/historical narrative, has seen its correction in the work of Eric Sundquist, Amy Kaplan, and Richard Brodhead; whether read in terms of ethnography or bourgeois consumption, the project of local color seems inevitably to resolve itself into that of the nation. Indeed, a recent volume on Jewett, edited by June Howard, takes as its project the articulation of the feminist, subcultural reading of Jewett with the historical narrative of nationalism.[16]

One thing to say of this talk about regionalism and the nation is that what it really has had in mind is the nation's place in the world. As Hans Kohn's classic argument suggested with regard to the historiography of political nationalism, the "age of nationalism represents the first period of

universal history" (at least to the extent that nationalism insists upon an outward comparison, a definition of the national against other nations).[17] As we
will see particularly clearly in the next chapter with William Dean Howells,
American local colorists like Jewett, Mary Murfree, Rose Terry Cooke, and
Mary Wilkins Freeman were heralded for marking what was best about
American writing, and for representing, in Howells's words, the "whole tendency of modern literature" toward regional representation.[18] The most
prominent spokesman for American literature during the period, Howells
looked to place American local colorists alongside the likes of the Russian
regionalist Ivan Turgenev and the Frenchman Alphonse Daudet. Local color,
the short story, the American magazine: even as early as 1871, these were
things in which *Harper's* critic George William Curtis could take solace, writing in a review of the country's seminal local colorists, Bret Harte and
James Russell Lowell, that the "most cynical critic will not despair of
American literature if American authors are to write such books" as they
do.[19] If compared with other national traditions, American writing stood up
nicely, thanks in large part to its local colorists.

Still, any such argument depended on an underlying sense that there
was, a priori, something particularly American about American regionalism—that literary regionalism offered a privileged point of access to the
nation. During this period, regionalism's nationalism worked by way of
synecdoche rather than analogy—by isolating literary texts as specimens of
the nation of which they were intrinsically a part rather than by pairing the
scenes described in regional fiction with an abstract ideal of America. For
example, when Hamlin Garland, American regionalism's most vociferous
proponent, defined his project, he called explicitly upon the work's "texture
and background," not upon its content: "Local color . . . means that it has
such quality of texture and back-ground that it could not have been written
in any other place or by any one else than a native."[20] It is as "indigenous as
the plant-growth"; it is "companionable and necessary, not picturesque"; the
writer "naturally carries it with him" (*Crumbling,* 54). As with folklore,
regionalism's representative quality depended on conceptualizing it as a
particular kind of text-object, something in most respects beyond authorial control, something conceptualized as being a representative part of a
larger whole.

In an excursus on "provincialism" published in *Crumbling Idols* in 1894,
Garland explicitly argued for the centrality of local color fiction to the establishment of an American national literature: "[T]he question for America to
settle is not whether it can produce something *greater* than the past, but
whether it shall produce something *different* from the past" (12). In making
"difference"—as opposed to quality—the crux of his argument against

America's continued "dependence upon England and classic models" (its "provincialism"), Garland's negative point of reference was clearly Matthew Arnold, whose influence drove the unhealthy persistence of conventional notions about "the ideal and the universal in literature"—notions that Garland held to be false (7, 10). Arnold surfaced as a counterpoint in the work from which Garland cribbed much of the chapter, Hutcheson Macauley Posnett's *Comparative Literature* (1886), wherein particularly Arnold's idea that aesthetic categories could in some way be "universal" was refuted:

> [N]either the art nor the criticism of the Greeks (or any other people) can possess that infallibility and 'natural' propriety which Mr. Arnold would admire. If we find a certain propriety in Greek classifications, it is not because they possess any universal 'nature,' but because . . . they fall in with modern modes of thought and conceptions of life.[21]

Arnold's universalism thus gave way to ideas about locality, to literature that "falls in" with "modes of thought and conceptions of life" particular both to the region from which it was produced and to the society that rekindled its reception. It needs to be understood that the comparative literature that Posnett imagined depended fundamentally on an evolutionary understanding; he was a firm proponent of the idea that literature reflected and was determined by the developmental stages of mankind. But at the same time, his interventions signaled a prescient readiness for pluralism—a pluralism as yet without any satisfactory descriptive vocabulary.

For Garland's essay, the more recognizable source was less Posnett than the French literary historian and philosopher Hippolyte Taine, who is mentioned in passing in the second paragraph. Taine should be remembered as having initiated the methodology that saw the study of literature broken down institutionally into the study of nations, as in departments of English, German, and French. He had provided the most influential midcentury statement of the relationship between literature and national character in the introduction to *Histoire de la littérature anglaise* (1863), where he argued for a reconceptualization of literature as the reflection of its author's "race, moment and milieu." Indeed, Taine placed the comparative study of national literatures (*l'étude des littératures*) at the heart of the revolution in historical practice that has also been shown to have formed Boasian anthropology—a practice new "within a hundred years in Germany, within sixty years in France"—because it "was perceived that a work of literature is not a mere play of imagination, a solitary caprice of a heated brain, but a transcript of contemporary manner."[22] Literature documented "the style of man's feelings and thoughts for centuries back," and in "these modes of feeling and thought . . . [are] embalmed facts of the highest kind." Literature is, essentially, the privileged site from which the historian can elaborate the primordial forces (*les forces primordiales*)—"la race, le milieu et le moment"—that define the elemental moral state (*état morale elementaire*) of a nation.[23] The language Taine used here is crucially important to understanding the reversal of the directionality between literature and nation. To read literature as an object in which facts are "embalmed," like reading it for its "modes of feeling and thought" (and not simply for its "feeling and thought") was to read it, as philologists did language and folklorists did tales, as a secondary artifact, a cultural specimen.

Wellek argued that Taine either did not understand or rejected the basic scientific method of other comparativist critics emerging at roughly the same time. Although Wellek's criticism may aptly signal Taine's limitations as a cultural critic in practice—Henry James remarked that Taine wrote without "that indefinable quality of spiritual initiation" into the English mind—it crucially misses the rhetorical significance of the Frenchman's formulation of the literary object.[24] For even if its application is lacking, one cannot help but be struck by the "thinginess" of literature in Taine's introduction to *Histoire*. Taine begins his argument with a wonderful series of metaphors, all of which draw attention to the artifactual kind of thing he must have imagined literature to be in order to be so bounded by race, moment, and milieu:

> Lorsque vous tournez les grandes pages roides d'un in-folio, les feuilles jaunies d'un manuscrit, bref un poëme, un code, un symbole de foi, quelle est votre première remarque? C'est qu'il ne s'est point fait tout seul. Il n'est qu'un moule, pareil à une co-quille fossile, une empreinte, pareille à l'une de ces formes dé-posées dans la pierre par un animal qui a vécu et qui a péri. Sous la coquille, il y avait un animal, et sous le document il y avait un homme. (iv)

> What is your first remark on turning over the great, stiff leaves of a folio, the yellow sheets of a manuscript—a poem, a code of laws, a declaration of faith? This, you say, was not created alone. It is but a mold, like a fossil shell, an imprint, like one of those shapes embossed in stone by an animal which lived and perished. Under the shell there was an animal, and behind the document there was a man. (1–2)

The materiality of Taine's images—"stiff leaves of a folio," "yellow sheets," "a mold," "a fossil shell," "an animal which lived and perished"—was coded to draw literature into two registers. The first was antiquarian, in the sense of the aesthetic value to be placed in old things. More dominant, however, was the second, which was the scientific and historical. Taine brought literature directly into the taxonomic categories that had been developed when recasting the study of language and folk art in the register of natural history. The materiality of Taine's literature made it analogous in most ways to words for philologists and tales for folklorists.

Taine's indebtedness to the new historical sciences coming out of Germany was explicit. His work leading up to the vaunted introduction to *Histoire* concerned itself with the philosophical problem of articulating two contrasting lines of thought coming out of Hegelian idealism and Comptean positivism. As Pascale Seys argues, Taine was swayed by positivist methodology but unsettled by its lack of interest in drawing conclusions, in looking for causal relations.[25] His solution, to find the social and historical origins of literary production, came not out of philosophy, however, but out of scientific developments in the study of philology and folklore initiated in the 1830s—from Franz Bopp and the brothers von Humboldt. Indeed, Taine specifically named these as *the* fields of historical study, to the exclusion of all others: "Nowadays, history, like zoölogy, has found its anatomy; and whatever the branch of history to which you devote yourself, philology, linguistic lore, mythology, it is by these means you must strive to produce new fruit" (6).[26] The history of ideas, of great men, or of governments, did not even enter into the new Tainian equation. Literature, rendered a strangely opaque and dense thing in the same way language and folklore had been, became a material artifact of the history of a people's origins and migration, of cross-cultural contact, conflict and acculturation, of the permanency and change of their character.

This objectification of literature underwrote Taine's historical project. Literature was of interest not for what authors actually said about their "race, moment and milieu," but for what they could not help but say about such things. Literature, like words and folklore, was the kind of thing you picked up, turned over, looked under and around, not the kind of thing you simply read. At its extreme, figurative limit, even the characteristics of the paper on which a book was printed could find its analogy in the characteristics of the people represented: "Qu'y a-t-il sous les jolis feuillets satinés d'un poëme moderne? Un poëte moderne . . . avec un habit noir et des gants, bien vu des dames" (v–vi).[27] Equated to the modern poet's satin gloves, texts were literally transposed as the fabric of society. One read the deeper meaning of words, their cultural signification, directly off the physical pages of the book.

At its core, Taine's method was linguistic, emerging most directly out of the work of Johann Gottfried Herder; and yet it differed from Herder's method in that it most often left to inference the linguistic genealogy so central to Herder's writing. Literature, not the language contained in the literature, became representative for Taine. In Herder, the primacy of language was signaled as early in his career as in the first "Fragment" of *On Recent German Literature,* where the directionality of the relationship was indicated when he deployed a syllogism whereby the *"genius* of its [a nation's] language therefore is also the genius of a nation's literature" (italics in original).[28] As confirmed in one recent study, Herder emphasized literature because he found documents of language in it—language, not literature, being "the treasury of the thought of an entire people."[29] By contrast, that moment of transliteration, from literature to culture via linguistics, went most frequently undocumented in Taine. Whereas Herder went to literature for something like data on a language, Taine turned over "les grandes pages roides d'un in-folio, les feuilles jaunies d'un manuscrit" and found on those pages something carrying its own figurative weight (iv). Like Boas fifty years later, Taine was interested in an author's "style," which might as easily be acquired by the step of the poet on the streets of seventeenth-century London as by his fluency in a culturally significant figurative language. He imagined literature functioning as the record of a people more than a record of a language. As such, literature was equivalent to language in its representational potential; both were symptoms of other, more primordial causes.

This version of literature as a synecdoche of the nation is strikingly different from that found in Washington Irving's sketches from earlier in the century. Irving is typically taken as the progenitor of American regionalism, but his work differed significantly from that of the postbellum period on these grounds. Throughout *The Sketch Book of Geoffrey Crayon, Gent.* (1819–20), the directionality of the linkage was either unspecified or exactly reversed. American literature, for example, did not come out of the native element, but rather "must grow up *side by side* with the coarser plants of native necessity."[30] Similarly, the exemplary man of letters, Roscoe, "is independent of the world around him" (18). Rather than national character being "embalmed" in the literary artifact, as Taine says, it was for Irving the role of literature "to strengthen and to embellish on national character" (*sic,* 49). Irving wrote frequently of the rural countryside in England, but what attracted him there was its aristocratic cultivation, "the influence of taste, flowing down from high sources, and pervading the lowest levels of the public mind" (52). The "rural feeling runs through British literature," he wrote, but it did so in terms of connoisseurship. The British poet makes "frequent *use of* illustrations from rural life": "A spray could not tremble in the breeze . . . but it has been *noticed by* these impassioned and delicate observers, and *wrought up into* some beautiful morality" (my emphasis, 63). The rural did not exert pressure on the type of literature being written; rather, it provided a source of inspiration for minds that were already highly cultivated.

Irving may have imagined America's own national character to be limited by the lack of evocative literary and historical associations, but that did not imply that the nation's literary production was similarly delimited by national character. The enchanting whimsicality of Irving's deployment of the character of Diedrich Knickerbocker both in *The Sketch Book* and *A History of New York* (1809) suggested as much by the way it parodied the very idea of an American historiography.[31] Especially with "Rip Van Winkle," Knickerbocker's presence confused any claims one might have wanted to make about the tale's actual connection to the Hudson River valley in particular or America generally: the tale may have come from Knickerbocker, or from his sources in the old Dutch settlements in the Catskills, or from the German superstition, or from the Native Americans who, we read, had their own somewhat similar legend. It is little wonder that no one bothered to trace its roots to German folklore until 1883. Irving made such an effort feel irrelevant, or even simpleminded. Some explanation came in the 1848 "Apology," attached to a new edition of his *History,* where Irving suggested that he layered both history and literature within the confusingly elaborate Knickerbocker framework in order to "clothe home scenes and places and familiar names with those imaginative and whimsical associations so seldom met in our new country, but which live like charms and spells about the cities of the old world, binding the heart of the native inhabitant to his home."[32] As such, the stories people told did not serve as specimens of the nation, but the stories people told about stories could help to cultivate one's attachment to it.

Later in the century, Garland and critics like Howells were striking a very different note. For Howells, the directionality described by Irving was exactly reversed. Rather than growing "side by side with the coarser plants" as in Irving, literature for Howells was, itself, a plant, "a plant which springs from the nature of a people."[33] "[L]iterature is from life" he wrote.[34] In an 1886 "Editor's Study," Howells too quoted from Posnett's *Comparative Literature* at length to the effect that, contrary to Irving's account of Roscoe, men of literary genius were nonetheless "workers in the language and ideas of their age and place," their imaginations delimited by "the associations of space and time."[35] By the time Howells wrote these lines, an entire scientific literature had developed around this point. Comparative literary methodology, both broadly nationalistic and evolutionary, had been worked out not only by Posnett but also by T. S Perry and H. H. Boyeson—all of whom were much appreciated by Howells in his *Harper's* editorials. Again, the genealogy for their positions passed back through Taine, and particularly through an epistemological shift also playing out in the emergent social sciences that reconceptualized literature as an ethnological thing, an object with a fossil-life.

The reconceptualization of literature described by Taine thus worked on a basic and widespread level to reshape literary style in the second half of the nineteenth century, but it is also interesting to note Taine's direct influence on American writers, especially the local colorists. For example, just months before writing *The Hoosier Schoolmaster* (1871), taken by many to mark the beginning of the post–Civil War local-color vogue in the United States, Edward Eggleston read Taine's *Philosophy of Art in the Netherlands* (1868) and reviewed it for *The Independent*. As Everett Carter argues, the introduction to Eggleston's second novel, *The Circuit Rider,* briefly but precisely evoked Taine's aesthetic principles. In it, the author excused what he feared some readers might have found to be the indelicacy of his treatment of the "rude as well as the heroic side of early Methodism" by claiming that his endeavor was "to produce the higher form of history, by writing truly of men as they are, and dispassionately of those forms of life that come within his scope."[36]

Almost all of the earliest American literature professors of the period have been suggested as likely "Tainians," but a clear line can be drawn between the likes of Fred Lewis Pattee (Penn State) and Moses Coit Tyler (University of Michigan), who made the socio-historical case that the American environment led to a "separate literary accent" for America (and even for the distinct localities within the United States), and Barrett Wendell (Harvard), who suggested that "our chief business concerns only the question of what contributions America has made, during its three centuries, to the literature of the English language."[37] The distinction was marked in the two accounts by the variation of keywords like American literature's "difference from" or "contribution to" literature in English. Pattee was perhaps closest to Taine, going so far as to classify his fundamental principles along the lines of race, milieu, and moment; he only changed Taine's problematically vague third term, "moment," into "epoch" and "personality." Taine's claims underwrote not only the nationalization of departments of literature in the early 1900s but also the paradigmatic strength of the "myth and symbol" school of Americanist work in the 1950s.[38] By that time, the centrality of Taine to American literary criticism had been well established, even if by 1965 Wellek could register the suspicion that "he is not read any more."[39] The nationalism carried in his objectification had the clear sympathy of local colorists like Garland and Eggleston, and as such provides us with a concrete genealogy by which to link the concerns of regionalism with those of an anthropology emerging from the new historical methodology of Herder's Germany. That link, however, came decidedly "before culture": it was less attuned to the provocations of circulation than to the romantic conflation of nation, race, and place.

RACE AND ENVIRONMENT:
THE PERSISTENCE OF LAMARCKIANISM
IN AMERICAN LITERARY THOUGHT

Taine's deployment of the categories of race, moment, and milieu as the "primordial causes" acting upon literature—and not, in a book about the history of English literature, the category of nation—should, for us, signal a kind of conflation. Not only for Taine but also for Garland and Jewett, race did not refer to a simple, biological essence, but rather to what might best be described as a Lamarckian doctrine about the inheritance of acquired characteristics. There were, as well, key differences in the way all three deployed the term race, especially when drawing distinctions between it and other categories, like the environment.

Given the type of connection between literature and national character that Taine was imagining, it is telling that he used the word "nation" very infrequently. In *Histoire,* he wrote of the nation adjectivally, as in *littérature anglaise,* instead of evoking the nation per se. In place of *l'Angleterre,* Taine generally used *le peuple* or, still more abstractly, simply *la littérature,* which followed from his triangulation of race, moment, and milieu as history's originary causes. The effect, as Anthony Appiah has pointed out, led him to begin his history of English literature not in England but Holland, along the coast of the North Sea between Scheldt and Jutland, from which place originated the Saxon race. England was not at issue because it, like literature, was a secondary product of the originary causes.[40] Taine's most explicit comment on the nation with regard to aesthetic production came in *Philosophie de l'art* (1865), where he was faced with the problem of explaining the superiority of Dutch to German painting, both being products of German racial heritage. Taine resorted to a biblical analogy: disperse your seeds in different soils and you will get different varieties of the same seed, "d'autant plus distinctes que les contrastes des divers climats seront plus forts."[41] Climate was the elemental cause, the nation the result.

The very same idea was explicitly stated by Howells, who became increasingly inspired by the scientific movement in comparative literary methodology and social scientific models of human evolution. In an 1891 "Editor's Study," he wrote that "the question is not whether this thing or that thing in an author is American or not, but whether upon the whole the author's work is such as would have been produced by a man of any other race or environment." For "all aesthetic purposes," he continued, "the American people are not a nation, but a condition. They are the old, well-known Anglo-Saxon race, affected and modified by the infusion of other strains, but not essentially changed by these, and not very different from the English at home except in their political environment, and the vastness of the scale of their development."[42]

With regard to Garland, it is interesting to note the manner in which Taine's work depended on a notion of "races" that Garland did not deploy. While new in many respects, Taine's study was formulated on a very old idea about race that linked biological and social theory. What he meant by race was similar to that old category of the *Volksgeist,* which was also consistent with the social-evolutionary notions of Lamarck.[43] Within the context of the period, this racial element proved of extreme importance to understanding the relationship of the region to the nation. Tracing his new vision back through Herder, Ottfried Müller, Goethe, Carlyle, and Sainte-Beuve, Taine used the category of race in *History* to impress upon his readers the fundamental diversity of human societies:

> They [of the preceding century] thought men of every race and century were all but identical; the Greek, the barbarian, the Hindoo, the man of the Restoration, and the man of the eighteenth century, as if they had been turned out of a common mold; and all in conformity to a certain abstract conception, which served for the whole human race. They knew man, but not men; they had not penetrated to the soul; they had not seen the infinite diversity and marvelous complexity of souls; they did not know that the moral constitution of a people or an age is as particular and distinct as the physical structure of a family of plants or an order of animals. (6)

Taine's marking of the boundaries between "a people or an age" defined in many respects the distinction between social communities that would come later with the pluralized notion of cultures. But his dependence on the category of race to mark these peoples was more than just a linguistic glitch. Shortly thereafter, he expounded on the idea that race was the most important of "[t]hree different sources [that] contribute to produce this elementary moral state," of which the other two were "the surroundings and the epoch"

(12). Taine's race concept, however, was as much social as biological. He depended on the idea of a biological transference of "aptitudes and instincts," which had been acquired in response to a "[d]ifferent climate and situation" in order to explain the pluralism of races (12). Taine was not, that is to say, strictly racist in the twentieth-century sense of pure genetics, but imagined the category of race as the conflation of social influence and biology.[44]

The wide scope and persistence in the late nineteenth century of Lamarckian thought with regard to race has been inadequately acknowledged, especially in literary criticism. It is of importance in thinking about regional literature because it allows us to see the paradoxical location of national unity in regional pluralities as part of a larger conflation of biological and social theory. As George Stocking has argued,

> The assumption that the processes of race formation were in large part social, and operated in the present through the biological mechanism of the inheritance of acquired characteristics, provided a theoretical rationale for the widespread casual misapplication of the term "race" to various national and cultural groups. If the English, the French, or the Jews were not "true" races in the strict physiological sense, they could still be spoken of as "historical" races, and as such they were in fact true races in the process of formation.[45]

This Lamarckian position—which, remember, was a forerunner *both* to a more strictly Mendelian racism (eugenics) and a more historically deterministic Boasian anthropology (cultures in the plural)—provides us with a logic for understanding the widespread belief held by late-nineteenth-century Americans that theirs was one of these "races in the process of formation."

In this respect, Garland's position should be recognized as being rather original in its quasi-total proposition of environmental determinacy. He was notably silent on the question of race in his chapter on provincialism except to the extent that he recognized the "mixture of races" as an apt topic for literary treatment; he was interested not in the German or Scandinavian races per se, but in "the marked yet subtle changes in their character" brought about upon them by the American environment (15). The assumption would seem to be that, even more profoundly than in Frederick Jackson Turner's formulation of the "crucible of the frontier," in which immigrants were "fused into a mixed race," a new "American race," Garland imagined regional environments to be directly forging a new American art.[46]

One gets Garland's environmentalism not only in *Crumbling Idols* (1894), but also in the way his short fiction from this period eschewed the development of characters who had any ability to act upon their environment. As in Jewett's *A Marsh Island,* Garland's most famous local-color sketch, "Up the Coolly," featured an urban artist, who in this instance returned to his natal village in rural Wisconsin. But unlike Dick Dale in Jewett's novel, Howard McLane found only misery upon his return. The story turns on the conflict between this older son, who had escaped the hardships of rural life for a successful career in theater, and his younger brother, who had been "crushed" by the circumstances of his agricultural existence.[47] The sketch resists, strenuously, the attribution of blame for the circumstances. As the successful older brother summarizes the case when trying to resolve the conflict with his resentful brother, "[l]uck made me and cheated you" (86). It is an analysis the story endorsed. The narrator frequently refers to events in terms of "epic" and "tragedy," presumably in the formal sense of resisting the possibility that mere human agency might have altered the situation.[48]

Jewett's work reveals a vastly different orientation in its embrace both of Arnoldian and Lamarckian doctrines about race, but is remarkably demonstrative, nonetheless, of the ineluctable power of the environment on regional plurality. As has often been noted, Jewett was devoted to Matthew Arnold both personally and intellectually.[49] But she was also a very visible Lamarckian. Her only historical work, *The Story of the Normans* (1890), was a classic in this sense, a long account of the Norman "race" and the "rich inheritance" it had bequeathed both to England and America.[50] Similarly, her most successful novel before *The Country of the Pointed Firs, A Country Doctor* (1884), explicitly staged the Lamarckian question of acquired characteristics, asking whether its heroine, Nan, could tame the clever but wild "traits of her ancestors."[51] "It seems to me," noted the country doctor who had adopted Nan,

> that up to seven or eight years of age children are simply bundles of inheritances, and I can see the traits of one ancestor after another; but a little later than the usual time she [Nan] began to assert her own individuality, and has grown capitally well in mind and body ever since. (212)

This most typical Lamarckian combination of social and biological traits—"mind and body"—carried over in all of Jewett's work, including *The Country of the Pointed Firs,* in which "French descent" was indicated as the source both of Mrs. Blackett's "appearance and her charming gifts" (body and mind) and of the Bowden family's "inheritance of good taste"; it was altogether in the Lamarckian vein that a "common inheritance" was celebrated as having priority over such "lesser rights" as birthright and custom (462, 465, 469).

Despite recent critical attention to Jewett's racial attitudes, this Lamarckian influence on her thought—the combination of social traits with biological inheritance—has not been acknowledged, a fact that leads to a misreading of the cloudy relationship between her Arnoldian allegiance to universalism and the particularity of the regional communities she sketches. Jewett deployed a Lamarckian doctrine, which helps explain her concomitant acknowledgment of "racial" pluralism and Arnoldian universalism. The evolutionary nature of Lamarckianism actually insisted on the unilinearity of progress through social or cultural stages.[52] Social evolutionary theory may strike us as distasteful, but it nonetheless insisted, in a way that more blatantly offensive race doctrines did not, upon the unity of man.

The key to understanding Jewett's sketches in this respect becomes the fact that social difference in her work was a difference between biological likes, the blood lines between rural and urban characters being the same, their Lamarckian inheritance shared. The natives of Dunnet Landing in *The Country of the Pointed Firs* repeatedly surface as individuals very much like individuals everywhere, "exactly the same types . . . as in the most brilliant city company," different only because "a narrow set of circumstances had caged a fine able character and held it captive" (466). The potential for universal similarity through shared "inheritance" was fortified by the stunning lack of morphological distinction in the characters inhabiting Jewett's Maine. Her communities were racially pure in a way that departed from the practice of her predecessors in New England regional fiction, most notably from Nathaniel Hawthorne as suggested by the historical centrality of the region's Indian tribes to *The Scarlet Letter* (1850). But there were no Indians in Jewett's New England, and there were but very few Indian relics, a stray allusion to Indians as early inhabitants of Shell Heap Island being the only notice of them in *The Country of the Pointed Firs.* Nor were there African Americans, not even as slaves on the ships so fondly remembered to be sailing out of Maine en route to what, historically, we know to have been the "triangle trade" along the African coast and in the Caribbean. Recent study has brought to light Jewett's Irish immigrant stories, and there remains the prominent example of racial difference in her Dunnet Landing story "The Foreigner," but among the core group of Maine folk on whom her interest fell, there were no significant racial barriers between populations.[53]

While one might read this racial delimitation as typical of the manner in which American regionalism worked to "forget" the more explosive racial conflicts taking place, it should also be recognized as isolating the sociobiological binary in such a way as to leave the environment as the sole cause of difference.[54] Of all her works, *The Country of the Pointed Firs* was the most particular about delimiting itself to a particular place. The first short chapter, for example, isolated Dunnet Landing by repeating the narrator's arrival in consecutive sentences: "After a first brief visit made two or three summers before in the course of a yachting cruise, a lover of Dunnet Landing returned. . . . One evening in June, a single passenger landed upon the steamboat wharf" (377). This repetition seems to signal a felt need to dislocate Dunnet Landing from the national infrastructure put into place by the tourist industry, the yachting circuit. Its isolation might be contrasted to the Maine of Elizabeth Stoddard's *The Morgesons* (1861), wherein the patriarch was a sea merchant and his home littered with exotic markings of the global economy—Turkish rugs and carvings of idols, talk of the slave and rum trades, exotic objects, *The Arabian Nights,* a library stacked with books of travel and adventure. Jewett's villages remained at all times postcosmopolitan, even when they were set far in the historical past, as in *The Tory Lover* (1901). The village life portrayed in this romance set in the year 1777 recalls that of Dunnet Landing, its "busy, quick-enriching days of the past seemed to be gone forever . . . the town must live long now upon their hoarded gains."[55] The cosmopolitanism of Maine's great shipping days were always one generation past in Jewett's work, her Maine serving always as a marker of geographical isolation.

From the anthropological perspective, what Jewett inevitably addressed in *The Country of the Pointed Firs* was a variation on the same question of interpreting the contrasts between the local and the universal when, in Lamarckian terms and in the interest of the nation, there should have existed none. This problem was raised explicitly in *The Tory Lover,* the plot of which turns on the question of how individuals of the same breeding can possibly hold different opinions on such a basic question as American allegiance to or independence from the British crown. In *The Country of the Pointed Firs,* this problem also seems to be behind Jewett's extended focus on three male characters—Captain Littlepage, William, and Elijah Tilley—who are, among Dunnet's isolated characters, particularly bereft. Captain Littlepage, arguably the most traveled and cosmopolitan of Dunnet's regular inhabitants, laments the way "that a community narrows down and grows dreadful ignorant when it is shut up to, its own affairs," but his own experience of travel has left him mildly insane, prone to, in his words, "comprehend the universe" in terms of "fog-shaped men" in a "waiting-place between this world an' the next" (389, 390, 396, 397). One sees even further the narrowing of "masculine possibility" in Elijah Tilley, one of the old fishermen who had never gotten over the loss of his wife, a man who in receiving the narrator at his home does not put down his "knitting of a blue yarn stocking" (476). Joanna Todd considers Tilley a "ploddin' man," but the narrator is more sympathetic to the environmental influences that created the "inner life and thought of these self-contained old fishermen" (483, 473). There is, Jewett's narrator seems to say, a local explanation for his failure to move about, to put down his knitting and acquire a broader, more diverse perspective.

But the contrast between the masculine possibility—that with universal potential—and the limitations of place is most poignantly produced in Jewett's treatment of Joanna Todd's brother, William, who though nearly sixty years old still lives out on Green Island with their mother. When the narrator goes on a visit to the island, William takes her to a promontory with a spectacular view "over all the island . . . the ocean that circled this and a hundred other bits of island-ground, the mainland shore and all the far horizons" (413). The narrator writes that:

> It gave a sudden sense of space, for nothing stopped the eye or hedged one in,—that sense of liberty in space and time which great prospects always give.
>
> "There ain't no such view in the world, I expect," said William proudly, and I hastened to speak my heartfelt tribute of praise; it was impossible not to feel as if an untraveled boy had spoken, and yet one loved to have him value his native heath. (413)

The paternalism of this passage speaks to the recognition that no matter how sympathetic, William's perception is marred by his inability to access other comparative views. His appreciation of the "liberty in space and time" evoked by this particular view is limited by his prolonged isolation on the island, his "untraveled" perspective. In Tainian terms, "space" as such becomes the antimilieu, the movement across perspectival frames that would provide other ways to process one's "native heath"—frames that, from Jewett's perspective, would free one from the deterministic outlook of Taine's historical methodology. Only the narrator could properly appreciate this view, for to appreciate the liberatory potential from space and time in the local requires something more than an "instinctive" sense of the category of beauty—and too, it needs something more than just travel. It is beyond both race and environment, beyond the register of natural history that Taine, following a line from Herder, had brought to the study of literature. What it needed, Jewett implied, was a sense for the literary, itself.

MOMENT: LITERARY STYLE IN THE
EMERGENCE OF THE CULTURE CONCEPT

Of Taine's primordial causes, *le moment* has been the least appreciated. Even if one disputes their presuppositions, race and environment make immediate sense as being determinative of the range of expression that might be open to an author, but moment is more difficult for the way it moves from the stage of production to that of circulation, reception, and retranslation. Wellek writes that moment brought a historical sense to the otherwise static race-milieu structure: "Its [moment's] main function is to serve as a reminder that history is dynamic while milieu is static."[56] But what it also brought was a more precise understanding of the effect of literature and the arts within the mix, which moved the analysis away from the natural forces delimiting the production of literature to something like the cultural forces stimulating it. Or, as Taine wrote, "for with the forces within and without, there is the work which they have already produced together, and this work itself contributes to produce what follows" (16).[57]

As such, moment was as close as Taine got to formulating an "elemental cause" that, given another conceptual frame, might have been taken as defining an anthropological idea of "culture." The particular attribute Taine gave to "moment," which was also most telling of its place in his system, was acquired speed, "la vitesse acquise" (xxviii). Taine's English translator thus made a mistake in translating it as "epoch": moment defined not so much "an age," for example the Renaissance, as the speed with which literature (and other arts, customs, beliefs, sayings) were taken up within a given society, the "momentum" that differentiated human input from natural scientific causes like race and milieu. The category of moment attended to the dissemination and collection of texts, and, as such, takes us back to the realm of fashion that Jewett was critiquing in *A Marsh Island:* to the delineation not simply of the folk living on the island but to Dick Dale's paintings of them.

The moment of local color was defined by its social scientific significance and by its fashionable aesthetics. And yet one would tend not to not want to hear of regionalism in terms of literary fashion if, as for Garland, the point was to access folk thought. Fashion would seemingly distance writing from the region by adding to it. The relationship between art and society could hardly be synecdochical if art "put in" more than the region, itself, provided. For Garland, there seems to have been an almost literal desire to collapse the book into the everyday life of the people it described. When he went to publish his manifesto, *Crumbling Idols,* he chose the Chicago fine-arts house of Stone and Kimball to bring it out. The volume made the case, with ample bravura, for a literature "rooted in the soil" and "rich in real utterances," one that might adequately treat such ethnographic topics as "the immigration of farmers . . . ; the mingling of races; the feudalistic ownership of lands; the nomadic life of the farmhands, the growth of cities, the passing of Spanish civilization" (50, 22, 23). These Tainian, broadly historical pressures were coupled in suggestive ways to the physical characteristics of the book. One reviewer of *Crumbling Idols* remarked on Stone and Kimball's fine handling of it only to suggest wryly that it "should have been printed on birch bark and bound in butternut homespun, and should have had for cover design a dynamite bomb, say, with sputtering fire-tipped fuse."[58] And as already mentioned, some books actually were. One bibliophile, in talking more generally about the excellence of cloth covers on American books, brought up the first edition of the local colorist George Washington Cable's New Orleans novella, *Madame Delphine,* olive with a floral decoration in red, in the context of how important it was for the cover of a book to "suit its complexion."[59] And so, that with which book covers were costumed became something like anthropological content, such that when you purchased a book you got not just the words on the page but the fantasy of fragments from the physical record of the peoples under textual observation.

Without making too much of these anecdotes, we might at the least say that they brought to light the pressures which, in a remarkably literal way, animated Jewett's treatment of Dick Dale's sketches of the rural maiden in *A Marsh Island.* Jewett was clearly against this move to objectify literature as an artifact. In the novel, she had Dick Dale set his mind to collecting Mrs. Owen's jug and also her daughter, whom he repeatedly imagines in terms of a local color sketch. "What a picture for a man to paint," he thinks with dawning appreciation of her in the opening chapters; and how, later, he might like to set the girl "in *its* rightful place, among the *books* and *pictures* and *silks*" in his New York studio, all of these *things*—the girl, books, pictures and silks—receiving his attention and appreciation equally (186, 257, my italics). This equivalency is clearly wrong, Dale's urge to objectify the girl getting in the way of what should be his romantic attachments. The point that the novel registers is not the impossibility of romantic love between the country and the city, the folk and the collectors of folklore; rather, it is of the need to scrutinize moves like Dale's, and like Garland's, to conflate lived life and writing, the raw and the cooked.

In order to insist upon their categorical discontinuity, Jewett staged regionalism as an aesthetically fashionable commodity. This move not only shielded the country girl from the wrong kind of gaze, but also set the aesthetic object, which was also Jewett's own book, in a different kind of relationship to her. Dick Dale's mistaken apprehension of the girl as a thing signaled Jewett's unease with the mistaken idea that her work was a thing like the girl, a mere consequence of race and milieu.

As if to assert itself disciplinarily, anthropology also moved against this trend, though in the other direction, in order to distinguish the ethnological from the fashionable. When Edward Sapir in the 1920s argued that a "genuine culture" was one in which the "immediate ends" of survival and the "remoter ends" of aesthetic development were connected, he revised in modernist terms a well established anthropological line of divide between what William Henry Holmes, a Smithsonian anthropologist who had also studied art in Europe in the late 1870s, called the "mechanical," "technical," and "nature-derived" elements and the "aesthetic forces of the human mind."[60] Although Holmes's conclusions were evolutionary and Sapir's relativist, they both started with the old, romanticist premise that while immediate ends and aesthetics had been proximate in primitive societies, they were divergent in modern ones. And as such, their formulation provided the same backdrop as *A Marsh Island,* where being fashionable ultimately limited a reader or collector's ability to connect with the folk, disqualifying synecdochical representational authority, sending Dick Dale home empty-handed.

These were the same terms that animated Franz Boas's 1903 discussion of "The Decorative Art of the North American Indians." Significantly, however, Boas contradicted Holmes and, preemptively, his future student, Sapir, in ways we saw him do in the previous chapter with the study of language and folklore. Boas began by acknowledging Holmes, among others, for the thesis that "the decorative designs used by primitive man do not serve esthetic ends, but . . . suggest to his mind certain definitive concepts."[61] But as with folklore, Boas's intervention insisted, instead, upon an appreciation of the detachability of art from any such "definitive concepts." In a move of extreme importance for seeing the emergence of the culture concept out of the romantic conflation of nation, race, and environment that proceeded it, Boas stressed the historical significance of the distribution of artistic designs across Indian tribes regardless of the specific ideas attached to them; more precisely, he found that the same design technique in different places could mean different things. Following an argument initially outlined by A. D. F. Hamlin, Boas argued that decorative technique was "carried across seas and lands, and in new hands receives still another dress in combinations still more incongruous with its original significance. It is no longer a symbol, but an arbitrary ornament, wholly conventional, modified to suit the taste and the arts of the foreigners who have adopted it" (547).[62] This pattern of dissemination would have challenged the idea that an isomorphic relationship attained between the meaning of decorative art and its supposed origins in primordial causes like the nation, race, and environment. Art was not necessarily "indigenous," as in Garland's formulation; instead, the rapidity (or in Taine's words the momentum) of its diffusion signaled the limitations of a conceptual apparatus that conceived of the relationships between the origins of a people and the origins of its art in terms of the natural sciences.

For Boas, this argument was always part of a two-step moving from diffusion to reception. The emphasis on diffusion in the first step defused racial and evolutionary claims; the second step attempted to understand how the particular re-expression of the disseminated element delineated real differences between peoples. In the case of decorative techniques, Boas's conclusions were striking in that they suggested that American Indians told themselves the same stories about indigenous origins and isomorphism that Hamlin Garland was telling himself. Although a uniform style of decorative elements was distributed across different tribes all over the western United States, the way they were explained varied from place to place—and within particular tribes from time to time. These explanations showed that there was generally an attempt to associate certain techniques to specific ideas, but that the explanations did little to show the actual history of the technique's origin. Rather, Boas concluded that the "idea which a design expresses at the present time is not necessarily a clue to its history. It seems probable that idea and style exist independently, and influence each other constantly" (562). To reframe Boas's claim but slightly, one might say he showed decorative art to be responsive neither to race nor to milieu, but rather to "moment," or to the manner in which people repeatedly found themselves living in worlds constructed from a fabric not of their own making.

In this vein, the object lesson that Jewett provided might be rewritten in terms of the access that the fashion for regionalism described in her books, as well as the fashion for her books as regional artifacts, provided to the emergent anthropological category of culture. It is telling that recent literary criticism has sought both to complicate and to ease back on reading regionalism for its "anthropological dimension." On the one hand is the resurgence of a feminist reading of regionalism, particularly in the work of Marjorie Pryse and Judith Fetterley, which insists against Kaplan, Sundquist, and Brodhead that regionalism worked "to dismantle and deconstruct hierarchies based on the categories of gender, race, class, age, and region." [63] And on the other is a line, expressed most convincingly by Carrie Tirado Bramen, which argues that "[t]here is no ideological position intrinsic to locality" by attending, instead, to the varieties of approaches to the writing and marketing of the form. [64] Recent work on Jewett has followed suit by drawing her later writing into the less ethnological, more aesthetic times of the fin de siècle art world. Sandra Zagarell has noticed changes in the covers of Jewett's novels, especially the increasingly aestheticized cover of *The Country of the Pointed Firs,* to argue that Jewett increasingly framed alterity as a cultural commodity.[65] Similarly, Laurie Shannon has analogized Jewett's approach to character with that of French *intimiste* painters like Vuillard and Bonnard.[66]

What seems to be taken as a given in all of these instances is the sentiment that in shedding, on occasion, its distasteful ideological baggage, regionalism is in some sense more recognizably distinct from anthropology. Indeed, as Tirado Bramen puts it, "local color is not a form of literary primitivism," as those associating it with anthropology might have it, but is rather "the apex of aesthetic development, because it captured the heterogeneous web of spatial dependencies characteristic of the modern moment" (126). As will become abundantly clear in the next chapter, I am far from thinking that Tirado Bramen is wrong either in her assessment of regionalism's "aesthetic development" or in her desire to link it to modernity. But neither am I ready to give up on what seems to become more than a mere analogy linking regionalism and anthropology. The turn to the aesthetic was no less an intervention in the anthropological, for what it suggested were those elements of the human subject that resided outside the categories of difference—nation, race, and place—by which they had been understood up to that time.

The Country of the Pointed Firs marks this aesthetic engagement with a wonderful excess of descriptive precision, not by cross-referencing the fashion for local color, as in *A Marsh Island.* There are many differences between the two texts, but perhaps the most striking stems from the qualitative sharpening of Jewett's language. Whereas *A Marsh Island* offers a third-person critique of fashionable collectors like Dick Dale, *The Country of the Pointed Firs* is a first-person synthesis of the position of the collector—a synthesis made possible by the narrative's fluency, delicacy, and exactness. In *A Marsh Island,* Dale's most acute observations offer at their best only a birch tree with "a touch of uncommon color on some of its leaves, which had been changed early" (4); similarly in *Deephaven,* the girls had found the "fresh sea air . . . welcome after the dusty day, and it seemed so quiet and pleasant" (13). In *The Country of the Pointed Firs,* by contrast, when the narrator takes on extra work for Mrs. Todd, it is because of "pennyroyal time . . . when the rare lobelia was in its prime and the elecampane was coming on" (383). The front of Mrs. Blackett's cottage is entangled in "portulacas all along under the lower step and straggling off into the grass, and clustering mallows that crept as near as they dared, like poor relations (408). On the way out to Mrs. Blackett's, Mrs. Todd "only stopped to underrun a trawl, for the floats of which [she] looked earnestly," and coming into shore she "took a firmer grasp of the sheet, and gave an impatient look up at the gaff and the leech of the little sail, and twitched the sheet as if she urged the wind like a horse" (403, 405).

There is an exquisite clarity of line in such descriptions, an ease in finding the names of the "rare lobelia" and "elecampane," or the verb to use when fishing along "trawls." Jewett's fluency makes this region pleasurably accessible to the "out-world" of readers, gives substance to the bibliophile's collection of books, a sense of "liberty and space" to the reader widely traveled enough to recognize its particularity. The point, however, is that such language was clearly the narrator's own, not that of the folk, and as such the access it provides to Dunnet Landing comes not *in* the writing, but *from* the writing. This may seem like an obvious point to make about a piece of fiction, but in the context of the epistemological confusion between ethnological and literary objects that I have been describing, it becomes significant of the subtlety of Jewett's play on category distinctions. She marked the literary as something that moved in time and circulated spatially in interesting and unique ways.

Rather than any direct access to the folk, *The Country of the Pointed Firs* always holds itself apart, not exactly trying to sequester itself from the region, but searching nonetheless for the proper balance between lived life and the aesthetic. From the start, this becomes an issue for the narrator as she negotiates between an "unwise curiosity" for the herbalist preoccupations of her host and the "long piece of writing, sadly belated now, which I was bound to do" (380). Privileging the latter implies, specifically, entering into a different perspectival orientation toward Dunnet Landing. Most immediately, the narrator must find seclusion during the day from Mrs. Todd's home, where "cheerful voices" and "friendly gossip" leave her with an "idle pen" (382). She rents out the "little white schoolhouse" high on "the brink of the hill" above the village, from which her access to the Dunnet folk is framed by "one of the seaward windows" (382, 383). We are not meant to miss this window, which is again drawn to our attention on the next page with the chapter title, "At the Schoolhouse Window" (384). It is through these windows, literally frames, that the narrator refigures not only her own relationship to Dunnet Landing but also that of *The Country of the Pointed Firs.*

This perspective manifests itself as she watches her friends and acquaintances passing below her in the distance for the funeral of Mrs. Begg, a scene that initiates the narrator's only prolonged reflection on her own writing. Mrs. Begg, having been "very much respected," was being followed to her grave by "a large company of friends"; the narrator, still in her Sunday dress from the church ceremony and watching the others from her schoolhouse, wonders if she had not better have stayed to walk with them (384). Not being there reminds all concerned, including herself, that she "did not really belong to Dunnet Landing" (386). But it also disrupts her writing, signaled in the text by a temporal double take on the scene. We read that,

> Now and then a bee blundered in and took me for an enemy; but there was a useful stick upon the teacher's desk, and I rapped to call the bees to order . . . or waved them away from their riots over the ink, which I had bought at the Landing store, and discovered too late to be scented with bergamot, as if to refresh the labors of anxious scribes. (385)

But then, as if to unwrite these lines, the narrator tells us in the next that "[o]ne anxious scribe felt very dull that day"; "The sentences failed to catch these lovely summer cadences" (385). Following on the earlier lines, these cadences are both written and erased. Jewett leaves us with lines on the riot of bees written as if over the palimpsest of lived life itself, as if reenacting on the page the liminality of belonging, but "not really" to the life of the village. Catching the summer cadences, but also failing to do so, the text advances in two temporalities, one of the book and the other of Dunnet Landing. When at the end of the chapter the narrator turns back to Dunnet time, she returns to a paper divided significantly between the written and the unwritten: "I sighed, and turned to the half-written page again" (386). The paper's equal division between unwritten and written signals, "again," the division between the scenes above and below, the temporality of *The Country of the Pointed Firs* and that of Mrs. Begg's funeral, the aesthetic and the lived life (385, 386).

As one would expect, the novel deepens its acquaintance with Dunnet Landing by entering into the scene of the everyday, such as the visits with Mrs. Todd's mother and friends, a voyage to the Bowden family reunion, a retired conversation with Elijah Tilley. But the moments of grand perspective that it highlights are equally significant for keeping attention focused on the text's own aesthetic maneuvering. The country road leading to the Bowden's reunion, for example, offers another view from "the top of a hill" that signals, oddly, that "the country" of the text is something of a perspectival mirage: "spread out before us [was] a wonderful great view of . . . distant shores like another country in the midday haze which half hid the hills beyond, and the far-away pale blue mountains on the northern horizon" (455). Similarly, as the narrator leaves Dunnet at the end of the summer, she watches from her "coastwise steamer" as the village sinks "back into the uniformity of the coast . . . indistinguishable from the other towns that looked as if they were crumbled on the furzy-green stoniness of the shore" (486, 487). One is left to wonder where Dunnet's distinction lies, what constitutes it as a place, how its borders are defined. If, at the beginning of the summer, the narrator had disembarked elsewhere along that "furzy-green stoniness," would her summer have opened out along a similar plane? Whereas one might be tempted to process such scenes in terms of the picturesque, the grandiloquent expanse of nature and the sublime that comes with the long view, *The Country of the Pointed Firs'* evocation of them serves, rather, to balance the lived life and the aesthetic—to return the text figuratively to the state of the half-written page. It distances the narration from folk life, showing that life to be determined, a priori as it were, from a frame that is essentially literary. The literary becomes the category of differentiation itself.

Nowhere is this aestheticist line pursued more explicitly than when the narrator and William mount the hillside behind Mrs. Blackett's home on Green Island. As the two come out over "an open bit of pasture at the top of the island," William picks a "a few sprigs of late blooming-linnaea," giving them to the narrator without speaking: "he knew as well as I that one could not say half he wished about linnaea" (413). This silence on the subject of linnaea, counterpoised as it is to the easy precision noted in many other aspects of the narrator's speech, is suggestive of "moments" in the text where narration fails to account for the meaning of things. One thinks, for example, of the "quicker signal" by which Mrs. Todd and her mother communicate, "heart on the shore to the heart on the sea," the wordlessness of that signal indicating their "deeper intimacy" (405, 381). Bill Brown notes such silences, especially as they attach to objects like the coral pin that Mrs. Todd gives to the narrator at the end of the novel, to suggest Jewett's suppression of the ethnological, her "attention to the human suffering and endurance that is neither regional nor national, that is neither rural nor cosmopolitan, that is irreducible to being Anglo-American or Native American, and for which there is no concrete evidence."[67] And, indeed, Jewett seems to play on just such a dynamic by having silence accrue specifically around "linnaea," a plant named after the eighteenth-century botanist Carolus Linnaeus, whose taxonomy is still used to classify plant and animal species in the natural sciences. "One cannot say half he wished about linnaea," the wish, itself, being that which is beyond the linnaean taxonomy, beyond words, ephemeral in is immateriality, and as such intensely human.

But the linnaea signals, as well, the connection between lived life and the literary, William and the narrator's painting of him. Linnaea, a flat, glossy evergreen that grows in mats with small, delicate leaves, is native to much of North America. It is also known as twinflower, having two bell-shaped blooms descending from a single stem. William and the narrator, twinned in the commonality of their sentiments, continue up toward "the highest point" from which they could see the ocean circling the island, a point described with a play on the novel's title as "there above the pointed firs" (413). And yet, as they approach this country above the pointed firs, the differences between them become pronounced. As noted before, looking out from this perspective, the narrator registers "a sudden sense of space . . . that sense of liberty in space and time which great prospects always give" (413). She describes not simply a taxonomic space, a place on a map, but a philosophy of art. From this perspective, which we know from its repetition elsewhere to be the point of access to the aesthetic, the "sense of liberty in space and time" signals the acquired speed that comes from the literary, the momentum that differentiates it from more stationary categories of affiliation, namely that of the geographical place of the region.

But for William, the flower to which the narrator is at this moment un-twinned, "[t]here ain't no such view in the world" (413). She looks on to him with affection, "it was impossible not to feel as if an untraveled boy had spoken" (413). The aesthetic perspective is defined here against the ethnological import of William's dialect. And yet the point is not in its difference but in characterizing the nature of that difference. Apparently William needs to do some more reading, for you do not get "above the pointed firs" by walking. But then we are left to ask where does that leave that half unspoken wish about linnaea? Surely it cannot be separated from the ethnological, but neither can its characteristics be understood without understanding its momentum within the fashion for local color, its speed acquired with its object-life as a book. And as such, even as she wrote against the impulse to the anthropological that would classify her book as linnaea—an isomorphic specimen of a fixed network of nation, race , and place—*The Country of the Pointed Firs* models the stylistic difference literature makes. In a sense, it models what was "beyond" the categories of natural history, that realm of human interaction that anthropology would later deploy the culture concept to describe.

CHAPTER FOUR

HOWELLSIAN CHIC

The Local Color of Cosmopolitanism

We who are nothing but self, and have no manner of being
    Save in the sense of self, still have no other delight
Like the relief that comes with the blessed oblivion freeing
    Self from self in the deep sleep of some dreamless night.

Losing alone is finding; the best of being is ceasing
    Now and again to be. Then at the end of this strife,
That which comes, if we will it or not, for our releasing,
    Is it eternal death, or is it infinite life?

—William Dean Howells, "Sphinx" (1894)

Had Sarah Orne Jewett's country maiden from *A Marsh Island* (1885), Doris Owen, decided to go off with the bohemian artist Dick Dale to a life of heady, urban aestheticism, she could have hoped for no better end than to have become William Dean Howells's Alma Leighton, from *A Hazard of New Fortunes* (1890). The two women's circumstances are remarkably similar, both of them familiar characters from the archives of New England regional fiction. Like Doris Owen, Alma Leighton grew up in one of those picturesque vacation destinations scattered someplace between Vermont, New Hampshire, or Maine; like Doris, her mother kept a summer boarder who happened to be a young bohemian artist who had come with the purpose of making some sketches of the local scene; and like Doris, she became romantically involved with him. The difference between them is that, rather than staying at home in rural Maine, Alma travels to New York. Like Doris, she ultimately rejects her bohemian suitor, but she does so not to remain true to her roots in the country but to become a bohemian artist herself. It is Alma's sketch for the cover of the novel's new illustrated magazine, *Every Other Week,* that sets the aesthetic framework for the novel. Her sketch was "chic," "awfully chic"—and, because she knows that it's "the nearest way to illustrating," and thus to making it as an artist in the big city, she's going to keep on "doing these *chic* things."[1]

"Chic" is not a word frequently attached to Howells, nor would one be prone to mistake him for a local-color writer. But what Howells formulated with his deployment of Alma Leighton in *A Hazard of New Fortunes* was a theory of taste that linked the American taste for the "ethnographic" aspects of local-color writing with the aesthetic arts movement—*Japonisme,* simple line drawings, languid women, flowered screens, art advertising, George Du Maurier's *Trilby,* lithography, posters, the blurring of image and text, little magazines, the French, cloying stamens, luscious pistils, and abundant cigarettes. Here, seemingly, we are further than ever from the culture concept, further afield on the drift begun with attention to folklore as a circulating, public object.

Alma's regionalism and her chic design are inextricably linked in the novel. She is a specimen from the local color movement that Howells and his readers would surely have recognized as a type—Jewettesque or Wilkins-Freemanesque. Her bohemian love interest, Beaton, who also hails from the locally colored rural northeast, would have known her as such from trips he had made to New Hampshire "sketching for one of the illustrated papers" (149). But she is also in circulation, moving about in Manhattan, producing covers and illustrations for the trendy new magazine, refusing to marry, making her way in the commercial mode of high aesthetics. Her Manhattan art instructor, something of a misogynist, despairs of her talent, but at the same time signals her out as an aesthete, a "case of art for art's sake" (212).

It is no secret that Howells promoted local-color fiction and local colorists—fiction with the ethnological content needed to "get the whole of American life into our fiction"—in his editorial writing.[2] However, his deployment of Alma in conjunction with *chicness* opens up questions about the parameters of that promotion and about an assumption held in common by the two prominent lines of contemporary critique of late-nineteenth and early-twentieth-century regionalism. Whether reading regionalism as an ideologically inflected geography of peoples and nations, or as an aesthetic commodity, critics have assumed that regionalism was about regions.[3] It has been taken as a given that both the form's ideological and market charge came from the way the fiction conceptualized and represented regional locales. However, even if thinking somewhat anachronistically, Alma's chic locality had very little to do with what we might think of as a "regional culture," a geographically isolated placed defined, either positively or negatively, by the integrity of its folk spirit or its pastoral attachment to nature.

Rather, it had to do with the aesthetic charge produced by the *dislocation* of Alma and her sketches from the region as they were routed through the urban, internationalist space of the fin de siècle art market. What made Alma chic was the confluence of the local and the cosmopolitan in her designs and in her mode of living; as such, regionalism in this account had less to do with a sense of place than with a dynamic of circulation.

In this chapter I want to argue that regionalism gains in aesthetic and theoretical interest, both for Howells and us, to the extent that it is (and was) seen to circulate in a transnational network of distribution. The point is to articulate the complicated relationship between circulating culture and the imagined isomorphism discussed in the previous chapters; in this instance, the relationship between the two projected regional fiction into the realm of a developing international market for ethnographic art. At the point when connecting with a region means picking up a book, and when an audience becomes conscious of regional writing as an object of art—or, even more crassly, as a cultural commodity—attention has already swung away from the locale described. Locality remains, but, like the origins of a folktale, only as a palimpsest over which new associations and meanings can be accreted. This point was reached in American local-color writing by the 1890s. What the character of Alma so nicely encapsulates is Howells's sentiment of localized forms and experiences that were all circulating, available to people who were also circulating, in newly conceived-of commercial, aesthetic, and ideological relationships.

But what Howells's development of her character might also reveal is a frequently overlooked characteristic of certain local colorists more properly defined, like Lafcadio Hearn, Alice Dunbar Nelson, or Kate Chopin. At least by this later phase of local color writing, in the 1890s and early 1900s, many people would have felt that the very idea of a discrete region being represented in writing would already have been transformed by the public taste for alterity. Even as he wrote it in 1893, Hamlin Garland's line on the isomorphic relationship between local color and a geographically homogeneous place was being recast in terms of the transnational fashion for local commodities; even more remarkably, local colorists had begun to deploy transnational aesthetic fashions to delimit in aesthetic terms a sense of regional places. Paradoxically, the local came to be defined by the deployment of artistic tropes that were, themselves, transnational in origin. And so, what Howells's definition of the local as the chic helps us recover is the chicness of later local-color writing *tout court*—a chicness making local color visible in a proto-primitivist mode, where its "anthropological dimension" would have evoked not its content but its point of departure, not what it was about but how far it was from its point of origin.[4]

LOCALISM'S GLOBAL PURCHASE

In one of the more theoretically savvy recent assessments of regionalism, Roberto Dainotto argues that the political, epistemological, and ideological concerns about race, gender, and the nation that have preoccupied recent assessments of the form are made visible by a different kind of problem altogether: "What, or where, in fact, is this 'region' where aesthetics and literature survive unchanged, undivided by social conflicts, and free 'despite political, religious, or psychological interference'?"[5]. Dainotto's response is that the region is no place at all, but rather is a "utopia" of "ideal places . . . from which we can begin to sanitize our present."[6] And in this, he is very much in line with critics who have argued more particularly in the context of American regionalism post-Reconstruction that the form stood ideologically for a nationalism out of repair, a nationalism troubled by the standardization of industrialism and the racial and ethnic impurity of the modern city.

It is certainly true that Howells's deployment of local color can be slotted into a model that understands the desire for regionalism in terms of an antimodernist nostalgia—a nostalgia that, as discussed in the previous chapter, literary critics have been too quick to associate with anthropology.[7] For example, Howells found, in his analysis of Mary Wilkins Freeman's local-color sketches, that a "[c]ommunity of character abounds: the people are of one New England blood, and speak one racy tongue."[8] To the extent that he would have known the territory of Wilkins Freeman to be more heterogeneous than suggested by such a phrase, Howells seemingly participated in the kind of practice that, as argued by Amy Kaplan, "effaced" more explosive urban and racial conflicts by "rendering social difference in terms of region, anchored and bound by separate spaces."[9] Elsewhere, Howells enacted the post-Reconstruction push for national reconciliation carried on mainly in the nation's elite literary monthlies when he wrote that "a great number of very good writers are instinctively striving to make each part of the country and each phase of our civilization known to the other parts."[10] With the word "instinctively," moreover, he suggested what became the more explicitly nativist conceptualization of local color that we saw working in Garland. As an instinctual way of being, or as a nativist birthright, this version of regionalism offered something of a therapeutic retreat from the transient uncertainties of modernity that many associated with immigration, urbanization, and mass culture. It is, notably, to this therapeutic region that Silas Lapham, at the end of another of Howells famous novels of the 1880s, goes to recover after the world falls apart around him in the urban metropolis.[11]

But even more strikingly, and in a way much less familiar to his critics today, Howells positioned the local as a highly aestheticized global commodity, one that was flung into a kind of transnational aesthetic where it traded on the visual and visceral pleasures attendant to a dislocation of the self. And here, I would insist, against Dainotto and Kaplan, that even if the region of regionalism did not correspond to any territorial locale, it does not necessarily follow that the category was one, simply, of naive nationalism and antimodernism.

For example, when introducing the preeminent local colorists, "Mrs. Cooke, Miss Murfree, Miss Wilkins and Miss Jewett," as among the best short story writers, Howells immediately brought into play the French mannerist writer Alphonse Daudet and the Russian regionalist Ivan Turgenev. Howells demarcated a transnational route for American regional writers by comparing them directly to Turgenev, who had achieved his status as a novelist largely on the quality of his regionalism.[12] He wrote that it was locality—incorrectly defined, in his opinion, by its critics as "narrowness"—that distinguished "the whole tendency of modern fiction": "A new method was necessary in dealing with the new conditions, and the new method is worldwide, because the whole world is more or less Americanized."[13] That the formal characteristics of local color became the worldwide method for literary modernity was a radical departure from a conceptualization of it as an artifact of nationalist cultural citizenship. This conceptualization of the local as the global in fiction ought to radically displace our own sense of where to locate Cooke, Murfree, Wilkins Freeman, and Jewett—not to mention Alma Leighton.

Howells's connection of Daudet to Turgenev and modernity in this worldwide Americanization of aesthetics had an extra purchase for his deployment of a character like Alma in *Hazard* because Daudet came to have the special symbolic role in the novel of being the benchmark for the chic. Not coincidentally, Daudet and Turgenev were famous acquaintances in Paris. Both were members of a very small and exclusive club of experimental realist authors who were meeting in Paris at the time—a group organized by Edmond de Goncourt that also included Émile Zola, and Gustave Flaubert.[14] Although it goes unmentioned in the novel, this group can be imagined as grounding Howells's fictionalized account of the coincidence of the local and the transnational, of Alma and chic aesthetics. It is to Daudet that Howells turned when trying to describe the effect of Alma's cover for the magazine *Every Other Week*. Beaton, a bohemian artist trained in Paris, immediately recognizes the mock-up of the magazine to be "like some of the *Tartarin* books of Daudet's," a reference to illustrated editions— which included, also, such works as Pierre Loti's decadent novel *Madame*

Chrysanthème (1888)—that had begun to appear in Paris in the 1880s under the influence of *Japonisme* and the aesthetics art movement. The magazine's publisher, Fulkerson, explicitly says that the process they want to use for its illustration is the same "that those French fellows gave Daudet thirty-five thousand dollars to write a novel to use with" (122). And the amiable socialite, Margaret Vance, confirms the pairing some hundred pages later when commenting that the new magazine is "as *chic*—that detestable little word—as those new French books" (212). Alma's illustrations, like Daudet's books, are poised to enter in the quickening current of the international trade in objects of art.

The issue for Howells, then, was specifically not that of getting local places defined as regional points on an American literary map, but that of understanding local color's charge within the space of the market—a space filled with mobile and consumable cultural forms, the picturesqueness of which was, itself, to be consumed. And it is here that Howells can be used to extend the other line on regionalism now emerging, which not only makes regionalism more visible in connection to the treatment of folklore as "circulating culture," but which also locates it much more directly in the context of an early-twentieth-century, modernist trade in exotic objects. Although Richard Brodhead's emphasis on local color as a strategy for suppressing the "radically heterogeneous" falls more directly into Kaplan's school of seeing regionalism as a form of nostalgia, he makes very clear that local color was part of metropolitan high culture.[15] Laurie Shannon has fit Sarah Orne Jewett into the world of French art, comparing her work to that of *intimiste* painters like Edouard Vuillard and Pierre Bonnard.[16] In the same vein, Bill Brown has argued that the nation is bracketed in her work, her attention to objects insisting instead on the dynamics of the global and the local.[17] Nancy Glazener and Carrie Tirado Bramen have both pointed to Garland's populism to argue that regionalism did not have a single political objective, while Stephanie Foote argues that "binaries that are assumed to constitute regional writing (rural/urban, native/stranger, simplicity/chaos, nostalgia/modernity) cannot hold up" to a more rigorous reading.[18] Gavin Jones, similarly, finds that the dialect speech of local-color writing was "not just a homogeneous act of repression" but was very capable of evoking "a worrying sense of linguistic and social disunity."[19] And Chris Bongie astutely places regional writing, especially by Lafcadio Hearn, at the center of discussions about creolization and hybridity.[20]

Howells's particular use in extending this line of analysis comes from the way he grounds the local as a commodity that accumulates value when put into circulation in an internationalist art market. His deployment of Alma marks and furthers what might best be understood as an aesthetics of circulation, or the production of aesthetic value via circulation. That circulation was, itself, multifaceted. On the one hand one might think of the way that American regional writing would have been traded in places like London and Paris. It was to this end that Howells promoted it in the way that he did, and there is some evidence that American regionalists did enter into the international art market. Hearn, for one, had books translated and published in France on several occasions in the early twentieth century, but was even more well received in Tokyo, where he moved in the early 1900s and where one can still find a memorial park honoring him. On the other hand, and it is here that this chapter will focus its energies, one can see the circulation of iconographic images from the aesthetic arts movement in local-color writing, such that the form became, in the 1890s and early 1900s, not so much about the local as about the color, not so much about regional places ethnographically defined as about the stylistic flair set off by the disassociation of the aesthetic object from its anthropological origins. In work by the likes of Hearn, Stephen Crane, and Chopin, the form emerged as one through which ideas about style and taste moved with particular ease. As such, the confluence of the local and chic insisted not simply on the multiplicity of local goods entering into the circuit of fashion and taste, but on the production of fashion and taste from within the rubric of locality.

HOWELLSIAN CHIC

The first impression Howells gives of Alma's artwork comes in the last stages of work on a new magazine—and about a third of the way into *A Hazard of New Fortunes*—when Basil March and Fulkerson are faced with the problem of deciding on the direction to take with the cover of *Every Other Week*. The question, as the businessman Fulkerson explains it to Beaton, a bohemian artist who has been brought in for a consultation, is whether to print the magazine with a paper cover, like the one decorating the mockup in "ivory-white pebbled paper," or whether it would be better off "in some sort of flexible boards, so they [the American public] can set them on the shelf and say no more about it" (120). It takes no time at all for the aesthetically cocksure Beaton to formulate his answer, which the Howellsian narrator puts forth in a tone characteristic of his male characters, boorish and seemingly but one step removed from a guffaw:

> Beaton had got done looking at the dummy, and he dropped it on the table before Fulkerson, who pushed it away, apparently to free himself from partiality. "I don't know anything about the business

side, and I can't tell about the effect of either style on sales, but you'll spoil the whole character of the cover if you use anything thicker than that thickish paper." (121)

There may be a certain specimen value in the pacing and ungrammaticality of this passage—"Beaton had got done looking," Fulkerson "pushed it away"—that could help us imagine what Kaplan has described as the conservative nature of Howells's "construction" of reality and the kind of muscularity needed for "controlling and ordering" it.[21] The narrative tone is abrupt but playful, showy but nonchalant, self-confident to the point of slang. Its voice is that of someone who can handle the hazards of modern life, who can negotiate its rhythms and emerge with his manliness intact. But coupled with this tone is an aesthetic question carried, almost by chance it would seem, in the slack reference to the magazine's cover. What *is* the "character of the cover" of *Every Other Week* that, contrary to our expectations of what might signify value in a literary publication, "anything thicker than that thickish paper" would spoil? And in what way might a better perception of the taste for covers complicate our reading of the tone in which the reference is made?

These questions are of particular interest for the way they frame the market context for the reception of Howells's own novel. Like *Every Other Week*, the fictional magazine around which the plot of *A Hazard of New Fortunes* circulates, the novel was published with a paper wrapper, relished by the critic Brander Matthews for its "decorative sobriety . . . with its sombre symbol of fate" (see fig. 4.1).[22] The key word, here, is "decorative." In the American 1890s, a paper wrapper was not a sign of an inexpensive or low quality publication, but rather of an experimentation with styles most recognizable as belonging to the British arts and crafts movement, the postimpressionist Nabis in Paris, and Japanese art. Matthews insists that the paper wrapper be associated with "the originality, the elegance, the freshness,—in a word, the art,—of the men who are making the things which encompass us roundabout."[23] More whimsically, Matthews quotes another writer to the effect that paper wrappers made fitting clothes for "summer novels":

> As certainly as the birds appear comes the crop of summer novels, fluttering down upon the stalls, in the procession through the railway trains, littering the drawing-room tables, in light paper covers, ornamented attractively in colours and fanciful designs, as welcome and grateful as the girls in muslin. . . . [I]n the summer, though the fiction be as grave and tragic as wandering love and bankruptcy, we would have it come to us lightly clad—out of stays as it were.[24]

4.1 *A Hazard of New Fortunes* in paper wrapper. The novel was no. 661 (November 1889) of the *Harper's* Franklin Square series, issued monthly at $5 per year. Yale Collection of American Literature, Beinecke Rare Book and Manuscript Library.

It is not, admittedly, to Matthews's evocation of the summer clothes of fiction that one might most immediately turn to elucidate *A Hazard of New Fortunes,* Howells's most direct, post–Haymarket Square critique of the inequities of market speculation. What I want to point out, however, is the extent to which these summer clothes—fluttering through railway trains, circulating out of stays, and cladding Howells's novel—should draw our attention to the aesthetic sensibility and visual iconography that articulates the novel's realist social agenda. That sensibility is of the chic, and it is connected in particular ways to the idea of the local defined as a commodity by its movement, "fluttering," "littering."

The chic permeates the novel, becoming its keyword for describing what is most aesthetically cutting edge in the world of Howells's realists. March can only smile when Fulkerson, too, mixes "American slang with the jargon of European criticism" in describing Beaton's success with the magazine's artwork as being "awfully *chic*": "He's caught on like mice. He's made the thing awfully *chic;* it's jimmy; there's lots of dog about it" (174). Beaton has a thing for the chic. Everything he touches seems to be so, as, for example, his architectural drawings, which are said to be "very striking, very original, very *chic,* very everything but habitable" (104). So too is the artistic nature of the woman to whom Beaton is most attracted, Alma Leighton, who designed the cover of *Every Other Week* that draws such stylistic praise. Her art teacher dryly recognizes her as the most talented of his students with the acerbic comment that because she's a woman "no amount of *chic* is going to help" (112). For her own part, Alma turns her teacher's criticism to a spunky self-affirmation: "He doesn't like my doing these *chic* things; but I'm going to keep it up, for I think it's the nearest way to illustrating" (94).

There was a kind of semantic doubleness about this word, chic, for while recognizable as a marker of "distinction" in the sense of Pierre Bourdieu, it clearly meant a real thing in the Manhattan literary world peopled in the novel—something with a sure referent and a sellable charm that also happened to be open in particularly loamy ways to those characters and objects with attachments to the local.[25] The chic denoted not simply a matter of style and taste, but an aesthetic modality that could be traded and traded upon. So what was the chic?

The *Oxford English Dictionary* suggests that the word only entered into English slang in the 1850s: "artistic skill and dexterity; 'style', such as gives an air of superior excellence to a person or thing." The first example is from 1856, but they multiply in the 1880s. Most tellingly for our purposes is the one from an 1888 *Pall Mall:* "Her voice is sweet and her delivery artistic, but she is wanting what the French call '*chic,*' an untranslatable word, denoting an indispensable quality."[26] At first glance, it would appear that the key determinant, here, was precisely that of place, and specifically of France. A *Harper's Monthly* article from 1892 confirms this sense, illustrating it with reference to "a Parisienne" in her dressing room, in which "there is no useless decoration, no excess of furniture . . . simplicity itself, a mere laboratory."[27] But this attention to a French, or more precisely Parisian place, is somewhat illusory. The chic for both the British and American magazines signaled not so much France itself as the dispersed network of distribution for chic things. As suggested by its frequent appearance in *Harper's,* the *Atlantic Monthly,* and the *Century Illustrated Monthly,* the term was connected not so much to the Parisienne in her dressing room as to the tableau of the Parisienne in the magazines—magazines that became chic, themselves, by trading on the image.

The particular style of the Parisienne was refinement, the minimalist elegance of the line that moved in the direction of art nouveau, and yet even there it would seem to be a style that deterritorialized the object. The *Pall Mall* suggested that chic was an untranslatable word, but an untranslatable word is most often one without a synonym in even its own language; and as such, one might imagine the chic's refinement—in the sense of its purification and precision—rendering it irreducible, foreign even to itself.

The chic suggested by the Parisienne in her dressing room was openly— even theatrically—sexualized: "the toilet of the Parisienne and the daily composition of her beauty are the result of taste, sentiment, and inspiration, even as a picture or statue. . . . Her toilet is perfect; her coiffure is a poem; and however surpassingly beautiful the one or the other may be, she wears them with absolute ease as if she had never worn anything else" (868). As a corollary, it was divorced from the domestic. Even at home, the chic woman was on stage, "each one play[ing] excellently the rôle that . . . she has assumed in the spectacle of the life of Paris" (871). Being chic entailed being at home everywhere and nowhere at once, life in either a "laboratory" or in one of Beaton's beautiful buildings that were "everything but habitable."

Always in circulation, the chic was also easily linked to commodification. It sold, and sold well, which may have been why in *Hazard* it was typically translated by way of its negative, as a symptom of false consciousness, as in Margaret Vance's half-hearted self-distancing from "that detestable little word." The chic was something both attractive and, because of its mass appeal, a bit clichéd. Charles Moore wrote of "an excess of what is called *chic*" in French portraiture, which he critiqued in particular for being "ungraceful and theatrical [in its] modes of conception."[28] The associated keyword in the novel is "decorative," and in this context it is not too much of a stretch to think more concretely of something like the New York apartments that the Marches spend so much time looking at during the first hundred pages of the novel. Going from one unsuitable apartment to the next, March finally breaks out with a diatribe against the "idiotic decoration" of their "French" aesthetic style: "No; the Anglo-Saxon home, as we know it in the Anglo-Saxon house, is simply impossible in the Franco-American flat—not because it's humble, but because it's false" (58, 59). The flat, as March imagines it, is society life as opposed to social life, confinement without coziness, no cider down in the cellar, the artificial. March goes so far as to sum it up as "the negation of motherhood," the elevation of a false, foreign, and flagrant taste over the humbler American sanctities (58).

March's outburst makes for a particularly fitting definition of the chic because of its applicability to Alma, who renounces both the Anglo-Saxon home of her New Hampshire childhood and the possibility of domestic motherhood in order to pursue her love of book illustration: "I'm wedded to my art," she tells her mother when explaining why she has turned away the romantic advances of Beaton, "and I'm not going to commit bigamy, whatever I do" (182). There is a great deal of whimsicality in Alma's declaration, but that should not divert the charge of her comment with regard to her play with the gendered expectations held for her as a young woman of rural background. As Christopher Diller has noted, Alma and Beaton are both cut loose from strict gender identifications; I would add that they would not be so chic were they not both to some extent androgynous.[29] For example, when Alma first uses the word, it is to describe an illustration she had just completed of a not quite manly man, about which she notes that "as soon as his back's turned I get to putting ladies into men's clothes" (93). But, of course, that is exactly what she has done when making the sketch. She was the model, as she just before "got up and took a pose before the mirror, which she then transferred to her sketch"—her sketch of what turns out to be a man (93). There is a thrill for Alma—and maybe for us when we find it, unexpectedly, in Howells—in her active, transgendered dislocation of herself from her body in a sketch that is chic. Indeed, what appears to be most chic about Alma's artwork—and what is chic about the association of it with Alma and Beaton—is that it signals both characters' inability to be pinned down. To be chic, they must inhabit a sensibility having no home, one that is ostensibly displaced from any comfortable locale, one that has to circulate.

The most prolonged assessment of Alma's art comes in reference to the cover she designed for the new magazine, the one compared to "those Tartarin books of Daudet's" by both Beaton and Margaret Vance.[30] Daudet, a French novelist of manners, published his first Tartarin book in 1872; but it, along with two others, was brought out in the late 1880s and 1890s in a series, *Collection artistique Guillaume,* that was illustrated by a group of artists, including Giradet, Montegut, de Myrbach, Picard, and Rossi, who

trained in the schools of open air painting and salon realism.[31] American
audiences would have known their work from the final installment of the
Tartarin series, *Port Tarascon*, that was brought out in *Harper's Monthly*
between June and November of 1890, just months after *Hazard* had completed its run in *Harper's Weekly*. The American magazine reprinted the
novel with the French illustrations. It was translated by Henry James,
who in an unusual preface noted, with some thought perhaps of the social
hazards described earlier by his friend Howells, that "the last moral of all is,
that however many traps life may lay for us, tolerably firm ground, at any
rate, is to be found in perfect art."[32] The chic, however, provided an
aesthetic ground that was firm perhaps only to the extent that it felt at
home, as James certainly must have, in the cosmopolitanism of the international art complex—one that had a sense for the perfection of Daudet and
his illustrators.

The books produced in the *Collection artistique Guillaume* were not
expensive, but their illustrations were notable because they achieved a quality of expression that was just coming into the art form. The most important
American illustrations for the decade leading up to 1885 were strikingly
pastoral. Winslow Homer's *Thanksgiving in Camp* (fig. 4.2), for example,

4.2 Winslow Homer, *Thanksgiving in Camp, Harper's Weekly,* November 29, 1862.
Mary Bartlett Cowdrey Bequest, Jane Voorhees Zimmerli Art Museum.

compresses different parts of narrative into one frame so that, as suggested by the art historian Diana Strazdes, "a single image would suggest past and future events, as well as the present."[33] The image fills the entire frame. The soldiers in the foreground seem to have struck a pose, and their placement does little to disrupt either the balance or the temporality of the composition. The *Tartarin* pieces, by contrast, depend much more on abstraction and quite literally break up the frame of the narrative by intruding into the text. Rather than illustrating a general mood, they tended to focus on particular scenes and points in the text that gave viewers a stronger sense of action and the characters' emotions (figs. 4.3 and 4.4, from *Tartarin*). They were, moreover, rather more sketchy, suggesting the speed and fleetingness of the modern moment.

An *Atlantic Monthly* review of *Port Tarascon* noted that the French artists "speak a French dialect of pictorial art which is not merely intelligible, but penetrates the sense with a pungency of meaning which is truly exhilarating."[34] One can imagine Fulkerson wanting similar exhilaration when he describes the "kind of thing that begins at one side, or one corner, and spreads in a sort of dim religious style over the print till you can't tell which is which" (122). One finds this especially in the illustrations by Rossi, where there is a strong emphasis on diagonal motion and an exploration of solid shapes to fill the background. Although getting a bit ahead of the argument, one might note at this point the same technique being picked up in the 1897 reissue of George Washington Cable's collection of local-color sketches, *Old Creole Days,* illustrated by Albert Herter (see fig. 4.5). Cable made use of the same technique in his own "little magazine" of the period, the aesthetically precious *Symposium* (see fig. 4.6).[35] What one sees in these instances is a process of merging word and text that led, once again, to the attribution of a certain materiality to writing, an "objectification" of narrative as something like a detachable commodity, something to pick up, look under and around, and transport to other places and contexts.

Howells's own engagement with the period's aestheticism was signaled even more directly after the publication of *Hazard,* when, in 1891, he began to publish his poetry in *Harper's Monthly*—poetry that *Harper's* began to pair with illustrations by the most well known artist/illustrator in the United States at that time, Howard Pyle.[36] Although beyond Howells's own control, *Harper's* decision to use Pyle was perfectly apropos of Howells's experimentation with both the cadences and cynicism of the aesthetic arts movement. "November—Impression," published in 1891, is one of the most remarkable examples:

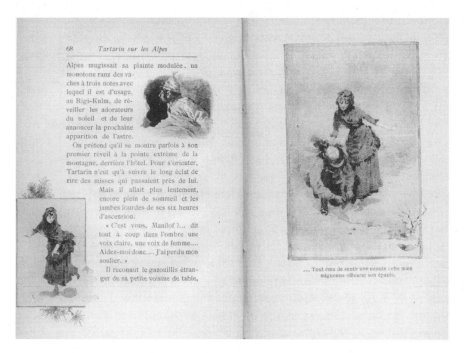

4.3 Rossi, Illustration for Daudet's *Tartarin sur les Alpes* (Paris: Collection Artistique Guillaume, 1886). Author's print.

A weft of leafless spray
Woven fine against the gray
Of the autumnal day,
And blurred along those ghostly garden tops
Clusters of berries crimson as the drops
That my heart bleeds when I remember
How often, in how many a far November,
Of childhood and my children's childhood I was glad,
With the wild rapture of the Fall
Thrilling from me to them, of all
The ruin now so intolerably sad.

Both the poem's darkness and its arhythmicality identify it as an engagement with the aesthetic sensibility associated with the Paris salons of Daudet and Turgenev, Flaubert, Zola, and Goncourt. The crux of the poem comes at the doubly-enjambed, heavily stressed, sixth line, "crimson as the drops/That my heart bleeds when I remember/How often . . ." With its transformation of crimson berries into the residue of a broken heart, the line becomes the hinge that holds the poem together thematically and (with five lines above and below it) numerically. The poem is an exercise in style. Howells's spry play with clusters of unstressed words in the rhymed opening, "against the gray/Of the autumnal day," give the poem a decidedly modern lilt. Similarly, Howells manipulates the rhyme pattern for dramatic effect, especially when pairing "my children's childhood I was glad" with "now so intolerably sad" in the last four lines. Although "glad" and "sad" offer an expression of emotion unfortunately reduced from that suggested with the earlier imagery, they still encapsulate the series of reversals that characterize the poem as a distinctly modern exercise in style.

The aestheticist line that Howells picked up here to explore his deceptions of the early 1890s was repeated in other poems from the same period, collected for their publication in monthly numbers of *Harper's* under distinctively modern titles, "Moods" and "Monochromes." Edwin Cady notes that "Monochromes" referred to "plastic art-work done in color, most often black-on-white"; coupled with the psychological depth of "Moods," he argues that the poetry immediately announced its "newness."[37] Howells's poetry extended his engagement, after the Haymarket Square episode and the death of his eldest daughter, Winnifred, not just with radical artists, like Crane, Garland, and Norris, but also with more exotic breeds, like the bilingual Franco-American poet, Stuart Merrill. Merrill had seemed

to be one of Howells's most promising young disciples during this period. According to Cady, Howells was very disappointed when Merrill moved permanently to France, yet the mutual influence between them continued. Merrill's 1891 publication of poems, *Les Fastes,* for example, was dedicated to Howells. And Howells wrote the introduction to Merrill's collection and translation of work by the most important

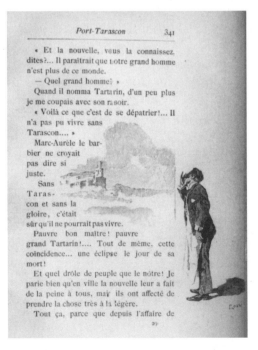

4.4 Rossi, Illustration for Daudet's *Port-Tarascon* (Paris: Collection Artistique Guillaume, 1890). Author's print.

BELLES DEMOISELLES
PLANTATION

HE original grantee was Count ——,
assume the name to be De Charleu;
the old Creoles never forgive a public
mention. He was the French king's
commissary. One day, called to France to explain the lucky accident of the commissariat having burned down with his account-books inside,
he left his wife, a Choctaw Comtesse, behind.

Arrived at court, his excuses were accepted, and
that tract granted him where afterwards stood
Belles Demoiselles Plantation. A man cannot remember everything! In a fit of forgetfulness he
married a French gentlewoman, rich and beautiful, and "brought her out." However, "All's
well that ends well;" a famine had been in the

4.5 Albert Herter, Illustration for George Washington Cable's *Old Creole Days* (Boston: Charles Scribner's Sons, 1897). Department of Rare Books and Special Collections, Princeton University Library.

French writers in the new style, *Pastels in Prose,* which came out at exactly the same time as *Hazard,* in April 1890. *Pastels* set up the French component of the constellation of artists that defined the aesthetic world in which the chic emerged, containing sketches by, among others, Charles Baudelaire, Joris-Karl Huÿsmans, Stéphane Mallarmé, Auguste Villiers de L'Isle-Adam, and, fittingly for the present discussion, Daudet. In his introduction, Howells added Turgenev to Merrill's group, noting that his work in "this irregular species of composition" shared "qualities . . . and traits common to them all": "beautiful reticence . . . brevity . . . simplicity; as if they felt the responsibility they were under to be even more laconic, more delicate, more refined than they might have been."[38] The description coincided directly with those qualities defining the chic. He noted their "freedom"; he admired that the authors resisted applying morals to their work, having instead the "most courageous faith in art"; and he ascribed to the form, as indeed to the title of the volume itself, *Pastels,* an "aerial delicacy" and "wonderful refinement, which is almost fragility" (vi, vii).

In this context, the most visually exciting possibility for understanding Howells's engagement with the aesthetic arts movement comes with the poster craze initiated in the United States by the literary monthlies in the mid-1890s. Brander Matthews, the American drama critic and author of local-color "vignettes" of Manhattan life, suggested the close link between picture posters and paper covers for

4.6 Will H. Bradley, Magazine cover illustration for local colorist George Washington Cable's "little magazine," *The Symposium,* 1896. Author's print.

books in an 1892 article for the *Century Illustrated Monthly,* calling the paper covers the "younger sister of the pictorial poster."[39] Starting in the late 1880s, but reaching its height between 1894 and 1896, the magazines promoted a generation of American artists who produced monthly posters to advertise for the major magazines. The first of these to come out were posters for the holidays by the children's magazine *St. Nicholas* and the *Century Illustrated Monthly* in 1883. *Harper's Monthly* commissioned its first Christmas poster in 1889, just as *Hazard* was reaching its conclusion in *Harper's Weekly,* and it proved so popular that they began having posters to advertise the magazine every month, as did the *Century, Lippincott's,* the *Chap-Book* and others.[40]

The style of these posters was an eclectic international mix of postimpressionist iconography of the Nabis, art nouveau, and *Japonisme* (see figs. 4.7, 4.8, and 4.9).[41] One sees this influence in such things as the palette, the *Japonisme* prints on the walls, the dependence on diagonals, the characters' costumes and postures, the immediacy of the moment that comes through with cropped figures, the use of strong outline, the excessive decorative flourishes that contrast with intense moments of flat spaces, the upward or downward perspective, the peacock feathers, and the erotically charged flowers. One can imagine what was chic about *Every Other Week*'s covers and illustrations, and thus what would have made the magazine sell, very much in these terms.

The craze for these posters hit after the initial publication of *Hazard,* yet that fact does not detract from the correctness of aligning Alma's art with it. The style here would seem to correspond most closely with what Howells described as chic, though it should be kept in mind that, in the context of American illustration, it was far from the only possibility. As many historians have noted, the rapid changes in the American magazine and newspaper industry led to "the Golden Age of American Illustration," and with it extraordinary opportunities for professional illustrators. Some surveys suggest that over 100,000 illustrations per year would have been published in the top thirty-four illustrated magazines alone, which does not even begin to account for the hundreds of other magazines Frank Luther Mott estimated were published during the period, or for the newspapers, which were actively publishing illustrations as well.[42] Most of this work would clearly not have been considered chic in the Howellsian sense; it would have been more descriptive and less decorative, more realistic and less abstract. But what I want to point to here is the way that *Hazard* seems to insist on Alma doing something different from the rest of the field, which of course would be necessary for the success of Fulkerson and March's new magazine.[43] Not only would the field have been ripe for an artist like Alma, but her own predilections suggest a precarious flirtation with the aesthetic avant-garde, which would make her immediately attractive to both Beaton and Fulkerson, the decadent artist and the businessman.

What makes *Hazard*'s engagement with this aesthetic style all the more interesting are the small ways it manifests what, from hindsight, we know to have been the history of the movement without ever naming it as such. To return to Howells's text, we can go back to the comment Beaton makes concerning Fulkerson's little Spanish book, that he was unlikely to find the kind of illustration he wants for the magazine in the United States. "'Do you expect to get such drawings in this country?' asked Beaton, after a glance at the book. 'Such character—such drama? You won't. . . . I can't think of a man who could do it; that is, amongst those that would'" (123). Although not altogether clear, what Beaton really seems to be after here is not so much verisimilitude in the illustration as the aesthetic flare tied up with this new internationalism—the sort of thing for which, prior to the 1890s, it would have made sense to look to Europe. Thus Fulkerson's response is all the more fitting. He replies, "Well, think of some woman, then," which, apparently, is what a large number of newspapers and magazines did (123). By the 1890s, the aesthetic arts movement began to have a particularly significant impact on a large number of women illustrators, foremost among them Elizabeth Shippen Green, Violet Oakley, and

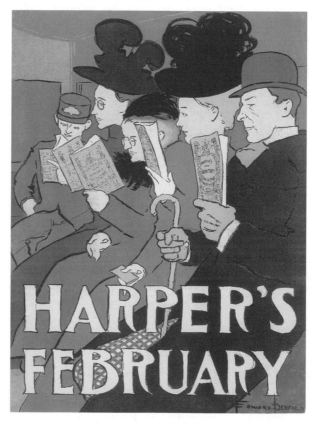

4.7 Edward Penfield, poster for *Harper's Monthly*, February 1897. Courtesy of Hirschl & Adler Galleries, Inc., New York City.

4.8 Louis J. Rhead, poster for *The Century Illustrated Monthly,* 1894. Courtesy of Hirschl & Adler Galleries, Inc., New York City.

Jessie Willcox Smith, all of whom studied with John Sloan in Philadelphia. Green is of particular note as being possibly the first woman to have had a regular contract illustrating for *Harper's Monthly,* where she worked into the 1920s. Book illustration and cover work were very much professions open to and dependent on women artists, and women artists were instrumental in pushing forward the new aesthetic formalism.[44]

But what this context also explains is the novel's surprising flirtation with the commercialization of sexuality. Creating the echo for Beaton's comments about "character" and "drama," Alma had earlier elicited a surprised response when showing her mother a sketch that seems to play with sexuality:

> "Go on—about the girl in the picture!" said Alma, slightly knocking her mother on the shoulder as she stood over her.
> "I don't see anything to her. What's she doing?"
> "Oh, just being made love to, I suppose."
> "She's perfectly insipid!"

(94)

4.9 Will H. Bradley, poster for *The Chap-Book,* 1894. Courtesy of Hirschl & Adler Galleries, Inc., New York City.

What Mrs. Leighton takes to be "insipid" was sure to have been recognized by Alma as something more akin to languid sexuality, a familiar image of woman as object of sexual desire in aestheticism. Again, reference to one of the poster artists inspired by art nouveau would seem to make sense here, for what Alma and her mother describe must be something like John Sloan's puzzle illustrations for the *Philadelphia Inquirer* in 1895 (fig. 4.10). Sloan, who in typical fashion moved fluidly between newspaper illustration and poster art, provided an image typical for the decorative nature of its work with lines, the floral pattern of the woman's chemise, the print pattern on the wall, the use of color, the strong vertical motion, and its intrusion upon the text. And, of course, with her "insipid" air, the woman pictured has that languorous femininity that Alma's more conservative mother, knocked on the shoulder by her daughter, might find offensive.

This context recalls, moreover, two rather unexpected flirtations with nudity in Howells's text, the first when Fulkerson talks about what to put on future covers of *Every Other Week,* and the second when the old and provincial Mrs. Dryfoos pronounces herself offended by the illicit nature of advertising posters in department store display windows. Indeed, Fulkerson goes so far as to describe what seven years later would become two of Maxfield Parrish's most famous magazine posters, an amazingly risqué 1897 midsummer piece for the *Century Illustrated* and a similar one for *Scribner's* (figs. 4.11 and 4.12). "Sometimes," Fulkerson proclaims excitedly, "we're going to have an indelicate little figure, or as much so as the law will allow. . . . Mr. Beaton here is going to supply the floating females, gracefully airing themselves against a sunset or something of that kind" (121). The style recalls most directly Gauguin's paintings from Martinique in 1889 and Tahiti starting in 1891. It was not coincidental that his image could be drawn so directly to those Gauguin-like nudes, to the extent that Gauguin represented in a nutshell both the exoticism and eroticism of the aestheticist movement. And yet, it remains difficult to gauge which comes as more of a surprise, the nudes on the cover of the notoriously prudish *Century*—which, remember, had not altogether given up its evangelical roots and which has always been held up in contrast to the decadent little magazines, like the *Chap-Book*—or a character of Howells's flirting with illicit images of floating females. Let us, at any rate, stick with Howells. The female artist and the female form; the commercial, the sexual, and the aesthetic; the local and the cosmopolitan; these references to the surprisingly forward artistic consciousness of the novel come, to say the least, as something of a surprise given what one expects from Howells. Could this be an undiscovered Howells . . . decadent, sexy, chic?

4.10 John Sloan, *The Snake Charmer Puzzle,* from *The Philadelphia Inquirer,* 1901. Courtesy of International Paper. Author's print.

4.11 Maxfield Parrish, poster for *Scribner's,* August 1897: "an indelicate figure, or as much as the law will allow . . . floating females, gracefully airing themselves against a sunset or something of that kind" (*Hazard,* 121). Courtesy of Hirschl & Adler Galleries, Inc., New York City.

4.12 Maxfield Parrish, poster for *The Century Illustrated Monthly,* August 1897.
Courtesy of Hirschl & Adler Galleries, Inc., New York City.

JAPONISME AND THE DISORDER OF THE MARKET

As suggested by the *Century*'s poster art and by Alma Leighton's social and professional mobility, across geographic and gender borders, the aesthetic offered access to a fluid, disordered sense of the self—to movement within and across geographically and socially located types—that came to signify something like the cosmopolitanism of the aesthetic arts movement of the 1890s. This image of guilty pleasures linked to aesthetic fluidity plays against the more doleful and conservative image of Howells constructed most prominently by Amy Kaplan's reading of him as a deeply anxious man, someone who urgently "exhorts, pleads, and proclaims the need to construct a familiar reality in fiction" in order to counter his fear of "modern life." Kaplan contrasts Henry James's reading of Howells as someone "animated by a love of the common, the immediate, the familiar and vulgar elements of life," with her own feeling of Howells's "lack of confidence in the existence of a common, familiar, immediate reality to which language can refer" and his fear of "emerging forms of mass culture."[45] Although my own tendency clearly is to side with James, Kaplan's characterization of Howells corresponds neatly with his deployment of a character who would otherwise seem to fit into the aesthetic constellation of the chic that I have been describing: Lindau, the novel's only true foreigner, an unmarried, German-born, anarchist intellectual who had been hired to translate stories from the international presses for *Every Other Week*. In the climactic scene in the novel, Howells kills off Lindau, letting him fall under the baton of a policeman as he protests at a streetcar strike.

The significant role Lindau plays at the end of the novel draws into sharp focus the risk associated with the aesthetics of circulation—a risk suggested in much lighter terms at the beginning of the novel when March decried the French flat, or when Alma sketched herself in men's clothing. It is a risk, staged in terms specifically applicable to the chic, between order and disorder. With Lindau, disorder has reached its limit, and yet deep sympathy remains for his plight. Despite his apparent taste in foreign literature and talent as a poetic translator, Lindau is the primary speaker of the novel's "violent words," an agent provocateur that Benjamin reading Marx has taught us to recognize as the original bohemian.[46] In the climactic scene in the novel, Lindau puts down his literature and takes to the streets, taunting a bevy of policemen who had come to break up the streetcar strike. But not only does Lindau die, he also causes the death of the saintly Conrad Dryfoos, who had come to minister to the Christian needs of the strikers. The ideological calculus seems to tip against Lindau at this point, his version of social disorder clashing too significantly with the disorder of the aesthetic realm. March admits so much to his son when he says, in response to a question, that "Mr. Lindau died in a bad cause":

> "Why yes," he answered; "he died *in the cause of disorder;* he was trying to obstruct the law. No doubt there was a wrong there, an inconsistency and an injustice that he felt keenly, but it could not be reached in his way without greater wrong." (my emphasis, 392)

And yet, there can be no mistake that March's response to his son comes with a great deal of moral complexity. He would not have even thought of the question without prompting: "He had always been so sorry for Lindau and admired his courage and generosity so much that he had never fairly considered this question" (392). Similarly, he avoids his wife's harsher critique of the international activist in the last pages of the novel, where she claims that the speculative capitalist, Dryfoos, "is a better man than Lindau." March turns the comment aside with a cynical rejoinder that Dryfoos, at least, "is able to offer us a better thing in *Every Other Week*" (423).

In effect, what Lindau has staged in his confrontation with the police is the social equivalent of Fulkerson's aesthetic flirtation with the limits of "what the law will allow" with regard to nudity on the covers of his magazine. Lindau crosses Howells's line, the line at which the chic does not find its analogy in the Paris barricades of Marx's *Eighteenth Brumaire of Louis Napolean* (1852). And yet he does not do so without Howells's evident sympathy.

March's ambivalence about Lindau registers alongside his experience, throughout the novel, of dizzying moments of psychic liberation coming directly as the result of another kind of disorder—that developing out of the aesthetic realm. March spends a great deal of time in New York as a flâneur, which Howells documents with a sense for the liberation that comes with the ease of movement and observation made possible in the city. At one point, March feels deep "relief" when watching a couple at a French café in Manhattan—a young couple who must be artists because "the wife had an aesthetic dress and defined her pretty head by wearing her back hair pulled up very tight under her bonnet; the husband had dreamy eyes" (257). His sensation when looking at them is described explicitly in terms of the disordering of the self:

> his immunity from acquaintance, this touch-and-go quality in their New York sojourn, this almost loss of individuality at times, after

the intense identification of their Boston life, was a relief. . . . March refused to explore his conscience. . . . [H]e said he liked now and then to feel his personality in that state of solution. (257)

This fluidity that March experiences, the movement within and across social and national borders, might provocatively be aligned with fin de siècle aestheticism. It is the pleasure arising from circulation, from not being at home anywhere, from the kind of liberated sense of sexuality that permits the married and middle-class March to look at the seductive young woman.

March's disorder, however, is not social but aesthetic. The parameters of this disorder is made explicit in another of Howells's poems, "Sphinx," wherein Howells writes of the "relief that comes with the blessed oblivion freeing / Self from self in the deep sleep of some dreamless night."[47] After the death of Lindau, Howells pulls March back, inscribing his response within a social reality that, we are led to believe, has to do with more than just a state of mind. What remains bracketed, however, is this flirtation with another mode of achieving disorder, one that Howells deploys as if it were the product of a different aesthetic genre—not the realist novel, but the poem or the colorful sketch of a young woman in a New York café. The novel is registered as being impermeable to this new subjectivity; it remains attached and coherent, while the short story, poem, and sketch are freed up for circulation.

Howells stages a similar flirtation with disorder with Beaton. Late in the novel, Beaton is contrasted to a younger and less impressive artist, Kendricks. Both men had been attracted to one of the awkward, locally colored Dryfoos girls for her "literary effect" (343). Unlike Beaton, though, Kendricks balks at pursuing her because doing so was incongruous in his mind with the "part of the gentleman" (344). There follows a bit of exposition that makes one question where Howells might come down on the implicit critique of Beaton's designs:

[Kendricks] could not have penetrated to that aesthetic and moral complexity which formed the consciousness of a nature like Beaton and was chiefly a torment to itself; he could not have conceived of the wayward impulses indulged at every moment in little things, till the straight highway was traversed and well-nigh lost under their tangle. To do whatever one likes is finally to do nothing that one likes, even though one continues to do what one will; but Kendricks, though a sage of twenty-seven, was still too young to understand this. (344)

It should be unmistakable that Howells's description of Beaton's wayward unselfconsciousness is modeled on the same aesthetic predilections pushing forward the line drawings of Aubrey Beardsley, the *Japonisme* influenced illustration of Sloan, and the flourishing of the American poster-period in the 1890s. With "wayward impulses indulged at every moment in little things," one is lost in the hair, in the dress, in the dislocating "tangle" of decorative lines framing the most interesting examples of this work. In life as in art, Beaton carries the complicated and inchoate world of aestheticism as close to decadence as anyone in the novel, spending his poor father's money on extravagant clothes and fine food while manipulatively pursuing both his art and three women at once. Howells's treatment of him, however, is remarkably indulgent. He excoriates Beaton for sexual wantonness in the last pages of the novel, yet Howells almost suggests that it comes with the territory of having a powerful aesthetic imagination. Fulkerson's assessment of him at the beginning of the novel is the one that seems to hold: despite being "the greatest ass in the solar system," he is an artist with a good deal of "substance," a "first rate critic," and the "best kind of teacher" (126). Howells, a sage of fifty-two at the time, seems to have had enough sense of the sentiment of aesthetic disorder to imagine it and luxuriate around it.[48]

It remains the case, nonetheless, that *Hazard* was not "Sphinx." Edwin Cady's biography of Howells suggests one way of understanding the disjuncture between them. Cady notes that Howells had been approached by *Harper's* in 1888, to do "a series of [local-color] sketches about New York . . . one based on the social meaning of such sketches."[49] Although Howells agreed, what he gave them instead (shortly after moving, himself, to New York) was *A Hazard of New Fortunes,* in which local color came in the form of March thinking about, but not producing, such sketches for *Every Other Week.* I would suggest that this story of Howells's production of his most impressive social realist novel has parallels to the split between order and disorder as portrayed by the characters of Lindau, March, and Beaton. That March never does directly produce his sketches of New York is not so much a conservative rejection of an aesthetic of circulation—of "the blessed oblivion freeing / Self from self in the deep sleep of some dreamless night" as he wrote in his poem from 1894—as it is a reflection of Howells's sense that such an aesthetic was more easily conceived of in the deployment of other genres. It was of no small significance that Howells gave the Harper brothers a novel, not a chic local-color sketch; that the novel found its serial publication not in the publishing house's more decorative monthly, but in *Harper's Weekly,* which at the time was a more politically liberal organ, publishing works by Garland and others also likely to be found in the left-leaning *Arena;* and that Howells personally selected W. A. Rogers, a staff artist at *Harper's* and well-known political cartoonist, to do the illustrations for his stories. All of these facts may be taken as a signal of his deepening concern with social and economic inequities.

But at the same time, in other genres, in his association with writers like Merrill, and in his fascination with characters like Beaton and the aesthetics of circulation represented by Alma's cover for *Every Other Week,* Howells indulged deeply in the more unruly sensibilities. Ultimately, the chic affect solicited by Fulkerson for the cover of *Every Other Week* is analogous to that suggested by the cover of *A Hazard of New Fortunes.* Despite the political imagination that could not abide the disorder of a Marxist bohemian, the aesthetic sensibility of *Hazard* was not antipathetic to the decorative stylistics of the feminine body "out of stays"—wearing what Matthews calls the "loosely fitting garments" of summer fiction.[50] They had a sellable charm, those summer clothes, with their tangled moral complexities and wayward impulses.

CHIC LOCALITY

There is more that could be said, at this point, about Howells's attention to the training of female art students and the international aesthetic of the chic—most notably that he takes up the issue directly three years later in the aptly named novel, *The Coast of Bohemia* (astoundingly, his seventh major publication after *Hazard*). But let me move instead toward the question of how one might hear the concept of locality as against that of the Howellsian chic within the specific context of the 1890s international art complex. One of the lessons of *Hazard*'s association of the chic with locality is that we should be hearing in local-color fiction the internationalist hum of the aesthetic arts movement. Marked by the ethnographic, this fiction emerged in ways that folklore never quite could as an object desired precisely for its detachability from local conditions. Indeed, the argument I want to make in conclusion is that what one sees in local-color fiction of the 1890s is not at all the assertion of integrated stasis and purity that one might imagine for it—a last gasp, as it were, of romantic nostalgia for a preindustrial past—but the assertion by artists, publishing houses, and perhaps even readers, of a rather hip participation in the dislocating, tangled complexity of the chic. Indeed, by the late 1890s, the status of local color had shifted increasingly toward the aesthetic, just as the objects collected by anthropologists became poised to fuel modernist primitivism. As Charles

Dudley Warner, the successor to Howells in *Harper's* "Editor's Study" column, wrote in 1897, "We do not hear much now of 'local color'; that has rather gone out. . . . But color is essential, and high color attracts even the uneducated taste."[51]

To start, let us return to the scene of the local in *Hazard*'s imagination of the aesthetics of circulation. The most chic characters in *Hazard* are also its most recognizably local. As we have seen, Alma comes to Manhattan from the country, and it might as well have been from Sarah Orne Jewett's "country of the pointed firs," St. Barnaby's, New Hampshire. As for Beaton, his study in Paris situates him in the world of aestheticism, but it does not make him nearly so chic as having a Syracuse stonecutter for a father, whose meager financial assistance funds Beaton's debauchery. Beaton now lives in a cluttered Manhattan studio with lots of tasteful things, among them a "lay figure simpering in incomplete nakedness . . . a Japanese dress dropped before it," a writing desk covered with "foreign periodicals—French and English," and on the mantel a "Japanese vase of bronze" (104, 104, 107). He moves like few other characters in the novel across the entire social spectrum—among socialites and the poor, from the Leighton's boarding house to the Dryfoos's mansion. He is dislocated from any one, particular sense of self; he can at will take "possession of one of those other selves of which we each have several about us . . . [becoming] the laconic, staccato, rather *worldlified* young artist" (my emphasis, 110). There is never any doubt that he is an extremely talented and superbly chic artist, one whose lifestyle seductively beckons to characters like Basil March. But our sense of his availability to the spirit of aestheticism cannot be disentangled from our sense of where he came from and what he is doing to his father to get it. He was not born "worldly" but must become "worldlified." Were he to go back to Syracuse, Beaton would be okay; but, being at home, he would never be chic.

Hazard brims over with similarly local characters whose circulation in the city gives them a new charge as aesthetic objects. The Dryfoos girls, though not by any means cultivated, are recognized by both Beaton and Kendricks as fascinating subjects for the production of chic art. In a similar vein, Alma proposes that Beaton use Miss Woodburn, a Southern belle who had moved to the metropolis with her unrepentant Old South father, Colonel Woodburn, for a sketch. "I should think you'd want to paint Miss Woodburn," Alma tells him. "Don't you think her coloring is delicious?" (116). Like Alma, Miss Woodburn's coloring is sharpened by being of the new school. She manages her aged father's finances and finds her way in the city, making her the representation of the "modern conditions . . . producing a modern type" (250). And in much the same way, the city becomes a stage for the transformation of the local into the aesthetic. March continually wanders the streets of New York contemplating the sights for the aesthetic bearing they might bring to some sketches he plans to do. To the extent that Howells provides local color in *Hazard,* he docs it in relating what March sees when riding in the elevated train, slumming in the colorful streets around Lindau's apartment, or strolling among "the young people of that region . . . the promenaders [who] looked New Yorky" (262). Fulkerson repeatedly comes to March asking for these sketches for *Every Other Week,* even suggesting during the streetcar strike that he and Beaton "go round together and take down its aesthetic aspects" (357).

The sentiment Howells develops of this connection between the local and aesthetic chicness was shared both by his most esteemed literary interlocutors and other writers of local color with whom he had but passing acquaintance. The most literal example of *Japonisme* in the movement came with Hearn, who moved to Japan in the early 1900s. Howells related Hearn directly to the visual arts, calling him "an impressionist who puts on pure color, and loves to render light in its fiercest and brightest and gayest tints."[52] After publishing a number of marginally successful novels about Martinique, Hearn finished his writing career in an even smaller, more aesthetically refined form. He took to collecting and retelling ancient Japanese folklore. Although not so successful as Hearn in the international market, other local colorists offered examples in the same vein. The African American local colorist, Alice Dunbar Nelson, has been unduly trapped in a very boring mode of criticism, which takes her to have been a minor and ethnically uninflected writer, yet her fictional recreation of the racial ambiguity of the carnival, coming out as it did in the same years as the Manicheanization of race in the United States with *Plessy v. Ferguson,* was remarkably sharp and, I would argue, suggested her engagement with the development of the short story as the preeminent genre for stylistic experimentation. Stephen Crane's *Maggie* (1893), while ostensibly about the ghetto, seems even more to be about blowing apart the contrived staging of reform journalism (especially Jacob Riis's *How the Other Half Lives*) with an exercise in pure aestheticism—"The girl, Maggie, blossomed in a mud pile."[53] And a plethora of art journals from the 1890s, working on the model of Beardsley's *The Yellow Book,* combine the forms, as in *The Echo, Moods, Two Tales,* and George Washington Cable's *Symposium* (figs. 4.13, 4.14, and 4.15).

Henry James worked out the same logic of the aesthetic value of dislocated locality in his 1892 short story, "The Real Thing," though the word chic does not come up directly. The story is about an illustrator who comes

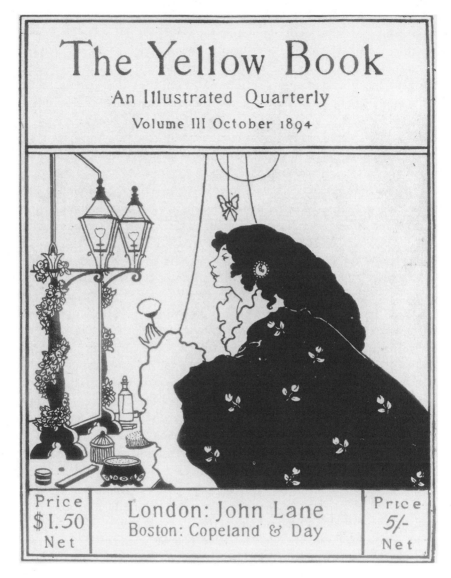

4.13 Aubrey Beardsley's cover for *The Yellow Book* (1894). Rutgers University Libraries.

slowly to grips with the fact that the only models he could use to produce the effect he wanted in his illustrations were those who were both distinctly local and displaced from any particular locale. His best two models are, like Alma and Beaton, distinctly localized types. One is a "freckled cockney"

4.14 John Sloan, cover for the "little magazine," *Moods* (1895). Author's print.

4.15 John Sloan, cover for *The Echo* (1895). Author's print.

named Miss Churm, and the other is an Italian who, "like other itinerants . . . had embarked [in England], with a partner and a small green handcart, on the sale of penny ices."[54] The artist scarcely ever saw Miss Churm "without thinking afresh how odd it was that, being so little in herself, she should yet be so much in others" (241). And the Italian, Oronte? "He was sallow but fair, and when I put him into some old clothes of my own he looked like an Englishman. He was as good as Miss Churm, who could look, when required, like an Italian" (247).

By contrast, James's illustrator can do nothing with a desperately poor aristocratic couple, who want desperately to serve for him as models of "aristocratic couples"—to model, in other words, "the real thing." In the words of his friend Jack Hawley, who had been abroad to "get a fresh eye," in good bohemian form, the aristocratic models simply "won't do": "Ce sont des gens qu'il faut mettre à la porte" (50). Hawley literally cannot translate the problem, but apparently the models are too much like themselves—too much like the aristocratic characters they are to represent. His sketches based on them always turn out in the same way: the man is a giant, while the woman is too perfectly formed. Unlike Miss Churm and Oronte, the aristocrats are not chic in what one commentator for the *Century Illustrated Monthly* might have called the "artistic" sense: "To use chic, in artistic parlance is to produce effects by means of the imagination and by means of analogy—as, for instance, to create from one model's face a dozen of different ages, or by a few skillful strokes to transform the cloth garment on the model into a fur one on the paper or canvas, or to make a straw hat over into a beaver."[55]

Perhaps even more to the point, though, is Chopin. No other American writer from this time period was more "out of stays" than she, and so the development of her work proves to be a remarkably useful example of the shift of local-color fiction toward the chic modernity I have been describing. Chopin was a stylist of the French school, as noted even in 1894 by William Schuyler, who remarked that she read Daudet and particularly Maupassant with pleasure.[56] She had, of course, translated Maupassant—publishing several translations of his stories in *St. Louis Life* in 1895—and, at least in the mind of Per Seyersted, had bettered his stylistic innovations.[57] One might thus imagine the chic influence on her of Maupassant, whom James, in his most decadent novel, *The Wings of the Dove* (1902), imagined as appealing to a passion of a "more imperturbably cerebral"—and thus undomesticated—kind.[58] But of particular interest is the way that, within her own work, one can begin to see a progression away from local-color fiction's early synecdochical fascination with the dimensions of national, racial, and environmental association and toward its emphasis on the disordered possibilities of an art for art's sake stylistics that came with its commodification. The point, of course, is that this style was also that of the then current vogue in the study of the diffusion and dissemination of "circulating culture." To see the epistemological preoccupations of both local color and folklore lining up is to signal the fiction as an emphatic instance—because "purely" artistic—of detachability.

Chopin published a story called "At the 'Cadian Ball" in the journal *Two Tales* in 1892 and after completing *The Awakening* in 1898, wrote a sequel, "The Storm," that she never tried to have published. In each, the description of the main female character, Calixta, is quite recognizable in terms of those qualities of insipid languidity that should by now be familiar. In 1892, she is "that little Spanish vixen," whose "slender foot had never touched Cuban soil . . . but her mother's had, and the Spanish was in her blood all the same."

> Her eyes . . . the bluest, the drowsiest, most tantalizing that ever
> looked into a man's . . . her flaxen hair that kinked worse than a

mulatto's close to her head; that broad, smiling mouth and tiptilted nose, that full figure; that voice like a rich contralto song, with cadences in it that must have been taught by Satan, for there was no one else to teach her tricks on that 'Cadian prairie.[59]

There was no one else to teach her tricks, except, perhaps, Aubrey Beardsley, whose interest in both tantalizing sexuality and the Satanesque were suggested as influences on Chopin by her first biographer, Daniel S. Rankin (fig. 4.16).[60] And they were sure to be recognized as such by the men who desired Calixta, especially the aristocratic rogue, Alcée Laballière, described by one of the old 'Cadian gentlemen, "who was in the habit of reading a Paris newspaper and knew things," as *"chic, mais chic"* (306).

Of particular interest, however, for understanding local color's movement toward aesthetics in these stories is its movement away from a more ethnological preoccupation with race. Take, for example, her attention to Calixta's hair, which in the first story "kinked worse than a mulatto's." In "The Storm," her hair still "kinked more stubbornly than ever," but far from any suggestion that those kinks have a racial antecedent, they are now identified as being "yellow."[61] The accents of race and heritage abound in "At the 'Cadian Ball": the ball, itself, is for a race other than white; the skin color of Bobinot, the 'Cadian farmer who at the end of the story wins Calixta's hand, is "brown"; Calixta has a distinctly Creole accent when she speaks French to the more purely bred aristocrat, Clarisse ("At the 'Cadian Ball," 302). Although by no means as dark as the "negro musicians" whose riotous music warms the 'Cadian ball, Calixta's tincture corresponds to the Caribbean ("At the 'Cadian Ball," 311). In "The Storm," by contrast, Calixta's skin whitens and her accent disappears. The racial markers of her desirability for Alcée are erased, and her Spanish blood is not reiterated as an excuse for her actions. She still has her "liquid blue eyes" and "a drowsy gleam that unconsciously betrayed a sensuous desire," but now she also reveals "her round, white throat and her whiter breasts" (928, 928, 929). Indeed, it is her whiteness that comes as a surprise to Alcée as he makes his way into her bedroom for the long-postponed coital experience: "She was a revelation in that dim, mysterious chamber; as white as the couch she lay upon" (929).

Moreover, "The Storm" engaged with those same markers of aesthetic stylization that began to displace the local in favor of the chic. Perhaps nowhere can this predilection for the deployment of iconic images of the aesthetic movement be seen more clearly than when Calixta's experience of the act of sex is described as being like "a creamy lily": "Her firm, elastic flesh that was knowing for the first time its birthright, was like *a creamy lily* that

4.16 Aubrey Beardsley, illustration for the provocative art edition of Aristophanes's *Lysistrata* (London: L. Smithers, 1896). Department of Rare Books and Special Collections, Princeton University Library.

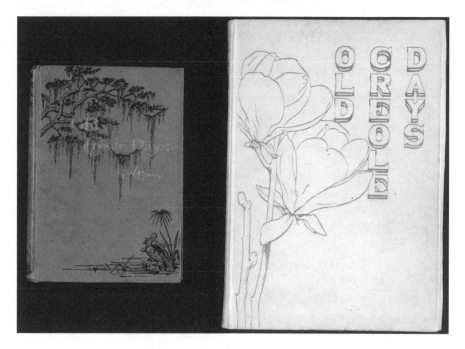

4.17 When a new edition of George Washington Cable's *Old Creole Days* (1879) was brought out in 1897, its cover was redesigned. Instead of drooping moss, a familiar symbol of nostalgia for the old plantation in the immediate postbellum period, the cover now displayed a Japanese-inspired line drawing of flowers, reflecting the association of local-color fiction with the aesthetic arts movement. Department of Rare Books and Special Collections, Princeton University Library.

the sun invites to contribute its breath and perfume to the undying life of the world" (my emphasis, 929). To draw on just a few examples, one sees something like that lily on the cover of the deluxe edition of Cable's *Old Creole Days,* reissued in 1896, on the cover of Beardsley's edition of *Le Morte D'Arthur* (1893), and on Crane's *The Black Riders* (1895) (figs. 4.17, 4.18, and 4.19). The lilies become poppies on the cover of Lafcadio Hearn's collection of Japanese folktales and sketches, *Kwaidan* (1904), but then Hearn always seems to push the cosmopolitan aestheticism of local color to the limit; he does not only deploy *Japonisme* in his writing, but actually takes it back to Japan (fig. 4.20). Calixta's name, itself, evokes these images, "calyx" being the whorl of leaves that sheathes the flower. But in "At the 'Cadian Ball," it had been Clarisse, the well-bred Creole woman whom Alcée eventually marries (and whom he cheats on with such harmless relish in "The Storm") who had

4.18

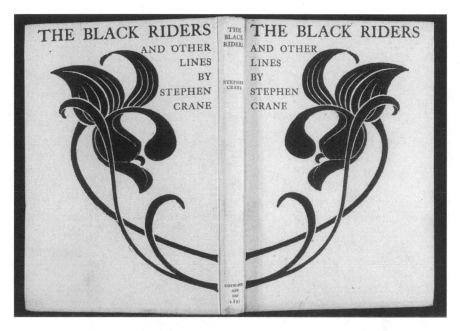

4.18, 4.19, and 4.20 More aesthetic arts flowers: Aubrey Beardsley's cover for the 1890s art edition of *Le Morte D'Arthur* (1893), Department of Rare Books and Special Collections, Princeton University Library; the cover for Stephen Crane's *Black Riders* (1895), Department of Rare Books and Special Collections, Princeton University Library; and the cover for Lafcadio Hearn's *Kwaidan* (1904), Rutgers University Libraries.

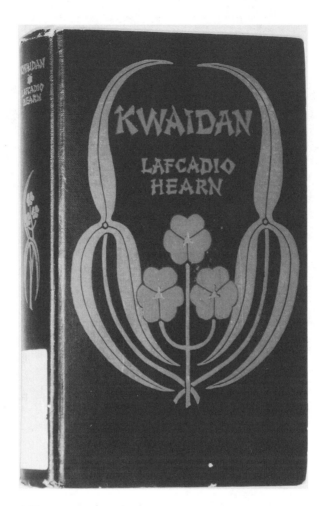

4.20

been described as being—somewhere between a Monet and a Van Gogh—as "[d]ainty as a lily; hardy as a sunflower; slim, tall, graceful like one of the reeds that grew in the marsh" (303). In "The Storm," the figure of the lily becomes Calixta, the most intensely dislocated character, the "Spanish vixen" of the bayou no longer. Chopin has gone postimpressionist: Van Gogh's sunflowers give way to visual icons of Gustave Moreau and Gustav Klimt.

Signaling an aesthetic sensibility that is located in neither any one place nor any one self, the chic became a singularly effective way for locally colored characters, like both Calixta and Alma, to inhabit modernity. But the real point is that neither they nor their work could have been recognizably chic in the aesthetic world Howells imagined without a primal connection to a locale from which they might be displaced. In her widely acclaimed work on American bohemianism, Christine Stansell notes early on the prevalence of "protoethnographic" sketches in the movement: "The notion of the bohemian reflected a nineteenth-century habit of mind already attuned to discovering and observing stock 'types' in their particular metropolitan niches."[62] What I am arguing for here is an understanding of the extent to which bohemianism and the chic do not just reflect but depend upon the *notions* of both "types" and "niches" such literature describes. The ability to localize, and thus, also, to dislocate them—the female illustrator from St. Barnaby's, the freckled cockney model—produced the possibility of their circulation as aesthetic commodities. This charge of the chic can be found in other local-color writing in the 1890s because what made local color chic is precisely the attention paid to its circulation—an attention that came when locality was deployed by practitioners of *Japonisme* and the aesthetics arts as a favored commodity to be circulated within and across the trade routes of taste. And while not at first glance recognizably "ethnographic" in the sense literary critics might have come to expect, this taste should by now be recognizable as the logical extension of the diffusionists' interest in folklore; what local color comes to trade on is the energy provoked by the dislocations of circulating culture.

THE ENDS OF CULTURE

W. E. B. Du Bois and the Legacy
of Boasian Anthropology

The bigotry of civilization which is the taproot of intellectual prejudice begins far back and must be corrected at its source. Fundamentally it has come about from that depreciation of Africa which has sprung up from ignorance of her true rôle and position in human history and the early development of culture. The Negro has been a man without a history because he has been considered a man without a worthy culture.

—Arthur A. Schomburg

The previous chapters have explained Alfred Kroeber and Clyde Kluckhohn's cultural lag in terms of the attention drawn to folklore and regional fiction as circulating objects—objects detached from traditional categories of difference not only by shifts in social scientific epistemologies but also by a changing racial politics and the emergent culture industry.[1] I want to conclude this book, however, by looking at a very old, Enlightenment version of conceptualizing difference that found new political life in the increasingly racialized context of early-twentieth-century social thought. The disruption of racial and nationalistic categories of difference that one might have anticipated emerging from dissemination, literary momentum, and marketplace *chic* faltered, then as now. But in its place, a modernist internationalism emerged that was broadly committed to the historical plasticity of race and to the ethical ideal of a pluralist universalism. As demonstrated in the life and work of W. E. B. Du Bois, this line suggests yet another element protracting, if not fundamentally challenging, the emergence of an anthropological concept of culture.

Most everything known about W. E. B. Du Bois in the period leading up to the publication of his first novel, *The Quest of the Silver Fleece,* in 1911, would lead us to expect that he would have taken up the long nineteenth-century tradition of collecting black folklore and carried it forward into a fully developed conceptualization of culture along the lines being pursued at the same time by Franz Boas and his students. Du Bois received his PhD in 1897 from Harvard, but not before coming within one semester of receiving the vaunted German doctorate in history, meaning that he would have been fully versed in the German historical and social scientific methodologies that were instrumental in the development of the fields of ethnology, folklore, and literature. He was a distinguished professor of sociology at Atlanta University from 1897 to 1910, during which time he arranged for Boas to make his now famous commencement address at the school in which he extolled the historical development of African peoples. Du Bois concluded what remains his most important work, *The Souls of Black Folk* (1903), with an inspired and inspirational reading of "the Sorrow Songs," the Negro spirituals, which would seem to take up the nineteenth century folklore tradition in direct terms. The connections between Du Bois and late-nineteenth-century social science were many; the point to be made, however, is that with his first novel, Du Bois said goodbye in no uncertain terms to the nineteenth century collection and study of black folklore, and also to the preliminary routes through which Boasian anthropologists had begun to formalize the anthropological concept of cultures.

A matriarchal old conjure woman figures prominently in *The Quest of the Silver Fleece,* but instead of recounting folk songs or stories, she prostitutes herself to several generations of white plantation owners. The heroine is her daughter, Zora, who literally shoos away the remnants of Joel Chandler Harris from the cotton field she has planted as a way out similar depredations. "Brer Rabbit—poor little Brer Rabbit, don't you know you must n't eat Zora's Cotton? Naughty, naughty Brer Rabbit," she scolds, while chasing the rabbits from her crop of "silver fleece," the cotton she hopes will lift her black sharecropping community out of dependence on the white landowners.[2] Rather than black folklore, Greek mythology underwrites the novel's aesthetic modality, as suggested by the allusion to Jason's "quest of the golden fleece" in the title. Zora needs to cultivate her cotton field, but she also needs to let the cultivation of high aesthetics course through her soul. Indeed, Du Bois reworked his famous image of the veil from *Souls* into the universalizing fabric of aesthetic cultivation at the end of the novel. The fruits of the cotton crop are stolen from Zora, but they come back to her in the form of "a bolt of silken-like cambric," which she weaves into a magnificent wedding "veil" for her white employers—"she wove in that white veil her own strange soul" (226). The fleece from the story of Jason and Medea is transformed by Zora's conjured, exotic soul into an aesthetic commodity of oddly transcendent value. The veil that separated white and black in *Souls* is not lifted, per se, but rather is brought into focus as a thing of intrinsic and complex beauty through which power struggles and overt manifestations of racism are positively reconfigured.

What *Quest* makes clear is that, far from marking the continuation of a nineteenth-century dynamic between the anthropological and the literary, Du Bois's intervention in the early 1900s might better be read as the end of what I have been calling the ethnographic imagination. Du Bois, moreover, never became the "Boasian" he seemed destined to become—even if, as I will be arguing here, neither did Boas. In the first part of this chapter, I will be using the relationship between Du Bois and Boas as a way of accessing another part of the story of why there was such a delay in the development of the culture concept. Although, as we have seen, the concept had been percolating in the United States since the 1870s, very old Enlightenment ideas about *Bildung* offered both Du Bois and Boas a surer route toward a cultural politics. The two remained, on the whole, on much more divergent intellectual trajectories than suggested by recent criticism, and yet their deployment of this *Bildung* ideal in addressing the race problem drew them together in unexpected ways around what had been a German-Jewish Enlightenment strategy.[3] This strategy differed from that of pluralizing culture in its focus on the historical plasticity of peoples and a harmonizing, universalistic ideal. The first half of this chapter explores the relationship between Du Bois and Boas's conceptualization of culture. The second half offers an extended reading from within this context of Du Bois's *The Souls of Black Folk* and his novels *The Quest of the Silver Fleece* and *Dark Princess* (1928).

DU BOIS AND THE CULTURE CONCEPT

Much of the recent critical attention to Du Bois has focused on what his deployment of the concept of race has to say to current trends in contemporary American racial, multicultural, and diasporic politics.[4] Less attention has been paid to his conceptualization of what, in the context of the evolving scientific debate of the early twentieth century, should be posed as its dichotomous other half: culture. Vernon Williams does the most to provide a thorough account of this history to date—of Boas and his students' problematic insistence on the inadequacy of biological descent to account for cultural differentiation, and of Boas's explicit rejection on cultural grounds of arguments for the hereditary inferiority of "the Negro."[5] More to the point is the absolute surety with which we can assert that Du Bois was familiar at an early date with the divorce Boas was attempting to adjudicate between race and culture. Boas's watershed statement to this effect took place on Du Bois's own invitation when, in 1906, Boas gave the commencement address at Atlanta University, where Du Bois had been teaching sociology and running the annual Atlanta University Conferences since 1898. In this address, Boas used the plural form of "cultures"—"it is . . . well to remember that there have been cultures different from ours and that the qualities that are today dominant and most highly esteemed . . . have not always had the same value"—and also stressed that "[t]here is no anatomical evidence available that would sustain the view that the bulk of the Negro race could not become as useful citizens as the members of any other race."[6] The contribution the graduates would make to society depended not on "race" but on their ability to "adapt [themselves] to the demands [and] . . . the conflicting interests of modern life" (62). In a precursor to more adamant statements— like that of 1930 in which he stated that it "does not matter from which point of view we consider culture, its forms are not dependent upon race"—Boas here argued that while there may be cultures different from the one in which the Atlanta University students found themselves, race was not an essential factor in determining their composition.[7]

It is thus important to note that Du Bois, throughout his long career—a career beginning at the genesis of an anthropological definition of culture and continuing well after it had been formally defined—never used the term, as Boas and particularly his students did, to define the characteristics of a given social group without reference to race. Du Bois's idea of culture remained remarkably consistent throughout his life, building in large measure on ideas that were evident in much of his earliest writing. As already noted, his most famous formulation of the term came in the first of several articles he published in the *Atlantic Monthly* in the late 1890s and later incorporated into *Souls* as the first chapter, "Of Our Spiritual Strivings": "This, then, is the end of his striving: to be a co-worker in the kingdom of culture, to escape both death and isolation, to husband and use his best powers and his latent genius."[8] As becomes clear as the article progresses, what Du Bois here harnesses are many of the Arnoldian connotations of the term, the intellectual and aesthetic aspects of "the kingdom of culture" carrying with them the sense of a shared human striving for "the best which has been thought and said in the world." Culture surfaces as the very work of "spiritual striving" about which Du Bois is writing; it marks the forward movement in "the training . . . of gifted minds and pure hearts." In two different instances, Du Bois refers to "higher culture" by way of suggesting a break

with the banalities of material existence and manual labor that were strad-
dling the prospects of the American Negro.[9] In so doing, his use of the term
recalls Matthew Arnold both thematically and grammatically. Not only does
it stand against the mechanization of human life, but also the noun and the
verb forms become almost interchangeable, the phrase "higher culture"
standing in at times both as the object of Negro education and the process of
achieving it.

   In contradistinction to the anthropological formulation, Du Bois maintained both the singularity of the term culture and the ethnographically
determining importance of race. Setting the stage in the *Atlantic Monthly*
article for his later formulations of both concepts, Du Bois on the one hand
charts race as the category by which he recognizes the peculiar characteristics of social groups, as when looking forward to the time that "some day on
American soil two world-races may give each to each those characteristics
both so sadly lack" (370). Culture, on the other hand, becomes one of a triad
of democratic principles—"[w]ork, culture, liberty,—all these we need"—by
which the Negro could forge a common bond with the rest of the world and
through which "that vaster ideal . . . the ideal of human brotherhood" may
some day be achieved (370). Keeping race as the ethnographic and political
marker of social organization, Du Bois turns to "higher culture" by way of
signaling both the common process of spiritual education and the common
ideal of universality to which all races should contribute. This higher culture
was, in turn, distinguished from the one traditionally evoked to perpetuate
racial discrimination, as when some would try to excuse prejudice as the
"natural defense of culture against barbarism" (368). At issue for Du Bois
was prejudice, not the pejorative category of barbarism: even if prejudice
were overcome, he suggests, the ideal would maintain its developmental
charge away from "barbarism" and toward "righteousness, and progress"
(368–69).

   It is in much this same sense that Du Bois uses the term when he gives
it his most direct definition thirty years later. Speaking on the theme of "cultural equality" in 1929, Du Bois explains that "By equality, I do not mean
absolute identity or similarity of gift, but gifts of essentially equal values to
human culture. By culture, I mean that organized tide which men call civilization."[10] In this formulation, it is the plural "gifts" that are relativized,
while "culture" maintains its singular attachment to ideas about development and civilization.[11] "Civilization," Du Bois continues, "is by the definition of the term, civilization for all mankind . . . the rightful heritage of
all"—it "cannot be monopolized and confined to one group" and will be
brought forth to "universal recognition and applause."[12] Similarly in the
Autobiography, written at the very end of his long life, Du Bois maintains

culture's universalizing, developmental association with civilization, speaking repeatedly of "human culture" and "modern culture" as that to which the striving of humankind should aspire.[13] Bemoaning, for example, the deleterious effects of "western acquisitive society," he worries that "private profit for the smart and unscrupulous in a world of poverty, disease, and ignorance" may have misplaced "the natural end of human culture."[14] Culture is imagined not anthropologically, as a descriptive term for distinct social units, but as the general forward movement of human civilization—a movement that, whether gained or lost, pertains universally.

By way of comparison, we might remark that Du Bois's alignment of culture and civilization recalls the much earlier formulation of E. B. Tylor at the beginning of his seminal tome, *Primitive Culture* (1871):

> Culture or Civilization . . . is that complex whole which includes knowledge, belief, art, morals, law custom, and any other capabilities and habits acquired by man as a member of society. . . . Its various grades may be regarded as stages of development or evolution, each the outcome of previous history, and about to do its proper part in shaping the history of the future."[15]

As George Stocking has aptly pointed out, the social evolutionary trajectory of Tylor's definition made it somewhat less revolutionary, somewhat less like a Boasian pluralist position, than even Arnold's.[16] Even with his insistence on imagining culture as a rough equivalent to "the organized tide which men call civilization," Du Bois added to Tylor's definition a remarkable level of multidimensionality. As opposed to categorizing "higher culture" by strictly known "stages of development," Du Bois imagined an ever-percolating cultural ideal that built on the racial plurality of its contributors, making room for voices arriving from outside the European juggernaut. Like Tylor, Du Bois imagined this ideal in terms of the forward movement of civilization, but he had in mind something more along the lines of Arnold, who wrote at one point that "culture is the study of . . . harmonious perfection."[17]

In addition to this primary use of the term, Du Bois also used culture on a general level to indicate education and uplift, as in the sense of "cultivation"; more specifically, he used it to refer to the material products of cultivation: "beauty," "truth" and "honesty" in literature, music, and the arts.[18] Culture, thus, was imagined as having an aesthetic trajectory; it entailed movement toward refinement and excellence, but it was entwined in a very specific notion of global inclusivity. For example, Du Bois proclaimed in "The Conservation of Races" (1897) that the American Negroes comprised "a nation stored with wonderful possibilities of culture," by which he meant to reference the potential for "the development of Negro genius, of Negro literature and art, of Negro spirit."[19] The ethnographic particularity marked here by race was given a universal direction by "culture," which imagined the Negro gifts as things that might "guide the world nearer and nearer that perfection of human life for which we all long" (819). One finds a similar use of the term, one that suggests the cultivation of the arts, in the 1928 novel *Dark Princess,* where Du Bois's hero naively finds himself at a Berlin dinner party among a select group of representatives from "the Darker World," where he "felt his lack of culture audible" (especially when trying to keep up with a discussion of "Shönberg's new and unobtrusive transcription of Bach's triumphant choral prelude").[20] Much of this novel was staged around the hero's need to discover that the European "culture" that he senses around the dinner table, and that later he discovers on his own in a Chicago art gallery, was but one chord in the universal harmonic—that only in developing the "eastern style" could a truly "harmonious perfection" emerge.

In 1940, when Du Bois published *Dusk of Dawn,* culture still generally meant progressive refinement, a sensibility to beauty, as in "above the average culture of his group" or "one of the obviously low culture groups in the United States."[21] "Wealth of work, wealth of commerce, factory and mine, skyscrapers. . . . This is what the white world means by culture," wrote Du Bois (148–49). But what Du Bois meant was best represented by his heavenly dark princess, Kautilya, and her geopolitical reorganization of the struggle of the colored masses against European and American capitalism: "In America is Power. Yonder [in Asia and Africa] is Culture, but Culture gone to seed, disintegrated, debased. Yet its re-birth is imminent" (*DP,* 285). Culture, in all these different manifestations, stood for social progress, moral and artistic accomplishment, beauty and truth, and the inclusive harmonization of the world's classes and colors, "Talent served from the great Reservoir of All Men of All Races of All Classes, of All Ages, of Both Sexes" (*DP,* 285). A particular racial group or region of the world may have possessed culture, but culture remained essentially a product of the human condition—not a demarcation of difference but a signal of universal humanity.

The sheer volume of Du Bois's literary production ensures that one can discover instances when he used culture in a way that sounds almost Boasian. In *Darkwater* (1920), for example, Du Bois wrote of the situation of colonized Africa where, within the recesses of European exploitation, "a fourth of the land and people [have] local self-government and native customs and might evolve, if undisturbed, a native culture along their own peculiar lines" (516). While the delimitation here is clear, there remains a problem with this usage from an anthropological standpoint in that it sounds like "the natives" are somehow existing without a culture as things currently stand—a fundamentally impossible condition from the anthropological perspective. Another case appeared in *Dark Princess*, where culture makes a very rare appearance in the plural when one of the Japanese dignitaries at the aforementioned Berlin dinner party claimed that "We [the Japanese] have our own carefully thought-out philosophy and civilization, while Europe has sought to adopt an ill-fitting mélange of the cultures of the world" (25). But again, despite the pluralization, culture here remains wedded to civilization, describing the evolutionary status of what people do as opposed to the underlying reason they do it.

Du Bois became most anthropological when using culture in its adjectival form, speaking in *Dusk of Dawn* of a "cultural connection" to Africa or in the *Autobiography* of "cultural patterns of American Negroes" (114; *A*, 318). "Culture" in and of itself, however, never emerged as an entity around which identity was formulated, never became the object of delimitation. It never attained the status that Boas laid out for it in 1906, nor the scientific reification it achieved with the publication of the seminal volumes of the 1920s and 1930s by the second generation of Boas's students, such as Margaret Mead's *Coming of Age in Samoa* (1928) and Ruth Benedict's *Patterns of Culture* (1934).[22] Despite Du Bois's training in and predilection for the social sciences, his use of culture remained firmly rooted in the realm of the humanities. Throughout his career, he continued to be much more in line with T. S. Eliot's conclusion that "Culture may even be described as that which makes life worth living" than with the construction of it proposed by an increasing number of social scientists.[23]

VÖLKERPSYCHOLOGIE: DU BOIS'S RACIALISM IN THE CONTEXT OF BOAS'S GERMAN JEWISH SCIENCE

To say that Du Bois did not use the culture concept is to highlight, in turn, the problems to be encountered by the critical project of assessing Du Bois's construction of the race problem. When Du Bois wrote "Strivings" and "The Conservation of Races" in the last years of the nineteenth century, he may not have had the critical vocabulary of "cultures" available to clearly distinguish between race and some other socio-historically delimited entity. However, by 1906, he did, and he chose not to put it into play. What this failure to deploy the concept suggests is that even if culture proved an effective category for conceptualizing the limitations of race, it nonetheless had a problem from an early date with racism. For even in its early versions, culture's potency as a descriptive tool limited its ability to account for either history or change. Change was not built into the cultural system, but would seemingly depend on such "external" forces as the economy or politics.[24]

In his rejection of this pluralization of culture, Du Bois was clearly no "Boasian." And yet, largely because of the success of George Stocking's seminal work on Boas's institutionalization of the culture concept in American anthropology, the Boasian legacy in this line of thinking is made difficult to chart. Any analysis of Du Bois's relationship to Boas needs to work against a caricature of Boasian thought streamlined from Stocking's finely nuanced arguments.[25] What we can say for certain is that Du Bois's shift away from social scientific methodology coincided with the generational shift in Boas's work that can be marked not only by his 1905 departure from the American Museum of Natural History to devote himself full time to teaching at Columbia but also by his failure in 1907 to secure funding from the Carnegie Foundation for a museum of African and African American material culture. This move from the museum to the academy can be read as one from the study of objects to the study of cultures, from the diffusion of things to the style with which they were received and reproduced. With this shift, the second generation of Boas's students entered upon the scene—among them Mead, Benedict, and Melville Herskovits; and with them came the commitment to a more static and descriptive notion of "cultures" as particularized wholes, the notion with which Boas has been most frequently associated.[26] Boas, however, was notoriously slow to come to any such formal synthesis; Du Bois, as we have seen, never did.

Du Bois never integrated with the second generation Boasians, and to that extent he was not, strictly speaking, a Boasian. But at the same time it is equally certain that a different Boasian line, occluded by an overemphasis on the culture paradigm, had profound similarities to Du Bois's project.[27] Boas's work on the extreme plasticity of cultures evident in his earlier attention to diffusion and his commitment to cultivation as a universalizing good had clear affinities with Du Bois's thinking, particularly that which has been taken by critics to come from his Hegelian historical idealism. As Matti Bunzl has begun to show in work that promises to revitalize the Boasian legacy, a significant line of Boasian thought came out of the Jewish German tradition of folk psychology that took as its central tenets the German Enlightenment notion of *Bildung,* self-perfection or the striving for betterment, and *Volksgeist,* group spirit.[28] These concepts, which had been deployed to address the Jewish problem in mid-nineteenth-century Germany, and which were being used in the same context in the United States in the early twentieth, prove extremely useful in making sense of Du Bois's conceptualization of the Negro problem in the United States.

To get a feel for this other Boasian line, it can help to go back to the persistence of racial thought in both Du Bois's and Boas's writing. One strategy for getting beyond the biological essentialism of race as a category, adopted by Jamesian cultural pluralists like Randolph Bourne and Horace Kallen more than by Boasian anthropologists, was to posit a socio-historical explanation of group differences in its place.[29] In one of the most convincing analyses of Du Bois's formulation of race, Anthony Appiah works to demonstrate Du Bois's failure to make just this socio-historical move. Concentrating on "The Conservation of Races," Appiah points out that while the social history of the Negro race was important to Du Bois's argument, it was not the basis upon which Du Bois constructed his definition of Negro identity; Du Bois failed to "complete the argument" against biological essentialism, in Appiah's phrasing, because black culture for Du Bois always came back to the biological transmission of Negro blood.[30] Du Bois, in effect, conceded the biological existence of race in order to argue that it set no determinative limits on the potential of the Negro to contribute to universal culture.

While right on the details of Du Bois's conceptualization of race, Appiah's analysis takes its centrality to Du Bois's cultural project in the wrong way. Du Bois's position on race may have been conservative with regard to biological essentialism, but it did exactly what he wanted it to do with regard to culture, which was to posit a long history of growth by the Negro race, both in Africa and with the vanguard in the United States. Du Bois's early commitment to race was actually a commitment to history, and, thus, to the ultimate plasticity of the category of race. As such, Du Bois's cultural project can be read in a much different way from that done by Appiah—not as a way to get beyond race but as a proof of what Du Bois, following Boas in a long tradition of German Jewish Enlightenment political engagement, may well have known as *Bildung*.

It should be remembered that Boas persisted in his use of race as a category of classification and, moreover, that he was not, strictly speaking, a pluralist.[31] Even in 1906, when Boas gave his Atlanta University commencement address, the anthropologist's challenge to the concept of race was, like Du Bois's, ambivalent. As Susan Hegeman notes, Boas's main line of argument depended not on the nonexistence of race but on its irrelevance to the formation of human cultures.[32] Like Du Bois in "Conservation," Boas conceded both the existence of a Negro race and its current state of inferiority in the United States, only to bring up the history of cultural development in Africa as proof that race was not determinative of achievement. Although allowing "the present weakness of the American Negro, his uncontrolled emotions, his lack of energy," Boas argued that the African development of "the art of smelting iron," the organization of "kingdoms which lived for many centuries," and "the beauty and daintiness of African" artwork showed that race and cultural development were not necessarily linked.[33] He had made the same move in an article from 1904 titled "The Negro in Africa," in which he avoided discussions of black people in America altogether, focusing instead on the achievements of black people in Africa, such as their development of "strict methods of legal procedure," their "power of organization," and their "ability to assimilate foreign cultures."[34] Far from being a move from "race into culture," as Walter Benn Michaels has fashioned the work of most cultural pluralists in the 1920s, Boas was willing to keep race around as a concept, but one without the potency to exert any determinative influence on a people's potential development.[35]

The significance of this ambivalence with regard to Du Bois comes from the way at least one line of it was clearly rooted in German Jewish scholarly work codified in the mid-nineteenth century by the *Völkerpsychologie* school (translatable as psychology of the peoples or folk psychology) established by Heyman Steinthal and Moritz Lazarus. To address race in the United States, Boas, in effect, drew keenly on a German Jewish ethnological strategy for confronting racism in Germany. Folk psychology was closely related to, but ultimately different from, the proto-anthropological work developing in Germany at the same time, with which Boas is more frequently associated because of his training with Rudolf Virchow and Adolf Bastian. Virchow and Bastian held the first university chairs in the field of ethnology in Germany and founded its leading periodical *Zeitschrif für Ethnologie.* Their work came directly out of the physical sciences; both men were trained as physicians, and their intellectual innovation came from their ability to wed natural history to the study of humanity. From Virchow, Boas learned a methodology for work in physical anthropology that formed the basis of his vast anthropometric work. From Bastian, for whom Boas worked at the Royal Ethnographic Museum in Berlin, he gained an appreciation for the urgency of the encyclopedic salvage from various geographic regions of artifacts of all kinds—from material culture to myths, from bones to religious beliefs and native grammars.

Bastian's methodology was radically inductive; the museum was imagined as an archive for the eventual reconstruction of cultural migration and diffusion. This approach can be seen permeating the first phase of Boas's ethnographic work, particularly in his museum-based research methodology, which focused on the collection of vast stores of material and also deferred broad conceptual claims in favor of inductive analysis. As noted earlier, Bastian's most immediate influence on Boas was made visible in the frequently cited debate with Otis T. Mason about classification strategies in museums.[36] That said, Bastian and Virchow may have had less of an impact on Boas's formulation of a cultural politics, like that of his early 1900s pieces on the Negro problem, than did reform-minded Jewish intellectuals in both Germany and the United States and his involvement with the German Jewish scientific discipline of *Völkerpsychologie.*

Völkerpsychologie drew on a historical line of response to the "Jewish problem" by upwardly mobile German Jews in the eighteenth century. The *Haskalah,* or Jewish Enlightenment, responded to the growing sense of the Jews as a degraded *Geist,* one that had suffered from cultural isolation in the ghettos and corrupt rabbinical instruction. Developed around the figure of Moses Mendelssohn, the *Haskalah* drew on the Enlightenment notion of *Bildung,* the notion of social and civic improvement related in many ways to the English idea of "cultivation." As such, the *Haskalah* argument is immediately recognizable in that deployed by Du Bois in "The Conservation of Races," where he argued for conserving race until such time that "Negroes inspired by one vast ideal, can work out in its fullness the great message we have for humanity" ("Conservation," 820). Emphasizing the plasticity of *Geist,* and the infinite possibility of improvement, the argument for *Bildung* conceded that the race had undergone centuries of deprivation, but that there were no natural limits on its ability to regenerate itself and grow on a moral and cultural level, ultimately contributing its particular genius to the universal brotherhood of man.

Steinthal and Lazarus took this basic Enlightenment insight about *Bildung* and looked to apply it to the situation of German Jews, their goal being the humanist one of understanding the complex inner workings behind the group's contribution to world culture. *Völkerpsychologie* was very much a kindred field to ethnology. Both disciplines drew on a shared intellectual tradition invested in historicism and cultural particularity, and their practitioners regularly published articles in each other's journals. And yet, folk psychologists defined their work in opposition to what they took to be the reductive materialism of ethnological work by Bastian and Virchow. As noted by Bunzl, Steinthal and Lazarus argued in the inaugural issue of their journal that the ethnologists' emphasis on external factors, like physiology and the environment, failed to take account of the "inner drive" of folk *Geist,* its historical plasticity, and its infinite capacity for development.[37] On numerous other occasions, Steinthal called for a more intense analysis of mythology and literature because of the way they provided an explanatory framework more suited to this exploration of *Bildung* than could be provided for by the natural scientific, classificatory methodology of the ethnologists.

As Bunzl argues, Boas would have been conversant with the Jewish reform movements of the *Haskalah* that underwrote *Völkerpsychologie's* deployment of *Bildung*. Moreover, he had direct contact with Steinthal and Lazarus in Germany, and credited their ongoing influence on his work in several of his key methodological texts. Bunzl notes Boas's citation of Steinthal and Lazarus's work in a number of his more important statements, including "The Aims of Ethnology" (1888) and "The History of Anthropology" (1904), as well as in a letter to Robert Lowie in which he explicitly remarked that his work on language had always followed "Steinthal's principles."[38] We might, additionally, see the *Völkerpsychologie* line in Boas's work on the dissemination of folk tales of the North American Indians, where he directly objected to his mentor, Bastian, on folk-psychological grounds. Writing on this subject, Boas noted that "I cannot agree with Bastian and Wundt" who considered the historical origins of the tales comparatively insignificant because of the supposed unity of psychological processes responsible for their creation and dissemination.[39] Rather, in line with what Steinthal and Lazarus had proposed, Boas held out as the very object of ethnological study the psychological variation that must accompany the historical development of cultural material in specific places at specific times. He argued not for the psychological unity of mankind but for an understanding of universality in terms of the psychological differences between peoples resulting from historical factors.

The political valence of such claims would have become particularly apparent in the New York cultural milieu of the early twentieth century, where Boas developed a close personal friendship with another German Jew, the founder of the Ethical Culture movement, Felix Adler. Ethical Culture, which still has offices throughout the United States, was organized around the ideal of humanity united in a common concern for ethical values. It was in many ways radically assimilationist, taking reform Judaism to its extreme by arguing for universalism as against Jewish particularity. And yet, at the center of its argument was a basic conceptualization of the plurality of cultural groups or races that *Bildung* could transform, reform, and emancipate. Significantly, Boas and Adler had met before Boas's immigration to the United States; once here, Boas sent his children to the school run by Adler to further the Ethical Culture movement's devotion to *Bildung*. While not at the fore of his anthropological work, the resonance of this German Jewish emancipatory vision can be heard in the overarching universalism of Boas's politics, his strong commitment both to the idea that differences were the result of the historically specific malleability of *Geist* and that these differences in no way placed limitations on the transformative possibilities of *Bildung*.

Not coincidentally, Adler was also an acquaintance of Du Bois, with whom he was a co-secretary of the First Universal Races Congress in

London in 1911—a conference that Du Bois greeted with a lofty verse, "A Hymn to the Peoples," beginning "Truce of God! And primal meeting of the Sons of Man, / Foreshadowing the union of the World! / From all the ends of the earth we come!"[40] The similarity of the two men's thoughts is immediately recognizable in a quote from Adler that Du Bois used as the epigraph to the 1913 Atlanta University publication, *Morals and Manners among Negro Americans:* "[W]e must depend for the peace and progress of the world upon the formation of a horizontal upper layer of cultured persons among all the more civilized peoples—a cross-section, as it were, of the nations, whose convictions and sentiments shall supply the moral force on which international arbitration courts and similar agencies will have to depend."[41] Adler's suggestion of internationalizing what Du Bois had famously called the "talented tenth" was surely to Du Bois's liking.[42]

To understand the Boasian legacy for Du Bois in light of their mutual respect for Adler is to add another layer to the critical interest in their racial thought, for on the one hand, by conceding race, both men might appear to have retained a notion of biological essentialism, while on the other, by challenging the determinative nature of race, their relativism seemingly suggests the real prospect of cultural assimilation. The point, however, is that from within the *Völkerpsychologie* framework, neither of these critiques of their racial positions hold, as can be seen by turning to Du Bois's own use of race in his early writings as a means, precisely, of demarcating the lines of Negro *Bildung,* or historical growth.

"GROWTH": RACE AND THE ACCESS TO HISTORY

Two modes of historical work were at play in Du Bois's writing. The first was inspired by Du Bois's adviser at Harvard, Albert Bushnell Hart and taken up by Du Bois in such works as *The Philadelphia Negro* (1899), *The Suppression of the African Slave-Trade* (1896), and even in much of "Strivings." Hart, like Du Bois's political economy professors at the University of Berlin, Gustav von Schmoller and Adolf Wagner, and like Virchow and Bastian, was a significant figure in the late-nineteenth-century methodological shift away from Hegelian idealism and Spencerian system-making to a more positivist study of material conditions—from a broadly deductive system working from the mind to a radically inductive one working from historical facts.[43] The second historical modality in Du Bois's work has been taken to be his Hegelian idealism, evident in "The Conservation of Races" with its sweeping pronouncements about the "vast historic race . . . but half awakening in the dark forests of its African fatherland" and projections about "the realization of that broader humanity." It is this second modality, historicism (as opposed to the "positivism" of the first mode), that is remarkably clarified by the German Jewish intellectual trajectory stemming from *Bildung.*[44]

The problem with understanding Du Bois's historicism in terms of Hegel comes from the difficulty one then has in explaining in what ways its universal history was neither accommodationist nor assimilationist on the race question.[45] Hegel, especially as taken up in American political philosophy of the late nineteenth century, was rendered in either one of these two strictly homogenizing cultural positions. Du Bois poignantly countered by insisting throughout his work, but especially in *Souls,* on a historical imagination that was "engaged in the direct confrontation of the actual and present world" and that was also rhetorically committed to large scale racial and historical claims for the "shadow of a mighty Negro past [that] flits through the tale of Ethiopia the Shadowy and of Egypt the Sphinx."[46]

As early as in "The Conservation of Races," Du Bois began to lay the grounds for linking a historicist reading of racial history with a demonstration of Negro *Bildung.* His explanation of the origins of the races was one of the more unique features of the piece—and one that remained remarkably consistent throughout his career, being reiterated, for example, in the opening pages of *Dusk of Dawn* (1940). This section of "Conservation," however, has received little critical attention, perhaps because of its signature insistence on the universality of the race instinct, but probably more so because of its wildly speculative historicism. Having set out "eight distinctly differentiated races," Du Bois outlined a theory for racial origin dependent upon what he called "a growth":

> The whole process which has brought about these race differentiations has been a growth, and the great characteristic of this growth has been the differentiation of spiritual and mental differences between great races of mankind and the integration of spiritual differences. (817, 818–19)

Here is, in fact, not only a nonbiological explanation of race, but also one intensely interested in marking a historicist trajectory. And again, it is very similar to Boas's conceptualization of the problem as suggested earlier in his critique of Bastian. In the earliest times, humans were spread out across the inhabited globe in nomadic tribes in which there was a uniform distribution of physical and spiritual differences. The growth pertains to a process by which people slowly separated themselves into groups sharing similar traits—traits that would eventually define the bounds of modern races and nations. Du Bois suggested a three-step sequence for this growth: first, the nomadic tribes; second, the city-state, in which the nomadic tribes slowly sift themselves out along race lines and differentiated *"ideals of life"*; and, finally, the coalescence of cities into nations, at which time the "sociological and historical races of men began to approximate the present division of races as indicated by physical researches" (819). Rather than a cosmopolitan model, in which civilization might have brought with it a mingling of the races, Du Bois here imagined the long history of growth as a sifting-out of racial differentiation.

When the plot of racial consciousness was rewritten forty-three years later, Du Bois once again argued for the need to understand race in terms of growth, but this time highlighted the particular problem posed by nineteenth-century racial ideology that consistently defined the Negro in terms of stasis. Growth in the opening pages of *Dusk of Dawn* represented the new idea powering the discourse of progress and development—"the revolution of conceiving the world not as a permanent structure but as a changing *growth* and then the study of man as a changing and developing physical and social entity had to begin" (my emphasis, 4). As in "Conservation," Du Bois argued that humanity grew into its awareness of "the difference between men . . . in their appearance, in their physique, in their thoughts and customs": "Culture among human beings came to be and had to be built upon knowledge and recognition of these differences" (4). The addition to growth in this account came when Du Bois argued that the labor structure of the industrial revolution was based on imagining the Negro race in stasis, the slave trade being rationalized by imagining that blacks did not participate in growth but were fixed in a low position on the evolutionary scale. The forces of industrial capitalism cemented racial differences outside the trajectory of progress, prohibiting nonwhite men from growing out of a situation of exploitation.

Quite remarkably, Du Bois did not discard a liberal humanist line of thinking in his analysis of this situation. Rather than arguing that racism was essential to Enlightenment ideology, he argued that it went against the central Enlightenment principle that the possibility of *Bildung* held for all of humanity. He did not argue with the general notion of human progress, but with the specific ideology of white America that, in gauging its forward movement against Negro "stasis," insisted upon the idea that the American Negro had no history (*Dusk*, 26).

But the problem history posed to Du Bois ran deeper than that suggested here. In his own positivist historical work, carried on in the methodology of Hart, Wagner, and Schmoller, Du Bois documented an extremely short timeline for Negro development in America—a timeline far too short for *Bildung*. Du Bois addressed the problem history posed to Negro *Bildung* as early as 1898 when, having completed his research for the volume on Philadelphia's seventh ward, he gave a talk at the American Academy of Political and Social

Science, outlining a more ambitious plan for sociological study. In his lecture, he suggested that the "great deficiency of the Negro . . . is his small knowledge of the art of organized social life—that last expression of human culture."[47] He went on to explain this lack of culture in terms of two histories: the history of slavery and the history of race consciousness. Du Bois argued that group life in Africa was "broken off by the slave ship" and that, once in America, the "talented slaves found large freedom in the intimate intercourse with the family which they enjoyed; they lost many traditions of their fatherland, and their ideals blended with the ideals of their new country" (109, 106). He further noted that along with this severance of social ties to Africa came the institution, along with stricter race codes designed to manage the threat posed by increasing numbers of freemen, of a "distinct beginning of group life among Negroes" in America (105).

These codes, argued Du Bois, had the effect of revising the slave question from a problem of labor to one of color, "changing the Slave Code into a Black Code, replacing a caste of condition by a caste of race" (105). As a consequence, Du Bois only dated "the first wavering step of a people toward organized social life" to the subsequent founding of the Free African Society in Philadelphia on April 12, 1787.[48] This explanation paralleled that made in *Dusk of Dawn,* where Du Bois maintained that race consciousness took on a "significantly and fatally new" aspect in the nineteenth century; it suggested, moreover, that the very notion of an American Negro group identity depended upon the legislation of racial difference and its consequent effect on the way black Americans related to their social environment. In this positivist mode, race became little more than white oppression, or, as he wrote in *Dusk of Dawn* in response to the question of his own relationship to Africa, the race was defined by having "suffered a common disaster."[49] As Du Bois understood it, American Negro culture had a problem with history because the self-consciousness of the American Negro had been "fatally" brought into being by white discrimination.

While organized group life may have begun among the freemen in the mid-1700s, it was not until after Reconstruction that American society radically reorganized itself along race lines, reconfiguring sectional differences as biological ones, federalizing racial segregation in a series of court cases culminating with *Plessy v. Ferguson* (1896), and repudiating the goals of political and social integration set out immediately after the Civil War.[50] By 1896, anything other than a specifically racialized Negro group life was no longer an option, which, of course, was the "problem" that Du Bois addressed most forcefully in the opening chapter of *Souls.* The chapter was first published as an article in the *Atlantic Monthly* in 1897, a year after *Plessy.* Du Bois's provocative evocation of the "two warring ideals" of the black intellectual can easily be read as a precise response to the unnatural Manicheanization of the races in the Court's decision. The problem came from the need, legislatively imposed upon people like Du Bois, to choose between black and white, the folk of the "black belt" chapters and the opera of "On the Coming of John." His famous meditation on "twoness" attested to the unnaturalness of having to make such a choice given what should be the universalizing harvests of culture. Indeed, what Du Bois in the 1898 address referred to as "group ideals," "group life among Negroes," and "a distinct [Negro] social mind" gained strength because of the reconceptualization of race that dated most specifically to the late nineteenth century, the time of Du Bois's own entrance on the public scene.

The paradox of Du Bois's historical orientation should be clear. Despite its substantiation in his own historical writings, he strongly resisted this short version of the social history of the American Negro, rejecting it on the grounds of an inadequate attention to growth. This short history of Negro life in America contrasted quite sharply with the centuries-long story of African tribal life on which he drew elsewhere.

Du Bois seems to have been well aware of the problem. In his 1898 speech to the Academy of Political and Social Sciences, for example, he argued, very much in line with Steinthal and Lazarus, that what had been lacking in the study of slavery was a historical sense of the group psychology of the Negro stretching back to Africa:

> The slave code of a state is given, the progress of antislavery sentiment, the economic results of the system and the general influence of man on master are studied, but of the slave himself, of his group life and social institutions, of remaining traces of his African tribal life, of his amusements, his conversion to Christianity, his acquiring of the English tongue—in fine, his whole reaction against his environment, of all this we hear little or nothing, and would apparently be expected to believe that the Negro arose from the dead in 1863.[51]

When Du Bois went this route, he signaled a moment of antithesis within the logic of his argument, a moment at which the positivist history of American Negro group life that he had already written was extended by a call not only to African origins but also to social evolution: "Yet all the testimony of law and custom, of tradition and present social condition, shows us that the Negro at the time of emancipation had passed through a social evolution which far separated him from his savage ancestors" (114).

Du Bois was well aware of the stigma attached to so-called African primitives and of the danger of making a connection with them, which perhaps explains why his first step in "The Conservation of Races" had been to suggest that his audience put aside their quick reactions and reflect on the question of race from the serenity of "calmer moments" (815). Similarly, he followed the tempered lead of the American Negro Academy (ANA) itself—an organization that had been renamed from its original "African Institute" or "African Association" on the insistence of Paul Laurence Dunbar—when he opted in "Conservation" to call his movement not Pan-Africanism but "Pan-Negroism" (820). But ironically, what this turn to racialism provided Du Bois was not distance from Africa but a connection to it—a connection by race if not by culture. This connection allowed, specifically, for a more Hegelian historicism for the Negro in America that could be measured in the thousands of years.

Africa, of course, was not where those sympathetic to black causes in the late nineteenth century wanted to go. When the question focused on the future of the Negro in America, commentators tended to discreetly avoid mention of Africa. For example, in a series of essays on "The Future of the Negro" published by the *North American Review* in 1884, ten leading statesmen and race men—including among them Joel Chandler Harris and Frederick Douglass—declined to spend any time considering the Negro's African origins. The same might be said of an article by the Harvard paleontology professor N. S. Shaler in the *Popular Science Monthly,* which managed to provide a social-evolutionist endorsement of Booker T. Washington's program in industrial training without positing any but an American starting point for American blacks.[52] Again, the president of Wilberforce University and ANA charter member, W. S. Scarborough, published an article in *The Forum* advocating higher education for the talented tenth and funding for Fisk University, but made absolutely no mention of Africa.[53] And, in arguably the most influential book on the topic of the American Negro published during the period, Frederick L. Hoffman's *Race Traits and Tendencies of the American Negro* (1896), discussion of Africa was once again slighted. Strictly social-evolutionary in ideology, Hoffman's tome, which concluded with the infamous remark that for the American Negro "gradual extinction is only a question of time," made no mention of Africa or African ancestry—except, perhaps, in its implied politics of Western imperialism ("When the ever increasing white population has reached a stage where new conquests are necessary, it will not hesitate to make war upon those races who prove themselves useless factors in the progress of mankind").[54] In his positivist historical writing, Du Bois was no exception. In his first major publication, *The Suppression of the African Slave-Trade* (1896), Du Bois avoided the topic of African origins and retentions, sticking strictly to the story of European and American legislation governing the Negro already on American soil and in the situation of slavery.[55]

The one consistent exception to this tendency came with the collection of Negro folk songs, superstitions, tales, and dialect forms, where the question of origins, and thus of Africa, did come largely into play. It is critical to note at this juncture the one significant variation that Du Bois played upon the conservation theme: his orientation forward to a vital future, and not backward upon a vanishing past. The constant refrain of the folk collections, from Joel Chandler Harris's famous introduction to the first volume of Uncle Remus tales in 1880 to the more lighthearted recounting of superstitions in popular magazines like *Lippincott's,* was that the quaint characteristics of Negro life were passing away. "We love him ["the old fashioned darkey"] because we know his end is fast approaching"; "It is unfortunate that the opportunity for study ["of our Negro dialects"] will soon be gone, for they . . . are fast fading from the memory of man"; "That the 'old-time negro' is passing away is one of the common sayings all over the South."[56] And so on and on was repeated this conservationist's lament—a lament all the more striking in that it refused to go stale over the course of decades, refused even to wane when applied beyond the Negro's case to the Indian, the Mexican, the forest, the coal mine, and the frontier.

However, Du Bois put conservation to a different use in his historicist writing, being interested not in the collection of artifacts fractured from the course of modern progress, but in modern progress itself; not in antiquarianism, but in a notion of race that could channel black history through Africa; not in Africa per se, but in Africa as a marker of growth. The logic of this conservation effort is highlighted in the passage cited previously from "The Study of Negro Problems," where Du Bois at once signaled and distanced the American Negro from his African origins by arguing that "the Negro at the time of emancipation had passed through a social evolution which far separated him from his savage ancestors" (114). If Du Bois stressed separation from the past here, his ultimate goal carried over into the future. Conservation made way for prophecy, as in "The Conservation of Races," where Du Bois predicted the coming of a "black to-morrow which is yet destined to soften the whiteness of the Teutonic to-day" (822). The historicist swings of this conservation logic—from an ancient past to a prophetic tomorrow—underscores the extent to which plotting a trajectory of growth became essential to Du Bois's cultural project. This tension between history and historicism signals the fact that Du Bois's commitment to race was not only meant to celebrate a unique African diasporic heritage, but also, and perhaps more crucially, to free up a historicist modality by which to understand Negro *Bildung,* a black contribution to the universal kingdom of culture.

THE SORROW SONGS: DU BOIS'S REVISION
OF FOLKLORE'S HISTORICAL TRAJECTORIES

To underscore this point, we might look at the way Du Bois deployed positivist history and *Völkerpsychologie* historicism in his treatment of the Sorrow Songs—at once both "primitive African music" and "the articulate message of the slave to the world"—in *The Souls of Black Folk* (539, 538). Often cited as the seminal text for the development of a black cultural politics, *Souls* contained Du Bois's most pronounced move toward understanding black group life as an ethnographic construction. *Souls* departed from the historical idealism of earlier pieces like "The Conservation of Races" to put a more firmly social-scientific, materialist history of racial character into circulation.[57] It located the psychology of the American Negro's "twoness" not via racial essentialism but in the sociological treatment of the Southern black belt, the cotton industry, the legal entrenchment of discrimination, and the development of the Negro church. The language Du Bois used to do so was evocatively poetic; however, one senses that the pathos thus generated was sanctioned by the authority of his sociological research at Atlanta University. The chapters in *Souls,* most of which appeared at an earlier date in article form, stuck to the main themes that Du Bois had already covered in the Atlanta University publications: "Efforts for Social Betterment," 1898; "Negroes in Business," 1899; "College-Bred Negroes," 1900; "The Negro Common School," 1901; "The Negro Artisan," 1902; "The Negro Church," 1903. It was surely because of this authority that the noted black critic and anthologist William Stanley Braithwaite, writing twenty years later, described *Souls* as "a book of tortured dreams woven into the fabric of a sociologist's document."[58] In this sense, the work was historical in the manner of Hart or Schmoller.

Du Bois seems, moreover, to have made a conscious choice to stress an almost Herderian formulation of black group life. He used the German-inspired words "souls" and "folk" in his title, concentrated his analysis on the black peasant-class and their "inner" feelings, and even went so far as to compare the "troubled sperrit" of a black Sorrow Song to a line he picked up studying German folk *Kultur* among peasants outside of Berlin in 1896 ("Jetz Geh i' an's brunele, trink' aber net," which translates as "Now go to the well, but don't drink it," is in German's Swabian dialect, from an area south of Stuttgart [543]).[59] Even his framing of many of the chapters—particularly

"Of the Black Belt" and "Of the Faith of our Masters"—might be imagined to anticipate the formulas of ethnographic fieldwork initiated by Frank Hamilton Cushing but institutionalized by Boas's students in the 1910s and 1920s: the lone traveler-ethnographer arrives in foreign surroundings, becomes disoriented, undergoes certain initiation rituals and learns the native's language—all this as a means to gaining the authority required for observation and interpretation.

Nonetheless, arguments about Du Bois's commitment to some form of racial essentialism still apply to *Souls*, for, at the same time that Du Bois did his anthropological culture talk, he passed rapidly over into a rich evocation of race instincts and unqualified assessments of "the real Negro heart" (505). And here, the German Jewish influence of Steinthal and Lazarus can clearly be heard. For example, in turning to consider the "inner ethical life of the [Negro] people," Du Bois repeated one of the racial stereotypes most likely to land Negro superstitions on the pages of the popular press and the minstrel stage: that the Negro was a "being of . . . deep emotional nature which turns *instinctively* toward the supernatural" (my emphasis, *Souls*, 499). The change in *Souls* came from what followed, namely an intuitive tracing of this "racial" trait back to a historicist source, the "rich tropical imagination . . . [of] the transplanted African [who] lived in a world animate with gods and devils, elves and witches" (499). Du Bois's attention, that is, turned specifically to a psychological history of race, a *Völkerpsychological* approach to the Negro *Geist*. In so doing, he was able to accentuate a long history of Negro *Bildung* stretching back to a long African history that could be opened up for black Americans only by way of the racial connection.

Du Bois worked throughout *Souls*, but especially in its final four chapters, to elucidate this racial history: "What did slavery mean to the African savage? What was his attitude toward the World and Life? What seemed to him good and evil,—God and Devil? Whither went his longings and strivings, and wherefore was his heart burnings and disappointments?" (495). Du Bois's answers to these classically anthropological questions were severely limited by his lack of specific knowledge about Africa, discussion of which appeared in *Souls* only by way of allusion.[60] And yet he departed from the socio-historical specificity of his treatment of the current conditions of the Negro in the United States in order to make the connection back to this historicist past.

It should be stressed that within the fabric of *Souls*, there seems no illogic to this discordance, the shift from a sociology of the American Negro to an ethereal link with "primitive Africa" being knit together within the text's poetic fabric. Nonetheless, the opposition at play here—between history and historicism, Hart and Hegel, Bastian and Steinthal, the economics of the black belt and the "shadow of a mighty Negro past [that] flits through the tale of Ethiopia the Shadowy and of Egypt the Sphinx"—signals the logic of Du Bois's approach, his intent to demonstrate the cultural vitality of American Negroes by playing on his audience's notions of the link between the humanist idea of culture and history (365). He looked to endow the relatively new social construct of "the American Negro" with an unassailable proof of its long history—of its growth, or *Bildung*. The African connection, authenticated by the biological inheritance of African blood and the category of race, provided it as much intuitively as scientifically.

Especially as deployed by Du Bois in his most ethnographic chapters, "Of the Faith of the Fathers" and "Of the Sorrow Songs," Africa specifically signals and substantiates the fact that the American Negro participated in the process of cultivation. He was neither frozen in a savage African past nor isolated in some kind of primitive stasis as the modern American world passed him by. Particularly when speaking of the spirituals—"the singular spiritual heritage of the nation and the greatest gift of the Negro people"— Du Bois plots Africa as a ground zero for growth:

> Sprung from the African forests, where its counterpart can still be heard, it was adapted, changed, and intensified by the tragic soul-life of the slave, until, under the stress of law and whip, it became the one true expression of a people's sorrow, despair and hope. (537, 494)

The stress here, as later, is on development, emendation, intensification, and sublimation. At its core, the attention is given to the plasticity of culture. These songs "sprang" from Africa; while they still find their "counterparts" there, they have gone beyond the African originals.

When Du Bois goes on to enumerate the "step[s] in the development of the slave song," he notes that "African music" originates the list:

> The first is African music, the second Afro American, while the third is a blending of Negro music with the music heard in the foster land. . . . One might go further and find a fourth step in this development, where the songs of white America have been distinctively influenced by the slave songs or have incorporated whole phrases of Negro melody. (540)

Again, Du Bois traces a genealogy of growth which delineates not merely a connection to Africa but development upon the African original—a "blending" still "distinctively Negro" but developed from the influence of both Negro and white America on each other (540). Most significant is the fact that, while race intrinsically defines this history, the cultural products are not racially essentialized: the slave song becomes a humanistically defined cultural object, transcending, complicating, and integrating distinctions between social groups. Indeed, the slave song would ultimately contribute to the *Bildung* of the American nation, white and black—not to mention to universal humanity.

Thus, in the final chapter of *Souls,* Du Bois brings his strategic positioning of Africa to a striking conclusion by suggesting that the ultimate power of the Sorrow Songs—their contribution to the kingdom of culture—resides in their long history of transformative culturation, and not in their essential blackness. Indeed, in the last three paragraphs of the book, he synthesizes his argument along the lines of history. Despite their sadness, Du Bois argues, the spirituals maintain faith in the future. But "[d]o the Sorrow Songs sing true?" he asks by way of leading up to his conclusion:

> The silently growing assumption of this age is that the probation of races is past, and that the backward races of to-day are of proven inefficiency and not worth the saving. *Such an assumption is the arrogance of peoples irreverent toward Time and ignorant of the deeds of men.* A thousand years ago such an assumption, easily possible, would have made it difficult for the Teuton to prove his right to life. Two thousand years ago such dogmatism, readily welcome, would have scouted the idea of blond races ever leading civilization. So woefully unorganized is sociological knowledge that the meaning of progress, the meaning of "swift" and "slow" in human doing, and the limits of human perfectibility, are veiled, unanswered sphinxes on the shores of science. (my emphasis, 544–45)

The cue to "Time"—signaled here by its capitalization—brings into focus the theme that punctuates much of the chapter, namely a questioning of a notion of history that depends for its measurement upon the stasis of the Negro race. From the chapter's beginning, Du Bois casts the Sorrow Songs in light of "the olden days": he celebrates the construction of Fisk University's Jubilee Hall, built with money raised by the concert tours of the Jubilee Singers among Northern whites, as a monument to "the blood and dust of toil" and "the voices of the past" (536). He argues that the songs themselves span time, that while they "still live in the hearts of those who have heard them truly sung and in the hearts of the Negro people," they are also "indeed the siftings of centuries" (538). To note the English words becomes important as a way of marking their ancient roots: the "music is far more ancient than the words, and in it we can trace here and there signs of development" (538). The best of the songs, in both melody and lyric, express "a depth of history and meaning" (542). Crucially, that historical depth is measure not in hundreds but, as at the beginning of the passage on Time, in the thousands of years. Du Bois's history of the Sorrow Songs works to blend them into this millennial framework, the universal time of *Bildung*.

Africa plays but an ephemeral role in this discussion, and yet in terms of the way Du Bois is working up to a conclusion about "Time," that role is essential. The African roots of the songs can only be acknowledged in a limited way. The first is by Du Bois's attestation of the unidentifiable African verse sung over the years in his family (and reprinted in each of his subsequent autobiographies), "Do ba-na co-ba, ge-ne me! / Do ba-na co-ba, ge-ne me! / Ben d' nu -li, nu -li, nu -li, nu -li, ben d' le" (539). The second is in the underlying melodies, the "primitive African music," that cannot be signified in words but are represented by the musical bars that head each chapter (539).[61] Despite their paucity, much of the force of Du Bois's argument works off of these markers, pushing against them in the elucidation of a historical trajectory. The chapter works to recognize the Sorrow Songs not only as inherently African but also as distinguishable from Africa—as being more or less African, more or less American: of a syncretic nature. Because the Sorrow Songs do have this link to Africa, Du Bois can posit them as a proof that the Negro race had also progressed, had also produced lasting examples of sublime culture. But perhaps more to the point, because the songs continue to grow once transplanted to American soil, because they are appreciated at distance and are also adopted and rearranged (for example by Dvorak in his Symphony No. 9, "From the New World"), Du Bois can use them to push forward an ideal of culture that is globally syncretic and universally inclusive.

BILDUNG AS QUEST

The problem raised by this reading of Du Bois is that of understanding how a figure who has been so firmly placed at the head of African American cultural thought could at the same time be resolutely committed to an ideal of culture in the singular. The preferred response of late has been to situate Du Bois in the Jamesian pragmatist intellectual milieu of the early twentieth century. Du Bois, of course, studied with William James at Harvard, and so it is natural to attribute the unconventionality of his thought with regard to racial affiliation to James. Ross Posnock uses Du Bois's Jamesian training as a way of placing him within the history of "the black creative intellectual" at the turn of the century—the intellectual, itself, being a category defined for Posnock by pragmatism and the anti-identitarian, anti-essentialist thinking catalyzed by the Dreyfus affair in France. Associating Du Bois with such internationalism, Posnock argues that the black intellectual "emerged as a social type by resisting the lure of the prevailing ideology of the authentic."[62] Carrie Tirado Bramen, by contrast, uses Du Bois's connection to James to argue for the significance of a "Jamesian pluralism" that was "sufficiently vague and 'muddled' to allow for an early form of identity politics, but a form that significantly differs from its postmodern counterparts. The Jamesian 'each-form' is ethnicized and racialized as an identity culture that is both connected to and independent from the dominant culture."[63]

The Boasian route that I have been suggesting offers a rather different explanation altogether for the version of universalistic pluralism that Du Bois develops—one less attuned to James than to social scientific thought coming out of Germany in the mid-nineteenth century, his brief contact with Boas, and his extended affiliation with German Jewish intellectual thought in New York. This context can be seen in Du Bois's direct rejection of the nineteenth-century folklore tradition, and in his adoption of something like a *Völkerpsychologie* model for political engagement. This reading aligns with that of Tirado Bramen, but insists on a different line of influence stemming from German anthropology rather than from James. Already apparent in the last chapter of *Souls,* this move is made perfectly clear in *The Quest of the Silver Fleece,* which is, explicitly, a fictionalized analogy of emancipatory *Bildung.* Of particular interest is the way that, as it had been in *Souls,* the problem Du Bois had with the nascent conceptualization of "cultures" proved to be that of accounting for history, and thus, too, for change.

Du Bois's most elaborate and engaging portrait of a cultural pluralist comes in *Quest,* where a Northern philanthropist named Miss Smith spends twenty years in Alabama trying to establish an experimental school for black children, only to end the novel physically wrought and evidently senile, hiding in a small room provided to her by one of her old students. Early in the novel, Miss Smith expresses the belief, often in terms analogous to those one might attribute to Boas, that it is important to understand "black folk" on their own cultural terms. She refuses to judge what she does not understand and explains at one point that "*I* am here to learn from those whose ideas of right do not agree with mine, to discover *why* they differ, and to let them learn of me—so far as I am worthy" (87).[64] But by the end of the novel, she has all but lost the school, and takes refuge in a room that Zora prepares for her that is nothing if not a shrine to the singularity of Western high culture:

The room was a unity; things fitted together as if they belonged together. It was restful and beautiful. . . . All round the room, stopping only at the fireplace, ran low shelves of the same yellow pine, filled with books and magazines. . . . Plato's Republic, Gorky's "Comrades," a Cyclopaedia of Agriculture, Balzac's novels, Spencer's "First Principles," Tennyson's Poems. (399)

Especially with the appearance of Herbert Spencer, a placeholder for Du Bois of the "synthetic" potential of the social sciences, we are ushered into the realization that what Du Bois rejects with the demise of his cultural pluralist is not just the nineteenth-century folkloric tradition, but also the very idea of cultural separatism as a solution to racial discrimination.[65]

The novel had begun in the swamp with Zora, and it is through her that change is plotted as a move away from the folkloric traditions of the proceeding century. Although structured on an analogy to classical mythology, Du Bois's novel begins with a scene familiar to traditional Southern black folklore—that of conjure and dangerous music. Bles Alwyn, the novel's hero on his way to the Ivory Towers of Miss Smith's school, is seduced into the swamp by the primal sounds of "human music, but of a wildness and weirdness that startled the boy as it fluttered and danced across the dull red waters of the swamp." He is led as if "by some strange power" to the home (later revealed to be a brothel) of an old conjure woman, where he looks on to see a strange "elf-girl" dancing "as on clouds of flame" for a group of vulgar white men:

She was black, and lithe, and tall, and willowy. Her garments twined and flew around the delicate molding of her dark, young, half-naked limbs. A heavy mass of hair clung motionless to her wide forehead. Her arms twirled and flickered, and body and soul seemed quivering and whirring in the poetry of her motion.

As she danced she sang. He [Bles] heard her voice as before, fluttering like a bird's in the full sweetness of her utter music. It was no tune nor melody, it was just formless, boundless music. The boy forgot himself and all the world besides. All his darkness was sudden light; dazzled he crept forward, bewildered, fascinated, until with one last wild whir the elf-girl paused. The crimson light fell full upon the warm and velvet bronze of her face—her midnight eyes were aglow, her full purple lips apart, her half hid bosom panting, and all the music dead. Involuntarily the boy gave a gasping cry and awoke to swamp and night and fire, while a white face, drawn, red-eyed peering outward from some hidden throng within the cabin.

"Who's that?" a harsh voice cried.

"Where?" "Who is it?" and pale crowding faces blurred the light. (14,15)

This scene of adulterated conjure wavers between cultural affirmation and debauchery. Its heavy sexuality arouses Bles, but it does so on a spiritual level, on the level of conjure, to "make his darkness light." Surely the boy is drawn to the nakedness of the "elf-girl"—her full lips and panting bosom, which Du Bois sketches with such a heavy hand (as is typical for him both in this novel and *Dark Princess*)—and yet his fascination is also for her birdlike music. A primitive bond is established that differentiates Bles's visceral reaction to this music, his orgasmic "gasping cry," from anything the white men, who are paying for their pleasure, might feel. However, the caginess of this scene makes it impossible to recuperate it unambiguously into any kind of healthy African American folk tradition. Rather, it speaks more directly to the problematic nature of black folklore's commercial success—to the ongoing, posthumous best-seller status of the Uncle Remus stereotype.

Arnold Rampersad suggests that Zora's swamp "symbolizes all that the author finds distressing about black life . . . ignorance, sloth, superstition, paganism, and moral delinquency."[66] Rampersad fails to take account, however, of the ambivalence of the swamp. Not only does it provide the rich loam out of which the "silver fleece"—Zora and Bles's first cotton crop— eventually grows but, as the home of the conjure woman, Zora's mother, it also provides the site for Du Bois to signify on the tradition of folk collecting epitomized by Harris. In making the swamp and the theme of conjure a central feature of the first half of the novel—the half that most closely dates to the turn of the century and the height of interest in the Uncle Remus series—Du Bois provided a running commentary on the relationship between the collection of Negro folklore and the emerging racial and economic conditions of the new South. But at the same time, he plotted a new position for the development of an aesthetics able at once to work through the constrictions of racial segregation and produce, out of that site, a model of cultural growth, or *Bildung*.

Before this reconciliation can occur, however, Du Bois insisted upon posing both of these aesthetic motifs, folklore and mythology, against what surfaces in the novel as a more weighty point of opposition: the materiality of race and industrial society. In other words, the novel lifts the impetus for change out of the cultural system, placing it instead in that of economic development. It does so primarily with the character of Bles Alwyn, the hero of the talented tenth who ultimately marries Zora. Counterpoised to the swamp are the Ivory Towers of Miss Smith's school, where Bles Alwyn learns of the story of Jason's quest for the Golden Fleece. Recognizing an alternative moral to the Greek myth, Bles reads Jason not as a hero but a thief. He identifies the aristocratic white landowners as the Greek Argonauts who stole (not rescued) the silver fleece from the black tenant farmers. Looking out over the dull cabins of the local black folk, Bles sees the Black Sea the Argonauts had rudely conquered.

Bles moves the question from the ideal to the real, from the historicism of myth and folklore to the more tangible context of the new Southern economy. Even in the opening scene of conjure in the swamp, in which Bles first witnesses the charmed debacle of Zora dancing, the oppositional reality of the material world is quick to surface. Terrified at having been discovered by the "pale crowding faces," Bles flees from the brothel into the swamp, "hearing strange sounds and feeling stealthy creeping hands and arms and whispering voices" (15). Escaping these most corporeal ghosts but still lost in the swamp, Bles soon stops running and falls into a dreamless sleep. When he wakes, he does not know if the girl and "that wondrous savage music" had been real or "some witch-vision of the night" (16). The conjure scene takes on for him an unsettling immateriality, which is hardly altered when Zora, who has found him asleep, starts talking about dreams that move right back to witch visions. Charting the local geography in mythlike terms, Zora tells him that "beyond the swamp" (in the direction away from the plantation and the school) are to be found "dreams . . . like big flowers, dripping dew and sugar and blood—red, red blood" (19). Beyond the swamp is beyond the reach of the aristocratic landowners, but, as Bles keenly recognizes, there is literally nothing there but dreams. No capital, no crops, nothing but Zora's unbridled visions. Although Bles does not see it yet, the solution to the problem of racial exploitation—"the Way," as Du Bois dramatically names it later in the novel—comes from buying the swamp and planting it with cotton. The dreams must be planted in the ground, given substance, and sold.

As such, "the Way" is very much a Booker T. Washingtonian one, but it becomes inflected by Du Bois's anthropological investment in the development of a racial *Geist*. When dealing with the term "culture" directly, the novel replicates early-twentieth-century notions that link culture with upper-class refinement. The scene occurs fairly early in the novel, setting up subsequent interventions on the subject, when a young teacher from Miss Smith's school goes north to Lake George to pass her summer vacation in genteel society. The teacher, named Mary Taylor, is the sister of an entrepreneurial Northern businessman who has plans to corner the cotton market by going into business with the Southern white landowners around Miss Smith's school, the Cresswells. But it is her extremely rich and refined host, Mrs. Vanderpool, a woman of exquisitely discriminating taste who will later hire Zora as a maid, who initiates the discussion of culture. In a conversation with the young teacher, Mrs. Vanderpool rejects the idea that the goal of Miss Smith's school should be to fulfill the modern mission of taking "culture to the masses." Mrs. Vanderpool scoffs at the idea, replying to Mary's naive endorsement of the plan with the remark that "Frankly, then, the modern idea is not my idea; it is too socialistic. And as for culture applied to the masses, you utter a paradox" (60). As becomes clear in the ensuing dialogue, Mrs. Vanderpool imagines culture to be incompatible with the masses and also with work, after explaining which she "stretche[s] her silken limbs, lazily," cultivating the posture of the leisure class (60).

Although the novel spurns the equation of conspicuous display with culture, it remains subtly ambivalent about the blurring of lines between spiritual and material cultural modalities. A woman representative of a more vulgar—"barbaric" as the novel terms it—version of culture soon arrives at Mrs. Vanderpool's "in her new red motor" (61, 60). Mrs. Grey, a woman of little discriminating taste, represents the new millions, brash displays of wealth, and "grim power" (61). As opposed to Mrs. Vanderpool's "silken" elegance, one finds Mrs. Grey loaded down with possessions, "mahogany and velvets that thrilled while it appalled" and "a Japanese vase that cost no cent less than a thousand dollars." Mary remains unaffected by the display; however, it has great attraction to her industrialist brother John Taylor, who "meant to be able to duplicate it some day" (61). The point, however, is that Du Bois does not delimit the conduits between wealth and aesthetic value, the "barbarism" of new money and cultural good form. Rather, he describes the economic and the cultural as blending together.

The Japanese vase signals the extent to which the novel takes pleasure in the commodification of a particular kind of aesthetic value—that of the exotic as it attaches to foreign people. Japan, in particular, should be registered as a potent symbol for Du Bois. As discussed in the previous chapter, the circulation of *Japonisme* in the form of cultural commodities very much defined an early modernist, "chic" aesthetic. It was one with which Du Bois's sweeping stylistics is very much in tune. Japan was repeatedly singled out in the early 1900s as one (perhaps the only) example of a highly civilized non-Western society, a cultured Other, one with significant *Bildung*. Theodore Roosevelt, for example, prefaced his case against the intermingling of the Japanese and American masses by explaining that neither "nation is inferior to the other": "The Japanese are one of the great nations of the world, entitled to stand, and standing, on a footing of full equality with any nation of Europe or America. . . . Their civilization is in some respects higher than our own."[67] Du Bois, of course, would later work to locate other civilizations worthy of this type of encomium, particularly in Africa; however, he seemed to recognize early on the purchase that alien cultural commodities have in a capitalist society—and, in turn, the requirement placed upon foreign cultures in America to justify their existence both spiritually and materially.

Such, at least, seems to be part of the moral of Zora's cultivation of the silver fleece. The exceedingly fecund seeds used for that first crop of cotton planted in the swamp had been brought directly from Africa on one of the earliest slave ships and are sowed by Zora's "hag" mother, "filthy of breath, dirty, with dribbling mouth and red eyes," in an electrifyingly barbarous ritual under the full moon (96). They produce a harvest of exceptional quality that, as a matter of course, is stolen by the new Southern landowners, the Cresswells—the Argonauts in the mythological register. But the fleece comes back into Zora's possession in the form of a commodity: "a bolt of silken-like cambric of wondrous fineness and lustre," which John Taylor had manufactured for his sister and fiancée's wedding gowns. Having been hired by Mrs. Vanderpool shortly before, Zora is put to work on the dress to embroider it with silken lace. Although she does not know that it is the silver fleece, her work branches off in "new and intricate ways" that unite menial work (she had been hired as a maid) with artistry and culture, positivist economics with *Bildung* and *Geist.*

As already noted, here is Du Bois's famous image of "the veil" reworked into the fabric of Southern cotton and Northern industry—the fleece being transformed by Zora's conjured, exotic soul into a cultural commodity vaguely reminiscent of the Japanese vase. "Willfully she departed from the set pattern and sewed into the cloth something of the beauty in her heart . . . she wove in that white veil her own strange soul" (227). Zora's soul melds aesthetically with the discriminating taste of Mrs. Vanderpool, who "watched her curiously, but in silence" (227). But this is not assimilation. Following her own "innate love of harmony and beauty," Zora produces a cultural object of such remarkable fineness that it overcomes the famous waste of "double aims" and "unreconciled ideals." The veil, so central to the Du Boisian imagery of the twoness of life for American blacks, becomes a material representation of the marriage of folk and myth elements—of the swamp and the silver fleece grown there—to an Americanized commodity produced under the sign of race prejudice and having global purchase. It signals, that is to say, a Negro *Bildung,* and its contribution to culture.

Fittingly, the greatest admirer of the Japanese vase also becomes one of the greatest admirers of the veil. Arriving in Toomsville just before his own marriage, John Taylor immediately asks to see Zora's handiwork:

> It lay uncut and shimmering, covered with dim silken tracery of a delicacy and beauty which brought an exclamation to all lips.
> "That's what we can do with Alabama cotton," cried John Taylor in triumph.
> They turned to him incredulously.
> "But—"
> "No 'buts' about it; these are the two bales you sent me, woven with a silk woof." No one particularly noticed that Zora had hastily left the room. "I had it done in Easterly's New Jersey mills according to an old plan of mine. I'm going to make cloth like that right in this county some day," and he chuckled gayly [sic].
> (228)

Although Taylor's brash materialism is clearly designed to upset the spirituality of Zora's handiwork, it should not, therefore, be concluded that Du Bois rejects it out of hand. It is true that Zora is repulsed by the implication and runs from the room. And Taylor conveniently overlooks both the fact that Zora alone could have worked such magic on the fleece and that seeds for the cotton from which it was spun came from Africa: "wonder seed, sowed with three spells of Obi in the old land ten tousand moons ago [sic]" (75). The young industrialist will have a very difficult time at being "able to duplicate it some day" (61). Nonetheless, Taylor's entrepreneurial valuation of this cultural object, like his valuation of the Japanese vase, lays out the path by which Zora eventually proceeds to recuperate the swamp.

On an aesthetic level, the mythological underwriting of the veil suggests the vulnerability of the union of a racist cultural commodification and a racialist spiritual *Bildung*. The veil recalls another cloth "of soft weave": that which Medea anoints with a deadly poison and sends on to Jason's new wife.[68] It is possible to read Zora as a foreigner in the Cresswell mansion—much like Medea in Corinth—weaving into the cotton cambric a poison intended for her employer, but also, by implication, threatening her own "cultural heritage." Indeed, Du Bois's choice of the story of Jason and Medea as the myth upon which to structure his first novel seems absolutely fitting, *The Quest of the Golden Fleece* being a tale of heritage gone awry, of the sacrifice of children and failed redemption. The golden fleece, which Jason is challenged to recover, had been woven from the wool of a ram sent to save two children from their stepmother. Jason himself had been sent away from his parents when his uncle usurped his father's throne. And Medea is famously dangerous with regard to family relations, siding with Jason against her own father, conspiring to have Jason's usurping uncle murdered by his own daughters, and exacting revenge on Jason by killing her own children. The myth, thus, fits neatly into the fraught aesthetic politics of Du Bois's novel, which contains within it not only the mystery of numerous other orphans and infanticides but also the central question of whether the spiritual offspring of rural black folk will find its place in the new cultural kingdom.

Du Bois offered something of a tepid but also optimistic answer in the affirmative at the end of the novel. Zora comes to recognize that Taylor's economic philosophy offers little resistance to her plans for cultivation. She correctly understands that Taylor's blueprint for turning Toomsville into a major mill town runs counter to the white aristocracy's irrational racism. Taylor "believed in an aristocracy of talent alone, and secretly despised Colonel Cresswell's pretensions of birth. If a man had ability and push Taylor was willing and anxious to open the way for him, even though he were black" (397). The narrator makes it clear that "Zora sensed fully the situation," and that it was this sense that encouraged her to buy the swamp, and also to press her claims against those of Cresswell in court (398). Crucially, Taylor provides the key testimony during a trial late in the novel to decide if Zora can own the swamp, a trial that pits Zora and a legally binding contract against the words and wishes of the aristocratic Cresswells. Taylor's "business game" may have been "utterly ruthless"; however, to the extent that it "respected no one," it opened the field to Zora's participation (413). Zora's newfound business acumen blurs the line between culture and work, racial liberalism and exploitation, folk spirit and the cultural commodity: one gives way to the other in a newly incorporated, commercial system.

When Zora first starts on "the Way," she is forced to give up some of her folk dreams. She gives up her conviction that her "people don't never work; they plays" and labors in the swamp until her hands bleed and her body wastes away (74). She also tames and harnesses her imagination, learning to direct it in new ways. As mentioned earlier, Du Bois references this transformation to Harris in a passage where Zora must redirect little "Brer Rabbit" from her cotton crop. Zora does not, however, give up all of her folk past to reach the successful denouement, as is most poignantly witnessed by two events. First, she depends on a conjure man, Old Pappy, to motivate the black masses to follow her vision of economic integration, which assures a continuation of African American spirituality, albeit one revised to meet the demands of industry. His arrival at Zora's side is announced by "a sharp cry

[from] far off down toward the swamp and the sound of great footsteps coming, coming as from the end of the world; there swelled a rhythmical chanting, wilder and more primitive than song" (373). As a sermon, however, he preaches work: "'God is done sent me to offer you all salvation,' he cried, . . . 'not in praying, but in works'" (374). The folk is thus regenerated by conjure in a new form, and folk belief becomes not a liability but a vital force for growth. Second, in the final scene in the novel, Zora returns to the swamp with the silver fleece. There, wrapped in the material representation of her artistically redeemed soul, Zora is granted a moment of illumination and clarity in which, significantly, she envisions the renaissance of the swamp: "living, vibrant, tremulous" (433). The growing cotton rejuvenates this home of conjure, bringing the black folk who live there into a living, striving, and commercially viable community. It also emancipates black folklore, imagining it not just as an ethnographic relic but as an integral part of a modern myth-literature, one not in opposition to but in harmony with the thousand-year historical tradition of classical Greek mythology. In the last line of the novel, Zora asks Bles to marry her, linking the two modalities into the future.

Zora's initial description of what is "beyond the swamp" has a curious resonance with a question Du Bois surely posed for himself as he completed *Quest* and contemplated leaving Atlanta University for the NAACP: "What's beyond the Ivory Tower?" One reason he desired to get beyond the Ivory Tower may have been his wish not to live his life in a dream: his dawning belief that the Ivory Tower was a place of dreaming, or dreaminess—a place with little ability to touch the material world of American society. But more exactly, his turn away from Atlanta University's Sociology Department offers a way to inject a certain dreamy idealism into his scientific work—a way for him to move, again, from history to historicism. The novel does so in large measure by reasserting a notion of race as *Bildung* and *Geist* that is at once hostile to the antiquarian line of the nineteenth-century folkloric tradition in the United States and sanguine about the prospects of aesthetic growth to promote universal citizenship of the kind Du Bois proclaimed alongside Adler at the Universal Races Conference. Against the politically impotent sympathy of Miss Smith, Du Bois imagines an aesthetic of discrimination capable of carrying the Negro race beyond the limitations of ethnographic collections and the dreams of an academically bound pluralism. He positions his own novel as propaganda for such a move—a novel that fastens upon the degradation of the black folkloric tradition as the site at which a transformative cultural aesthetics might take root, at which Negro *Bildung* might find entry into the kingdom of culture.

FROM GERMANY TO HARLEM AND "BEYOND"

Although Du Bois's own ideas about culture did not dramatically change over time, the country's ideas about the concept did. Perhaps most notable in this respect is the fact that, by the 1920s, minority groups began to adopt the concept as one around which to organize politically. Indeed, it was as a political move that cultural pluralism received, early on, its most public attention in the work of Kallen, Bourne, and Alain Locke—none of whom, it should be said from the outset, were particularly close with Du Bois.[69] Gone from the idea of culture were many of the evolutionary implications of late-nineteenth-century anthropology and high society; in their place was an optimistic sense of the cultural contributions to be made by vital, new minority communities. Writing about American blacks, for example, Alain Locke celebrated the renaissance in Harlem, where "Negro life is seizing upon its first chances for group expression and self determination." Continuing, he championed the idea that Harlem has "the same rôle to play for the New Negro as Dublin has had for the New Ireland or Prague for the New Czechoslovakia" (7). As with the Irish and Eastern Europeans, this "new" cultural vitality in the United States must be seen as having been widespread among minority groups other than just Harlem blacks, most notably American Indians. For example, just as Locke plotted Harlem as a "race capital" that would positively reassess "the Negro in terms of his artistic endowments and cultural contributions, past and prospective," so too did Oliver La Farge in *Laughing Boy* (1929) locate the Navajo reservation as a center for the revaluation of traditional American Indian cultural forms.

The establishment of culture as an anthropological concept, and with its pluralization the slow decline of social-evolutionary thought, clearly had something to do with this change. However, the ascendancy of an anthropological notion of culture does not offer the simple explanation of the culturalist movement's popular ascendancy that we might expect. For, much in the vein of Du Bois at the time he wrote both *Souls* and *Quest,* the notion of culture underwriting optimistic declarations like Locke's remained wedded to a universalizing, humanistic singularity, not to mention to a strong idea of race. Far from being supplanted by the anthropological pluralization of cultures, something like *Völkerpsychologie*'s position on *Bildung* took on new importance as a touchstone for critics sharing the goal of a mutual striving toward a "kingdom of culture." Du Bois's commitment to aesthetic discrimination—a commitment to beauty and truth as a means of redirecting racial discrimination—remained the gauge by which a call for the revaluation of "cultural contributions" was to be measured. In turn, what emerged here was not so much pluralism as a universalism dependent on the redefinition of cultural taste.

Du Bois in the 1920s was much less interested in the history of integrated whole cultures than in situating the *Bildung* of *Quest* in terms of a race struggle that had been internationalized. Again, it is in a novel, *Dark Princess,* that Du Bois made this *Bildung* philosophy most readily apparent. Although not so taken with mythology, Matthew, the novel's appropriately Arnoldian-named hero, is drawn once again to the altar of high culture. He reaches a personal epiphany at a Chicago art gallery, having spent a week "bathed . . . in a new world of beauty," viscerally experiencing the colorful paintings of Van Gogh, Cézanne, Brangwyn, Cottet, Derain, Gauguin, Pisano, and especially Monet. "I saw in Claude Monet what sunrise and sunset on the old cathedral at Rouen might say to a human soul, in pale gold, white, and purple, and in purple, yellow, and gold," he writes in a letter to his lover, the dark princess Kautilya (280). Emerging a week later from this colorful repast of early European modernism, he felt himself "a more complete man—a unit of real democracy," and shortly thereafter he is able to formulate more clearly than ever before in the novel the problem facing the black race and all of America:

> We Americans are caught here in our own machinery; our machines make things and compel us to sell them. We are rich in food and clothes and starved in culture. . . . All delicate feeling sinks beneath floods of mediocrity. The finer culture is lost, lost; maybe lost forever. (280, 284)

With the exception of his claim for "real democracy," Du Bois's hero returns us to the classical formulation of Arnold, which seems to have lost little of its potency throughout the decades. The sweetness and light of "delicate feeling" stands against the ongoing menace of machinery—machinery that leaves man "arid, artificial, vapid, so charmed and distracted by the low, crude, gaudy, and vulgar" (284).

From a critical standpoint, it is perhaps necessary to concede that the hyperbolically earnest characters of *Dark Princess* did not bring Du Bois's own art any closer to the cultural ideal that is held out here. It is, however, important to note the evolution in his conception of the relationship of culture to the political environment. For Du Bois makes it clear that Matthew's equation of culture and "real democracy" has gotten a number of things wrong. For one thing, Matthew begins to beatify labor, imagining in it a way out of the mechanical darkness: "But this at least I do know," he writes to Kautilya, ". . . Work is God" (272). Unlike *Quest,* however, where work surfaces as a possible solution, this novel spurns such banality. The dark princess quickly sets Matthew straight by insisting on a more spiritually transcendent ideal than work: "Work is not God," she writes. "Love is God and Work is His Prophet" (279). With this love, Kautilya proves intent on transcending the local situation of work in Chicago (which in many respects is what work in *Quest* would have been without the redemptive aesthetic work on the silky cambric veil) in order to unite the colored people of the world against white economic exploitation. She urges Matthew to take his place on the "High Command" of "The Great Central Committee of Yellow, Brown, and Black"—a committee that has a precise twenty-five-year plan: "Ten years of preparation are set. Ten more years of final planning, and then five years of intensive struggle. In 1952, the Dark World goes free" (296–97). Rather than work, what seems to be needed is Adler's Ethical Culture movement, a spiritual harmonization of the "Dark World" by means of a global conference of inspired intellectuals.

A similarly transcendent formula is deployed with regard to aesthetics. The figure of Kautilya, a native of India and daughter of a deposed Maharajah, insists upon the fact that Matthew's taste for European art is also off the mark. When Matthew finally goes to be joined with her at his mother's farm deep in Virginia, she is "dressed in eastern style, royal in coloring, with no concession to Europe" (307). Rather like the African sculptures celebrated throughout *The New Negro*, the "eastern style" of cultural objects here circulates across both geographic and ethnographic borders. Discriminating taste still applies, yet it is one in a distinctly non-European, non-Virginian flavor: "a king's ransom lay between the naked beauty of her breasts; blood rubies weighed down her ears, and about the slim brown gold of her waist ran a girdle such as emperors fight for" (307). Having thrown off the garb of Western civilization (indeed having thrown off most everything but jewels), Kautilya presents Matthew with a son, a son the American did not know existed, still named after Arnold but inflected by what the Indian princess calls "our softer tongue": "Madhu." As signaled by the proliferation of impersonal pronouns used to describe him, this son, proclaimed a "Messenger and Messiah to all the Darker Worlds," is spoken of as an object of cultured beauty, "its little feet, curled petals; its mouth a kiss; its hands like waving prayers." The boy is pointedly, however, an eastern beauty, crowned by a "turban with that mighty ruby that looked like frozen blood" (311). Du Bois perhaps means to recall Zora's Africanized dreams about what lay beyond the swamp, those "dreams . . . like big flowers, dripping dew and sugar and blood—red, red blood" (19).

By the end of this pageantlike novel, Du Bois's point about culture aesthetically defined seems clear: the end all in the fight for racial justice will bring with it a high aesthetic culture, but it, like the unified darker races, will be defined globally. The novel, which Du Bois famously identified as "my favorite book," offers a completion of the vision Du Bois first noted in "The Conservation of Races" thirty years earlier.[70] Having served as a category for colonialist exploitation, the "common consciousness" of race here signals a colorful new avenue for cultural production—one that is both universalizing in the Arnoldian and Boasian sense of *Bildung* and *Geist,* and global in the sense of having been touched by and worked through European and American colonial capitalism. It is an avenue, nonetheless, with origins winding clearly back into the period "before cultures."

AFTERWORD

On Literature and Anthropology

—•—◄◊►—•—

I n 1952, Alfred Kroeber and Clyde Kluckhohn published their encyclopedic volume on the culture concept, *Culture: A Critical Review of Concepts and Definitions,* in which they noted the humbling effect for anthropologists of the fifty-year "cultural lag" in the popular application of the term.[1] By their account, it had only been since the early 1940s that one could assume that "educated Englishmen" would be fairly familiar with the anthropological sense of culture.[2] Kroeber and Kluckhohn tended to read this lag in terms of a general "moral" for scientific disciplines; they implied that there was, frequently, such a "half century lag" between the specific sense of words developed in scientific communities and the common sense meanings confirmed by dictionaries.[3] Given words developed contemporaneously to culture—Darwin's version of evolution, say, or Einstein's special relativity—the moral would seem not to hold; but perhaps worse, and somewhat paradoxically, this particular reading of culture's emergence is unfortunate for the way it suggests the inevitability of a general consensus around a definition of culture. Developing consensus was the ostensible goal of *Culture,* but, if history is any lesson, consensus on culture should not be the goal. It was not achieved then, nor has it been since. Indeed, I would argue that the definitional failure is largely why culture has remained a salient and conspicuous concept for both anthropologists and others, for that failure has been remarkably productive.

There remains more to be said about the history of the culture concept, and the study of literature provides a particularly compelling angle from which to say it because the work that remains to be done involves understanding that what has made culture such an unavoidably important concept is the slippage between humanistic, scientific, ideological, and epistemological registers. If there were a moral to be drawn from the history of the culture concept, it would not likely be that there was a "cultural lag" in the translation of the word from specific scientific to more broadly humanistic communities; rather, it would be that the edgy purchase of the term has come from the problematic of its translation between these communities. Indeed, had a consensus definition formed around the concept, it would probably not have become the preferred explanatory architecture for understanding difference. Culture has been appealing because it has been a correlative term, one suggesting—even if not always delivering on—the profundity of connections between the arts and the sciences, and between the stylistic peculiarity of particular groups and elements common to them all. Disciplines, publics, and interdisciplinary projects all keep producing accounts of these correlatives, and yet these accounts can never stand because the particularities and commonalties they describe are always on the move.

As such, the current trend on the part of some critics and theorists to get "beyond culture" suggests not so much the inadequacy of the concept as a supposed arrival at the longed-for consensus about what it means. What culture means in these consensual circumstances has usually not been good: it has been taken to be just another word for race, or nation, or ethnicity.[4] If we finally knew what culture was, and if it really was just a substitute for these other categories, it might indeed be time to get beyond it. We are not yet there.

From a historical perspective, at least, we still do not know the full story of what culture was not. This book has described the controversies surrounding the relationship between key modes of understanding difference in the period "before cultures," and particularly those caused by the recognition of circulation as the central challenge to theories attempting to link together who people were, where they came from, what they believed, how they behaved, and the kind of things they produced. I have argued that such controversies have been occluded by the overriding emphasis on the culture concept in the history of anthropology, but that they merit our attention because of the way they speak to the antinomies and critical preoccupations motivating contemporary theoretical moves toward the study of such things as flow, disjuncture, diaspora, and cosmopolitanism.

It is telling that such controversies persisted well into the period described by Kroeber and Kluckhohn, in which the anthropologists, for a brief term before the onset of postmodernism and cultural studies, had their way with the word culture. Even into the 1940s, and particularly when the term came up in the context of race and nationalism, there remained an emphasis by many critics on the need to dislocate culture from race and language. At the very time that the anthropological concept would seem to have been fully popularized, there were ongoing calls to problematize it. As discussed in the previous chapter, the difficulties in understanding history and change from within a paradigm of culture were already made visible in the attention to "growth" that the *Völkerpsychologie* school made available to Franz Boas and W. E. B. Du Bois. These problems persisted during the period of culture's ascendancy, as did challenges posed by the prevalence of circulation and contact—by the diffusion of peoples, ideas, books, paintings, stories—to the desire to think of culture in terms of anything like complex, stable wholes.[5]

Nowhere is the ongoing debate over the culture concept more evident than in the work of Alain Locke, the anthologist of the Harlem Renaissance who emerged in the later 1920s as one of the main intellectual rivals of Du Bois. Whereas Du Bois's internationalist politics led him ever further away from the field of anthropology, Locke is of interest because of the way he continued to find and promote in Boasian anthropology that line of thought devoted to circulation that would pose problems to a static, integrated notion of culture. This line was evident in Locke's work during the Harlem Renaissance, especially in his seminal anthology, *The New Negro* (1925), in which he followed the logic of Boas's early line on diffusion to point out that what was happening culturally in Harlem could not be thought of as a "separatist" movement, for it simply was not possible to "encyst" a race or a culture within a given set of parameters, even if so doing were desirable.[6] In his work from the 1920s, Locke frequently drew on Boasian-trained anthropologists like Edward Sapir, Clark Wissler, and especially Robert Lowie, to fundamentally challenge popular conceptions about race and culture. In 1924, for example, he cited Lowie when arguing for the nullification of two "popular and scientific fallacies" that, already then, had been attributed to the culture concept: "the ascription of a total culture to any one ethnic strain, and the interpretation of culture in terms of the intrinsic rather than the fusion values of its various constituent elements."[7] Although Locke promoted what he called "a revised notion of ethnic race" throughout this period, he was always clear to note its "quixotic" nature.[8] In *The New Negro,* he argued that the racialism of Harlem was not intrinsic, but came externally from the fusion of American segregationist legislation, black migration to Harlem, and the "world phenomenon [of] . . . wider race consciousness."[9]

Even more impressive, however, was a much later volume Locke edited with the sociologist Bernhard Stern, *When Peoples Meet: A Study in Race and Culture Contacts,* first published in 1942. By then a well-established professor of philosophy at Howard University, Locke provided most of the notes to this wide-ranging "source-book," which attempted to "show what characteristically happens when peoples meet, and what interests, attitudes and policies condition their subsequent relations."[10] For the volume, Locke and

Stern culled from eighty-two different authors—including Boas, Ruth Benedict, Randolph Bourne, Sterling Brown, Raymond Firth, Melville Herskovits, Margaret Mead, Ralph Linton, G. H. L. F. Pitt-Rivers, Edward Sapir, and Clark Wissler—material that made way not simply for "culture," as one might expect given the contributors, but for understanding contact and transculturation. For example, they turned to the section of Benedict's *Patterns of Culture* (1934) in which she makes the point that the diffusion of cultural material and people has been the constant norm across the globe, despite the Western sense that other societies lived in relative isolation: "[T]he great spread of white civilization is not an isolated historical circumstance. The Polynesian group, in comparatively recent times, has spread itself from Ontong, Java, to Easter Island, from Hawaii to New Zealand, and the Bantu-speaking tribes spread from the Sahara to southern Africa."[11] For Boas, they turned to the section of *The Mind of Primitive Man* (1911) in which the point is made that the advances of any race or civilization are predicated upon the exchange of ideas with others, such that "none of these civilizations was the product of the genius of a single people."[12]

This emphasis on contact, as opposed to culture, is not surprising given Locke's work twenty years earlier in *The New Negro*. However, the sophistication of the introduction to the volume's first section, written by Locke, is remarkably prescient given the concerns that continue to be raised about culture today. In this introduction, Locke argued that the persistence of romantic racialism was a problem, and that the anthropological concept of culture was also a problem. In fact, it was a "fiction":

> Racism is only one of the fictions involved in current false perspectives of human history, all of which need to be examined and corrected in a sound and balanced view of human civilization. The prevailing notion of separate, distinctive and ethnically characteristic cultures is another example, and it, too, is shown by broad, historical analysis to be contrary to fact. Culture is not related functionally to definite ethnic groups or races, but varies independently. Races change their culture on many historic occasions and various culture advances are made independently by different racial stocks. Each culture, also, upon examination is discovered to be dynamic and constantly changing, with an increasing tendency, on the whole, to become more and more composite, in the sense of incorporating aspects of other cultures with which it comes in contact. Thus, even as the tradition of a characteristic group culture develops, the less true it is apt to be to actual fact, since the older a culture, the more composite it usually is.[13]

In this passage, which I quote at length because of the extraordinary challenge it would seem to pose to received histories of the culture concept's rise to theoretical prominence, Locke again engaged the debates motivating what I have called the ethnographic imagination. His position rigorously insisted not only on the disjuncture of race and culture but also on the varied and disjointed process of dissemination, which as we know from reading Locke elsewhere would include the way that works of art might easily leap the imagined bounds of race, language, and nationality.[14] Moreover, in criticizing the culture concept specifically—and with the nod to "function" Locke would seem to have had Bronislaw Malinowski and, perhaps, Pitt-Rivers in mind, even while moving Kroeber and Kluckhohn's adoption date of the culture concept by the "educated Englishman" forward a decade or so—Locke turned to none other than the Boasian idea of secondary explanations in order to forecast how culture became political. The argument for secondary explanations suggested that popular explanations for the origins of elements in a culture were frequently different from the historical origins discerned by anthropologists doing research into historical dissemination, and as such that such "speculation[s]" should be treated as psychological, not historical material.[15] Locke recognized that once culture became a word around which groups could organize themselves, as had been the case during the Harlem Renaissance, self-explanation would begin to play a larger role, obfuscating the routes of origin for given practices or art forms that were beyond the reach of the particular culture's historical self-competence. Such obfuscation, of course, could be purposeful. While obscuring the avowedly disinterested "actual fact" of ethnographic history, secondary explanations could also be read as having shaped—and been shaped by—a history of strategies that were not only psychological but also political and ideological. The popularization of the culture concept made it a word available for description, and for mobilization.

It seems to me to make little sense to try moving "beyond culture" if one is only to end up with a new set of terms by which to misunderstand the historical and systemic nature by which people share a sense of things.[16] Rather than moving beyond culture, it would be better to go back and work out the complexities of what was already there, both "before" and "during" the period of culture's sway. As suggested by Locke's take on Boasian anthropology, the problems with culture were never so monolithic as we may now believe. Indeed, from the period just before the culture concept's so-called emergence, what has been most fascinating—and perhaps most indicative of the humanity it supposedly describes—has been the way systems of meaning that came to be called cultures were shot through with races, languages, and even literary texts not initially associated with them.

The period before cultures is ripe for reexamination because of the enormous flux in these categories and for the way the categories, themselves, came to be challenged by the circulation of the people and things they supposedly delimited across their conceptual borders.

There has been enormous slippage between humanistic and social scientific registers for thinking through the culture concept. Throughout this book, I have tried to draw attention to the peculiar epistemological shifts in the kind of evidentiary relationship imagined to exist between literary texts and cultures—shifts that have been a constant source of production for each field. My goal in so doing has been to trouble the genealogies of culture both fields assumed they knew. As such, it is my hope that this book will have served as a catalyst for keeping the imagined relationship between literature and anthropology—and between their relative, commingled notions of culture—open and fluid, in effect promoting the desirability of an ongoing definitional disconsensus.

NOTES

INTRODUCTION

1. W. E. B. Du Bois, *Dusk of Dawn: An Essay Toward an Autobiography of the Race Concept,* reprinted in *Writings* (1940; New York: Library of America, 1986), 549–802, 555–56.

2. W. E. B. Du Bois, *The Souls of Black Folk,* reprinted in *Writings* (1903; New York: Library of America, 1986), 357–548, 545.

3. See George W. Stocking Jr., "Lamarckianism in American Social Science, 1890–1915," in *Race, Culture, and Evolution: Essays in the History of Anthropology,* Phoenix edition (1968; Chicago: University of Chicago Press, 1982), 234–69. A quick literary example can be found in Sarah Orne Jewett's fondness for the Normans, visible in much of her best short fiction and also in her popular history for children, *The Story of the Normans, Told Chiefly in Relation to Their Conquest of England* (New York: G. P. Putnam's Sons, 1887).

4. Critical work on the history of whiteness is of relevance here: David Roediger, *The Wages of Whiteness: Race and the Making of the American Working Class* (New York: Verso, 1991); Ian Haney-Lopez, *White by Law: The Legal Construction of Race* (New York: New York University Press, 1996); and Matthew Frye Jacobson, *Whiteness of a Different Color: European Immigrants and the Alchemy of Race* (Cambridge, MA: Harvard University Press, 1998).

5. For "beyond" books, see Richard G. Fox and Barbara J. King, eds., *Anthropology beyond Culture* (New York: Berg, 2002); Victoria E. Bonnell and Lynn Hunt, eds., *Beyond the Cultural Turn: New Directions in the Study of Society and Culture* (Berkeley: University of California Press, 1999); Paul Gilroy, *Against Race: Imagining Political Culture beyond the Color Line* (Cambridge, MA: The Belknap Press of Harvard University Press, 2000); Werner Sollors, *Beyond Ethnicity: Consent and Descent in American Culture* (New York: Oxford University Press, 1986); Bruce Robbins and Pheng Cheah, eds., *Cosmopolitics: Thinking and Feeling beyond the Nation* (Minneapolis: University of Minnesota Press, 1998); Robert N. Bellah, *Beyond Belief: Essays on Religion in a Post-Traditional World* (Berkeley: University of California Press, 1991); Neera Chandhoke, *Beyond Secularism: The Rights of Religious Minorities* (New York: Oxford University Press, 1999); Sander L. Gilman et al., *Hysteria beyond Freud* (Berkeley: University of California Press, 1993); E. San Juan Jr., *Beyond Postcolonial Theory* (New York: Palgrave, 1997); and Sherry B. Ortner, ed., *The Fate of Culture: Geertz and Beyond* (Berkeley: University of California Press, 1999).

6. Raymond Williams, *Keywords: A Vocabulary of Culture and Society*, rev. ed. (1976; New York: Oxford University Press, 1983), 87. The point is also made by Marc Manganaro, *Culture, 1922: The Emergence of a Concept* (Princeton, NJ: Princeton University Press, 2002), 2.

7. As I discuss in more detail in chapters 2 and 5, the centrality of this episode in Boasian historiography has come to obscure what I consider to be Boas's more significant work during this period on diffusion and in the field of *Völkerpsychologie*. The museum debate is cited as one of two or three key texts in most articles on Boas's work in the 1890s. See 210n36, below.

8. Curtis M. Hinsley, "The World as Marketplace: Commodification of the Exotic at the World's Columbian Exposition, Chicago, 1893," *Exhibiting Cultures: The Poetics and Politics of Museum Display*, ed. Ivan Karp and Steven D. Lavine (Washington, DC: Smithsonian Institution Press, 1991), 344–65.

9. Raymond Williams, *Culture and Society, 1780–1950* (1958; New York: Columbia University Press, 1983), 161.

10. Alfred L. Kroeber and Clyde Kluckhohn, *Culture: A Critical Review of Concepts and Definitions* (New York: Vintage, 1952), 11.

11. See, for example, Susan Hegeman, *Patterns for America: Modernism and the Concept of Culture* (Princeton, NJ: Princeton University Press, 1999); Adam Kuper, *Culture: The Anthropologists' Account* (Cambridge, MA: Harvard University Press, 1999); Christopher M. Hann, "All Kulturvölker Now?: Social Anthropological Reflections on the German-American Tradition," in *Anthropology beyond Culture*, ed. Fox and King, 262; Michel-Rolph Trouillot, "Adieu, Culture: A New Duty Arises," in *Anthropology beyond Culture*, ed. Fox and King, 42; and Manganaro, *Culture, 1922*.

12. This trajectory is now well documented. See especially George W. Stocking Jr., ed., *Volksgeist as Method and Ethic: Essays on Boasian Ethnography and the German Anthropological Tradition*, History of Anthropology Series 8 (Madison: University of Wisconsin Press, 1996).

13. Norbert Elias, *The Civilizing Process* (1939; Cambridge, MA: Blackwell, 1994).

14. Trouillot, "Adieu, Culture," 45.

15. The phrase is Walter Benn Michaels's, "Race into Culture: A Critical Genealogy of Cultural Identity," *Critical Inquiry* 18 (1992): 655–85.

16. Granted, "racialism," the conflation of biological and social characteristics, continued into the twentieth century, just as it continues today. Michael Silverstein, for one, recalls in a recent article on Boas that the nativism of the mid-1920s, against which much of the anthropologist's research was directed, continued to rely on a "cluster of folk concepts that racialize(d) virtues" deemed characteristic of the United States, such as self-reliance and independence. Michael Silverstein, "Boasian Cosmographic Anthropology and the Sociocentric Component of the Mind," in *Significant Others*, ed. Richard Handler, History of Anthropology Series 10 (Madison: University of Wisconsin Press, 2004), 131–57. For more on this history, see also recent work on "whiteness": Roediger, *Wages of Whiteness*; Haney-Lopez, *White by Law: The Legal Construction of Race*; and Jacobson, *Whiteness of a Different Color*.

17. I explain this point in more detail in chapter 5.

18. See Homi Bhabha, "DissemiNation," in *The Location of Culture* (New York: Routledge, 1994), 139–70, and Boas's 1891 article, "Dissemination of Tales among the Natives of North America," reprinted in his *Race, Language and Culture* (1940; Chicago: University of Chicago Press, 1982), 437–45.

19. Washington Irving, "Rip Van Winkle," in *The Sketch Book of Geoffrey Crayon, Gent.* (1819–20; New York: Penguin, 1988), 28–42, 41. Future references will be cited parenthetically.

20. John B. Thompson, "The Genesis of the Rip Van Winkle Legend," *Harper's New Monthly Magazine* 67 (1883): 617–22.

21. Irving, *The Sketch Book,* 9, 10. For a summary of critical attention to the German source, see Henry A. Pochman, "Irving's German Sources in The Sketch Book," *Studies in Philology* 27 (1930): 477–507, especially fn. 47. On the "autochthonous" myth, see Thompson, "The Genesis," 621.

22. Thompson, "The Genesis," 618–19.

23. The American Folklore Society was founded five years after the appearance of Thompson's article in *Harper's.* For an extremely useful overview of their method and thought, see "On the Field and Work of a Journal of American Folk-Lore," *Journal of American Folk-Lore* 1 (1888): 3–7.

24. Thompson, "The Genesis," 621.

25. Adolph Bandelier, preface to *The Delight Makers* (1890; New York: Harcourt Brace Jovanovich, 1971), xxiii. Future references to the novel will be cited parenthetically.

26. *The Delight Makers* became a classic among scientists and students of American Indians and was in print for over thirty years. However, it was far from becoming "popular" among the general public. See Jovanovich's introduction of the novel's 1971 edition (only the second edition in the text's history) for more details.

27. Hamlin Garland, *Crumbling Idols* (1894; Cambridge, MA: Harvard University Press, 1960), 9.

28. See Daniel F. Littlefield Jr. and Lonnie E. Underhill, "Renaming the American Indian, 1890–1913," *American Studies* 12, no. 2 (Fall 1971): 33–45; and Daniel F. Littlefield and Lonnie E. Underhill, eds., *Hamlin Garland's Observations on the American Indian, 1895–1905* (Tucson: University of Arizona Press, 1976).

29. William Dean Howells, "Dialect in Fiction," *Harper's Weekly,* June 8, 1895, reprinted in *Selected Literary Criticism,* vol. 2 (Bloomington: Indiana University Press, 1993), 219–23, 220. On the construction of cultural identity around objects, see Richard Handler, *Nationalism and the Politics of Culture in Quebec* (Madison: University of Wisconsin Press, 1988).

30. Garland, *Crumbling Idols,* 54.

31. There are, of course, exceptions. As I will discuss in chapter 3, the most evident is Sarah Orne Jewett, who wrote largely against this trend in the conceptualization of local color's relation to the world.

32. Walter Benn Michaels, *The Gold Standard and the Logic of Naturalism* (Berkeley: University of California Press, 1987), 27.

33. Hippolyte Taine, *History of English Literature*, trans. Henri Van Laun (1863; New York: A. L. Burt Co., n.d.), 18.

34. See René Wellek, *A History of Modern Criticism, 1750–1950*, vol. 1 (New Haven, CT: Yale University Press, 1955), 197.

35. See Stephen Greenblatt, "The Touch of the Real," in *Fate of Culture*, ed. Ortner, 14–29; and Catherine Gallagher and Stephen Greenblatt, *Practicing New Historicism* (Chicago: University of Chicago Press, 2000).

36. Hamlin Garland, *A Son of the Middle Border* (New York: Macmillan, 1923), 307.

37. Henry James, "Taine's English Literature," *Atlantic Monthly* 29 (1872): 469–72, 472.

38. Henry James, "The Art of Fiction," reprinted in *Literary Criticism, Volume One: Essays on Literature, American Writers, English Writers* (1884; New York: Library of America, 1984), 44–65, 52.

39. Franz Boas, "The Ethnological Significance of Esoteric Doctrines," originally published in *Science* 16 (1902); reprinted in Boas, *Race, Language and Culture*, 312–15, 312, 314.

40. Otis T. Mason, "The Natural History of Folk-Lore," *Journal of American Folk-Lore* 4 (1891): 97–105, 102.

41. Joel Chandler Harris, *Uncle Remus, His Songs and His Sayings* (1880; New York: Penguin, 1986), 39. Harris quotes Herbert H. Smith to make, albeit indirectly, the claim about Africa, 43. A more thorough discussion of this problem follows in chapter 2.

42. And, of course, the same holds true for other cultural objects and elements. Wai Chee Dimock, "Non-Newtonian Time: Robert Lowell, Roman History, Vietnam War," *American Literature* 74 (2002): 911–31, 920.

43. This claim is consistent with a recent wave of "neo-Boasian" thought about cultural theory. See the special issue of *American Anthropologist*, vol. 106, no. 3 (September 2004), edited by Richard Handler, and in particular articles there by Matti Bunzl, "Boas, Foucault, and the 'Native Anthropologist': Notes Toward a Neo-Boasian Anthropology," 435–42, and Ira Bashkow, "A Neo-Boasian Conception of Cultural Boundaries," 443–58. See also Michael Silverstein, "Boasian Cosmographic Anthropology and the Sociocentric Component of the Mind," in *Significant Others*, ed. Handler.

44. One of Boas's most forceful statements on this issue comes in his introduction to *The Handbook of American Indian Languages* (1911): "An attempt to correlate the numerous classifications that have been proposed shows clearly a condition of utter confusion and contradiction. If it were true that anatomical form, language, and culture are all closely associated, and that each subdivision of mankind is characterized by a certain bodily form, a certain culture, and a certain language, which can never become separated, we might expect that the results of various investigations would show better agreement. If, on the other hand, the various phenomena which were made the leading points in the attempt at classification are not closely associated, then we may naturally expect such contradictions and lack of agreement as are actually found" (Washington, DC: Georgetown University Press, 1963), 3.

45. See Silverstein, "Boasian Cosmographic Anthropology," and Bashkow, "A Neo-Boasian Conception."

46. It also led to the "four-fields approach" in anthropology—the separation of physical, linguistic, archaeological and cultural approaches—which remains the discipline's dominant structuring paradigm.

47. Ira Bashkow has described something similar when considering the lingering status of certain items as "foreign," even once they had been fully subsumed within cultural systems. He suggests attending to what he calls "the zone of the foreign": "a zone of things that from the perspective of the people's folk boundary concepts are regarded as foreign, but that from the perspective of the analyst might nonetheless be interpreted as internal to their culture" (447).

48. See George W. Stocking Jr., "Matthew Arnold, E. B. Tylor, and the Uses of Invention," in *Race, Culture, and Evolution,* 6991.

49. Michael A. Elliott, *The Culture Concept: Writing and Difference in the Age of Realism* (Minneapolis: Univ. of Minnesota Press, 2002); James Clifford, *The Predicament of Culture: Twentieth-Century Ethnography, Literature, and Art* (Cambridge, MA: Harvard University Press, 1988), 121.

50. Manganaro, *Culture, 1922,* 2.

51. Richard G. Fox and Barbara J. King, "Introduction: Beyond Culture Worry," in *Anthropology beyond Culture,* 1–19, 2. Trouillot writes that "[e]ven within academe we are losing ground to cultural studies in the debate over the appropriation of the word culture, a loss that seems to irritate anthropologists more than the political capture of the word in the world outside" (55).

52. Robert Brightman, "Forget Culture: Replacement, Transcendence, Relexification," *Cultural Anthropology* 10 (1995): 50946.

53. There are some significant exceptions, including Christopher Herbert, *Culture and Anomie: Ethnographic Imagination in the Nineteenth Century* (Chicago: University of Chicago Press, 1991); Walter Benn Michaels, *Our America: Nativism, Modernism, and Pluralism* (Durham, NC: Duke University Press, 1995); and Ross Posnock, *Color and Culture: Black Writers and the Making of the Modern Intellectual* (Cambridge, MA: Harvard University Press, 1998). They are, however, in the minority.

54. The concluding chapter of Susan Hegeman's wonderful book, *Patterns for America,* offers one of the best examples of such a defense; she is, clearly, an exception to the critics who rely on a naive definition of culture that I describe below.

55. John Carlos Rowe, *The New American Studies* (Minneapolis: University of Minnesota Press, 2002), 12. As evidence of the broader trend, one might consult the *PMLA*'s special issue on "America: The Idea, the Literature," *PMLA* 118, no. 1 (2003).

56. See Terry Eagleton, *The Idea of Culture* (Oxford, UK: Blackwell, 2000), 15.

57. The most humorous and crisp version of this critique comes in the pamphlet, *Waiting for Foucault, Still* (Chicago: Prickly Paradigm Press, 2002).

58. See especially Brightman, "Forget Culture"; and Bashkow, "A Neo-Boasian Conception."

59. Richard Handler, "Cultural Theory in History Today," *American Historical Review* 107, no. 5 (2002): 1512–20, 1514. I take it that Marshall Sahlins was making a similar point when he argued in *Culture and Practical Reason* (Chicago: University of Chicago Press, 1976) that capitalist systems were also culturally constructed.

60. William Sewell, "The Concept(s) of Culture," in *Beyond the Cultural Turn,* ed. Bonnell and Hunt, 35–61, 39, 40.

61. Sewell, "The Concept(s) of Culture," 44.

62. Of course, it should be noted that the semiotic systems are, themselves, transformed when objects come to light in them.

63. Fredrik Barth, "Toward a Richer Description and Analysis of Cultural Phenomena," in *Anthropology beyond Culture,* ed. Fox and King: 23–36, 32. Bonnell and Hunt suggest something similar in their introduction to *Beyond the Cultural Turn,* see especially 11–12.

64. For examples, see Catherine A. Lutz and Jane L. Collins, *Reading National Geographic* (Chicago: University of Chicago Press, 1993); Barbara Kirshenblatt-Gimblett, *Destination Culture* (Berkeley: University of California Press, 1998); and Andrew Zimmerman, *Anthropology and Antihumanism in Imperial Germany* (Chicago: University of Chicago Press, 2001).

65. Richard H. Brodhead, *Cultures of Letters: Scenes of Reading and Writing in Nineteenth-Century America* (Chicago: University of Chicago Press, 1993), 125.

CHAPTER ONE

1. *Letter Epigraph. Cushing at Zuni: The Correspondence and Journals of Frank Hamilton Cushing, 1979–1884,* ed. Jesse Green (Albuquerque: University of New Mexico Press, 1990), 281.

2. By Cushing: "The Zuni Social, Mythic, and Religious Systems," *Popular Science Monthly* (June 1882): 186–92; "The Nation of the Willows," *Atlantic Monthly* 50 (1882): 362–74, 541–59; "My Adventures in Zuni," *Century Illustrated Monthly* 25 (1882–83): 191–207, 500–511, and volume 26 (1883): 28–47. By Sylvester Baxter: "The Father of the Pueblos," *Harper's* 65 (1882): 72–91; "An Aboriginal Pilgrimage," *Century Illustrated Monthly* 24 (1882): 526–36.

3 "A Word to the Readers of the Century," *Century Illustrated Monthly* 26 (1883): 951.

4. George Stocking first made the argument that the genealogy of cultures could be traced to Boas in *Race, Culture, and Evolution: Essays in the History of Anthropology,* Phoenix edition (1968; Chicago: University of Chicago Press, 1982), 195–233. Joan Mark provides the rejoinder on behalf of Cushing in "Frank Hamilton Cushing and an American Science of Anthropology," *Perspectives in American History* 10 (1976): 449–86. On Cushing's significance not only for the culture concept but also for the development of fieldwork methodology, see works by Curtis Hinsley, and in particular "Ethnographic Charisma and Scientific Routine: Cushing and Fewkes in the American Southwest, 1879–1893," in *Observers Observed: Essays on Ethnographic Fieldwork,* ed. George W. Stocking

Jr., History of Anthropology Series 1 (Madison: University of Wisconsin Press, 1983): 53–69.

5. For the success of Boas's students in obtaining department chairs, see Stocking's *Race, Culture, and Evolution*, 296, and Regna Darnell, *The Development of American Anthropology 1879–1920: From the Bureau of American Ethnology to Franz Boas*, (PhD diss., University of Pennsylvania, 1969), 263. See also Darnell's more recent books: *And Along Came Boas: Continuity and Revolution in Americanist Anthropology* (Philadelphia: John Benjamins, 1998); and *Invisible Genealogies: A History of Americanist Anthropology* (Lincoln: University of Nebraska Press, 2001).

6. Matthew Arnold, *Culture and Anarchy*, ed. Samuel Lipman (1869; New Haven, CT: Yale University Press, 1994), 5.

7. See Lawrence W. Levine, *Highbrow/Lowbrow: The Emergence of Cultural Hierarchy in America* (Cambridge, MA: Harvard University Press, 1988); John F. Kasson, *Rudeness and Civility: Manners in Nineteenth-Century Urban America* (New York: Hill and Wang, 1990).

8. Joel Chandler Harris, "At Teague Poteet's," *Century Illustrated Monthly* 26 (1883): 137–50, 185–94; Edmund Clarence Stedman, "The Constant Heart," *Century Illustrated Monthly* 25 (1883): 512; C. E. S. Wood, "Among the Thlinkits in Alaska," *Century Illustrated Monthly* 24 (1882): 323–39; Richard Grant White, "Opera in New York," *Century Illustrated Monthly* 24 (1882): 31–44, 193–211; Charles G. Leland, "Visiting the Gypsies," *Century Illustrated Monthly* 25 (1883): 905–12; John Burroughs, "Henry D. Thoreau," *Century Illustrated Monthly* 24 (1882): 368–79.

9. I am very much in sympathy, for example, with Ira Bashkow's argument that the border in the work of many second-generation Boasian anthropologists was never as hermetic as often described. See "A Neo-Boasian Conception of Cultural Boundaries," *American Anthropologist* 106, no. 3 (2004). On the border, see Akhil Gupta and James Ferguson, eds., *Anthropological Locations: Boundaries and Grounds of a Field Science* (Berkeley: University of California Press, 1997), in which Clifford published "Spatial Practices: Fieldwork, Travel, and the Disciplining of Anthropology." For "flow," see Arjun Appadurai, *Modernity at Large: Cultural Dimensions of Globalization* (Minneapolis: University of Minnesota Press, 1996).

10. Donald Weber, "From Limen to Border: A Meditation on the Legacy of Victor Turner for American Cultural Studies," *American Quarterly* 47 (1995): 525–36, 526, 533. Similarly, see Arnold Krupat, who was one of the first to retheorize borders in American cultural history when he argued that the "frontier" as an important new critical term, the frontier being defined as "that shifting space in which two *cultures* encounter one another." Arnold Krupat, *Ethno-Criticism: Ethnography, History, Literature* (Berkeley: University of California Press, 1992), 5.

11. The most prominent example is Gloria Anzaldúa's *Borderlands/La Frontera* (San Francisco: Spinsters/Aunt Lute Press, 1987).

12. See John Carlos Rowe, *The New American Studies* (Minneapolis: University of Minnesota Press, 2002); and José David Saldívar, *Border Matters: Remapping American Cultural Studies* (Berkeley: University of California Press, 1997). The

ascendancy of this paradigm can elsewhere be marked by the appearance of the tenor of the "special topic" issue of the *PMLA* in January 2003 (118, no. 1) devoted to "America: The Idea, the Literature" and by a new journal, *Comparative American Studies.*

13. From Powell's 1885 Bureau of American Ethnology (BAE) report on "Indian Linguistic Families of America North of Mexico," quoted in Curtis M. Hinsley, *The Smithsonian and the American Indian: Making a Moral Anthropology in America* (Washington, DC: Smithsonian Institution Press, 1981), 180.

14. I undertake this rethinking of the "border" or "contact zone" for the purposes of understanding how Cushing's adventures were received by a magazine audience, which was, itself, denying borders. The claim might be made that in so doing I, once again, circumscribe minority voices. Rather, I want to add to work like that done by Green and Hinsley a more complex understanding of the logic by which these voices were at once silenced and celebrated, and that means understanding the historical period on its own terms. For information on how the Zunis saw Cushing and other anthropologists, see Triloki Nath Pandey, "Anthropologists at Zuni," *Proceedings of the American Philosophical Society* 116 (1972): 321–36, and Phil Hughte, *A Zuni Artist Looks at Frank Hamilton Cushing* (Zuni, NM: A:Shiwi A:wan Museum and Heritage Center, 1994).

    The recent emphasis on "borders" and "frontiers" threatens to insist on borders in just about any situation at all. To cite but one example, Annette Kolodny starts off a recent essay on the subject with what seems like a reasonable set of frontier situations meriting a more complex, inclusive understanding—border events represented by texts like Columbus's "Letter to Lord Sanchez," William Bradford's *History of Plimmoth Plantation,* James Fenimore Cooper's Leather-Stocking series, and Leslie Marmon Silko's *Ceremony.* However, by the end of the essay a little over ten pages later, that list has undergone cascade failure, ballooning to include everything from moral dialogues composed by mendicant friars in the Nahuatl language to all forms of dialect fiction and diaries composed by Chinese and other Asians brought to labor in the United States. Such an impulsive claim for borders lays itself open to charges of historical and theoretical sloppiness. For the border to work as an analytic tool, it needs historical and contextual specificity. I would argue that there are simply situations of transculturation, like that of Cushing, where the "border" is the wrong metaphor—where the paradigm is, in fact, historically misleading. Not all sites of transculturation present the same situation, and the idea of a border is not, per se, specific enough to account for economic, cultural, political, linguistic, geographic interactions. See Kolodny, "Letting Go Our Grand Obsessions: Notes toward a New Literary History of the American Frontiers," in *Subjects and Citizens: Nation, Race, and Gender from* Oroonoko *to* Anita Hill, ed. Michael Moon and Cathy Davidson (Durham, NC: Duke University Press, 1995): 9–26.

15. Jesse Green, introduction to *Zuni: Selected Writings of Frank Hamilton Cushing* (Lincoln: University of Nebraska Press, 1979): 3–34; and introduction to *Cushing at Zuni* (1990): 2–27. Hinsley, *The Smithsonian and the American Indian;*

"Ethnographic Charisma and Scientific Routine"; "Zunis and Brahmins: Cultural Ambivalence in the Gilded Age," in *Romantic Motives: Essays on Anthropological Sensibility,* ed. George W. Stocking Jr., History of Anthropology Series 6 (Madison: University of Wisconsin Press, 1989): 169–207; "Authoring Authenticity," *Journal of the Southwest* (Winter 1991): 462–78; "Collecting Cultures and Cultures of Collecting: The Lure of the American Southwest, 1880–1915," *Museum Anthropology* 16 (1992): 12–20; and introduction to *The Southwest in the American Imagination: The Southwestern Writings of Sylvester Baxter, 1881–89* (Phoenix: University of Arizona Press, 1996).

16. See volumes by Green and Hinsley cited above.

17. E. V. Smalley, "Features of the New North-West," *Century Illustrated Monthly* 25 (1882–83): 529–37, 533.

18. Alan Trachtenberg, *The Incorporation of America: Culture and Society in the Gilded Age* (New York: Hill and Wang, 1982), 3–4.

19. See Arthur John, *The Best Years of the Century: Richard Watson Gilder, Scribner's Monthly, and Century Magazine* (Urbana: University of Illinois Press, 1981).

20. *Century Illustrated Monthly* 24 (1882), 200. For Kellogg's fond recollection of the Gilder's salon, see her *Memoirs of an American Prima Donna* (New York: G. P. Putnam's Sons, 1913), 280–83.

21. Although it is not the focus of this work, I would point out that the border metaphor might also distort the ways in which Native Americans and African Americans were *part of* cultural life in the city and salons of Boston; without cultural borders, the idea of cultural assimilation, too, would need to be read differently. As the century drew to a close, race was used to inscribe segregation, but that happened regardless of anything like culture.

22. Richard H. Brodhead, *Cultures of Letters: Scenes of Reading and Writing in Nineteenth-Century America* (Chicago: University of Chicago Press, 1993), 125. Brodhead's argument accounts well for regional literature's popularity with the leisure class, but his insistence that it is a form strictly limited to a leisure class is not altogether convincing. Cushing, it should be remembered, also wrote for somewhat less prestigious magazines like *Popular Science Monthly,* and even for a trade journal, *Millstone* (in which he published what is widely considered to be his best ethnographic work, "Zuni Breadstuff," in 1884). Local color was also a regular feature in newspapers and the less expensive magazines. Moreover, the museum program of the Smithsonian Institution, for which he was collecting, clearly had in mind the education of a broader audience than Brodhead seemingly imagines. For a related argument, see Bill Brown, "The Popular, the Populist, and the Populace—Locating Hamlin Garland in the Politics of Culture," *Arizona Quarterly* 50, no. 3 (1994): 89–110, in which he shows that Garland positioned regionalism as an emerging popular form.

23. Henry James, "Venice," *Century Illustrated Monthly* 25 (1882): 3–24, 3.

24. See Cushing's letter of October 15, 1879, to Colonel Stevenson, excerpted in a footnote below.

25. Baxter, "Aboriginal Pilgrimage," 527, 529.

26. For the numbers, see Nancy J. Parezo, "The Formation of Ethnographic Collections: The Smithsonian Institution in the American Southwest," *Advances in Archaeological Method and Theory* 10 (1987): 1–47; and, more generally, see Steven Conn, *Museums and American Intellectual Life, 1876–1926* (Chicago: University of Chicago Press, 1998).

27. See Sarah J. Blackstone, *Buckskins, Bullets, and Business: A History of Buffalo Bill's Wild West* (Westport, CN: Greenwood Press, 1986).

28. This zone of eccentricity is similar to what Bashkow, in his article about rethinking borders in Boasian anthropology, calls the "zone of the foreign." Bashkow, "A Neo-Boasian Conception,"449. The point in this context is that while exotic, the items initiating this zone are precisely not *foreign* but *American*.

29. Baxter, "Father of the Pueblos," 74.

30. For the most explicit explanation of this project, see the draft of Cushing's letter to Colonel Stevenson, the head of the 1879 Southwest collecting expedition, dated October 15, 1879: "You remember that our instructions were to remain as long at the Pueblo we should choose as typical as I should deem it necessary, after the collecting was done, for measuring and research relative to the sociological organization of these people. You remember that Major Powell said to me, 'Find out these points by all means, as they are of primary importance, and if you can't do it in one month, *take six,* or even more. I would much prefer that one Pueblo be investigated thoroughly than that all the twenty-seven should be seen and collected from superficially.' The object, therefore, of the Expedition, as I understand it, is not merely collecting, which in itself is of great importance, but observing as well, which work I believe I have the honor of being trusted with." *Cushing at Zuni,* ed. Green, 42–43.

31. Sylvester Baxter, "Zuni Revisited," *American Architect and Building News* 13 (1883): 124–26, 125.

32. Baxter, "Father of the Pueblos," 74.

33. In effect, Cushing's articles stage in a very public fashion and medium what Roy Wagner has described as "culture shock," the process by which culture "first manifests itself to the anthropologist through his own *inadequacy;* against the backdrop of his new surroundings it is he who has become 'visible.'" Roy Wagner, *The Invention of Culture,* rev. and exp. ed. (Chicago: University of Chicago Press, 1981), 6–7.

34. The "gaze," of course, has acquired a vast theoretical apparatus; for readings of the gaze pertinent to the particular historical period treated here, see Catherine A. Lutz and Jane L. Collins, *Reading National Geographic* (Chicago: University of Chicago Press, 1993); and Shawn Michelle Smith, *American Archives: Gender, Race, and Class in Visual Culture* (Princeton, NJ: Princeton University Press, 1999). My thinking on the subject began with Laura Mulvey, *Visual and Other Pleasures* (Bloomington: Indiana University Press, 1989).

35. We might read some added significance into this name, the healing flower, when reading in Cushing's letters the extent to which he physically suffered due to his living conditions at the pueblo. Later photographs and paintings of him show the

extent to which his body was emaciated and scarred by his "adventures"; he seems never really to have recovered his health even after leaving Zuni.

36. Renato Rosaldo calls this duality "imperialist nostalgia"; it might be contextualized as part of what Mary Louise Pratt would identify as the poetics of "anti-conquest." See Rosaldo, "Imperialist Nostalgia," in *Culture and Truth: The Remaking of Social Analysis* (1989; Boston: Beacon Press, 1993); Pratt, *Imperial Eyes: Travel Writing and Transculturation* (New York: Routledge, 1992).

37. Hinsley, "Zunis and Brahmins," 187, 204.

38. Editors, *Century Illustrated Monthly* 23 (1881): 144.

39. Norbert Elias, *The History of Manners,* trans. Edmund Jephcott (1939; New York: Pantheon, 1978), 5.

40. Draft of a letter from Cushing to Baird and Powell, February 18, 1880, in *Cushing at Zuni,* ed. Green, 95.

41. R. W. Gilder, "The Century's First Year under Its New Name," my italics, *Century Illustrated Monthly* 24 (1882): 939.

42. Cosmo Monkhouse, "Some English Artists and their Studios," *Century Illustrated Monthly* 24 (1882): 553–68, 553.

43. It should be noted that advertising is becoming a major source of revenues for magazines during this period. In December 1880, the *Century* carried forty-nine pages of ads (to roughly 150 pages of print); by 1891, they carried 150 pages of ads. From Frank Luther Mott, *A History of American Magazines* (Cambridge, MA: Harvard University Press, 1938).

44. There is a notable byproduct, which could be the subject of another kind of study than this one, namely the objectification of the Zunis as nonconsumers.

45. On the Eakins portrait, see Judith Zilczer, "Eakins Letter Provides More Evidence on the Portrait of Frank Hamilton Cushing," *American Art Journal* 14, no.1 (Winter 1882): 74–76. One final anecdote about Cushing's return from Zuni, once again highlighting the eccentric: Cushing was recalled after a dispute with a well-placed senator over a land claim in which Cushing, defending Zuni territory in his role as a priest of the bow, shot the senator's son's horse; later, there were also some disputes about Cushing doctoring some of his "finds" in archeological work in the Southwest and in Florida. Again, for biographical information see the recent work by Green and Hinsley.

CHAPTER TWO

1. Simon Bronner, *Following Tradition: Folklore in the Discourse of American Culture* (Logan: Utah State University Press, 1998), 97.

2. Perhaps with this quiescence in mind, Barbara Kirshenblatt-Gimblett has called the folklore of the early 1900s an "academic relic area for the practice of an outmoded philology." See "Folklore's Crisis," *Journal of American Folklore* 111, no. 441 (1998): 281–327, 289.

3. See, for example, Thomas Wentworth Higginson, "Negro Spirituals," *Atlantic Monthly* 19 (1867): 685–94. Ronald Radano discusses this tradition in "Denoting

Difference: The Writing of the Slave Spirituals," *Critical Inquiry* 22 (1996): 506–44, especially 509–13.

4. William Wells Newell, "Additional Collection Essential to Correct Theory in Folk-Lore and Mythology," *Journal of American Folk-Lore* 3 (1890): 23–32, 26.

5. Joel Chandler Harris, introduction to *Uncle Remus: His Songs and Sayings* (1880; New York: Penguin, 1982), 40.

6. Joel Chandler Harris, introduction to *Nights with Uncle Remus: Myths and Legends of the Old Plantation* (Boston: Houghton Mifflin, 1883), xxviii.

7. This appropriation of Indian mythology for that of the American nation can be seen to begin with Jefferson in his section on the "Aborigines" in *Notes on the State of Virginia* (1787), if not earlier. See in particular Curtis Hinsley, *The Smithsonian and the American Indian: Making a Moral Anthropology in Victorian America* (Washington, DC: Smithsonian Institution Press, 1990); Richard Slotkin, *Regeneration through Violence: The Mythology of the American Frontier, 1600–1860* (New York: Harper Perennial, 1973); and Brian W. Dippie, *The Vanishing American: White Attitudes and U.S. Indian Policy* (Lawrence: University Press of Kansas, 1982).

8. Although not one of its stated purposes, Hans Aarsleff's seminal work, *The Study of Language in England, 1780–1860* (1967; Minneapolis: University of Minnesota Press, 1983) makes this point abundantly clear. See also Julie Tetel Andresen's discussion in *Linguistics in America, 1769–1924: A Critical History* (New York: Routledge, 1990).

9. T. Frederick Crane, "The Diffusion of Popular Tales," *Journal of American Folk-Lore* 1 (1888): 8–15, 12.

10. Unsigned, "Negro Minstrelsy—Ancient and Modern," *Putnam's Magazine* 5 (January 1855): 72–79, 72.

11. See E. Cobham Brewer, *Dictionary of Phrase and Fable* (Philadelphia: Henry Altemus Co., 1898).

12. W. F. Allen, "Southern Negro Folk-Lore," *The Dial* 1 (1880–81): 183–85, 183.

13. W. S. Scarborough, A. M., "Negro Folk-Lore and Dialect," *Arena* 17 (1896–97): 186–92, 186.

14. Annie Weston Whitney, "Negro American Dialects," *The Independent* 53 (1901): 1979–81, 1979.

15. See Michel Foucault, *The Order of Things: An Archaeology of the Human Sciences* (New York: Vintage, 1994).

16. On this point in Hobbes, see Ian Hacking, *Historical Ontology* (Cambridge, MA: Harvard University Press, 2002), especially 115–39.

17. Matti Bunzl, "Franz Boas and the Humboldtian Tradition: From *Volksgeist* and *Nationalcharakter* to an Anthropological Concept of Culture," in Volksgeist *as Method and Ethic: Essays on Boasian Ethnography and the German Anthropological Tradition*, ed. George W. Stocking Jr., History of Anthropology Series 8 (Madison: University of Wisconsin Press, 1996), 17–78; see especially 29, 31.

18. In Bunzl, "Franz Boas and the Humboldtian Tradition," 32.

19. Foucault, *Order of Things,* 282.

20. Johann Gottfried Herder, "On the German-Oriental Poets," *Selected Early Works, 1764–1767,* ed. Ernest A. Menze and Karl Menges, trans. Ernest A. Menze with Michael Palma (University Park: Pennsylvania State University Press, 1992), 179.

21. George Lyman Kittredge, introduction to *English and Scottish Popular Ballads Edited from the Collection of Francis James Child* by Kittredge and Helen Child Sargent (Boston: Houghton Mifflin, 1904), xi–xxxi, xi.

22. William Owens, "Folk-Lore of the Southern Negroes," *Lippincott's* 20 (1877): 748–55, 748. Future references will be cited parenthetically.

23. Steven Conn, *Museums and American Intellectual Life* (Chicago: University of Chicago Press, 1998).

24. Otis T. Mason, "The Natural History of Folk-Lore," *Journal of American Folk-Lore* 4 (1891): 97–105, 99.

25. Daniel G. Brinton, ed., *The Maya Chronicles* (Philadelphia: D. G. Brinton, 1882), 6.

26. George Bird Grinnell, *Pawnee Hero Stories and Folk-Tales* (1889; Lincoln: University of Nebraska Press, 1961), 6.

27. Jeremiah Curtin, *Creation Myths of America* (1898; London: Bracken Books, 1995).

28. Lafcadio Hearn, introduction to *Gombo Zhèbes* (1885; Bedford, MA: Applewood Books, 2000), 3.

29. See A. Gerber, "Uncle Remus Traced to the Old World," *Journal of American Folk-Lore* 6 (1893): 245–57, 251.

30. Quoted in Crane, "Diffusion of Popular Tales," 10, 11. Originally from Lang's introduction to Hunt's *Grimm's Household Tales,* vol. 1 (London, 1884), xi, xliii.

31. Daniel G. Brinton, *Aboriginal American Authors and Their Productions, Especially Those in the Native Languages: A Chapter in the History of Literature* (Philadelphia, n.p., 1883), 48, 47, 46.

32. William J. McGee, "Fifty Years of American Science," *Atlantic Monthly* 82 (1898): 317–19. Quoted in Bronner, *Following Tradition,* 98. For more on McGee, see Hinsley's chapter on him in *The Smithsonian and the American Indian.*

33. Moreover, he appears to have guessed correctly about how diffusion actually worked. In perhaps the most exciting work on folklore to date, drawing on the wealth of cataloguing information being ushered in by the switch to digital technology, folklore scholars are now beginning to understand the extent to which these tales were spread in inexpensive, chap-book editions. See, for example, Ruth B. Bottigheimer, "Luckless, Witless, and Filthy-Footed: A Sociocultural Study and Publishing History Analysis of 'The Lazy Boy,'" *Journal of American Folklore* 106 (1993): 259–84.

34. Linda Dowling, "Victorian Oxford and the Science of Language," *PMLA* 97, no. 2 (1982): 160–78, 162.

35. Franz Boas, "The Occurrence of Similar Inventions in Areas Widely Apart," and "Museums of Ethnology and Their Classification," *Science* 9 (1887): 485–86, 587–89; reprinted in Franz Boas, *A Franz Boas Reader: The Shaping of American*

Anthropology, 1883–1911, ed. George W. Stocking Jr. (Chicago: University of Chicago Press, 1974), 61–67.

36. George W. Stocking Jr., *Race, Culture, and Evolution: Essays in the History of Anthropology* (1968; Chicago: University of Chicago Press, 1982), and especially "The Basic Assumptions of Boasian Anthropology," in Boas, *A Franz Boas Reader,* ed. Stocking, 1–20, especially 1–5. For other citations of the debate, see Hinsley, *The Smithsonian and the American Indian,* especially 98–100; Ira Jacknis, "Franz Boas and Exhibits: On the Limitations of the Museum Method of Anthropology," in *Objects and Others: Essays on Museums and Material Culture,* ed. George W. Stocking Jr. (Madison: University of Wisconsin Press, 1985), 75–111, especially 77–83; Michael A. Elliott, *The Culture Concept: Writing and Difference in the Age of Realism* (Minneapolis: University of Minnesota Press, 2002) especially chapter 1; Marc Manganaro, *Culture, 1922: The Emergence of a Concept* (Princeton, NJ: Princeton University Press, 2002), 9; and Bill Brown, *A Sense of Things: The Object Matter of American Literature* (Chicago: University of Chicago Press, 2003), 88–89.

37. In Stocking, "Basic Assumptions of Boasian Anthropology," 5.

38. See Stocking's note in Boas, *A Franz Boas Reader,* ed. Stocking, 130.

39. "The Mythologies of the Indians," part II, *International Quarterly* 12 (1905): 157–73, reprinted in Boas, *A Franz Boas Reader,* ed. Stocking, 135–48, 146.

40. The *Handbook* was produced as a supplement to the map of Indian languages that had been the centerpiece of John Wesley Powell's tenure at the BAE.

41. E. B. Tylor, *Primitive Culture* (Boston: n.p., 1871), 1.

42. For "literary style," see Boas's 1914 article, "Mythology and Folk-Tales of the North American Indian," reprinted in his *Race, Language and Culture* (1940; Chicago: University of Chicago Press, 1982), 451–90, 466, 479.

43. Zora Neale Hurston, *Mules and Men,* reprinted in *Folklore, Memoirs, and Other Writings* (New York: Library of America, 1995), 1–267, 13.

44. Anonymous, "Word Shadows," *Atlantic Monthly* 67 (1891): 143–44, 143.

45. Gavin Jones provides an excellent survey and analysis of white anxiety about the contamination of the English language in *Strange Talk: The Politics of Dialect Literature in Gilded Age America* (Berkeley: University of California Press, 1999).

46. Some of the best work on this subject has come in Regina Bendrix, *In Search of Authenticity: The Formation of Folklore Studies* (Madison: University of Wisconsin Press, 1997), and Radano, "Denoting Difference," 506–44.

47. Eric Sundquist, *To Wake the Nations* (Cambridge, MA: The Belknap Press of Harvard University Press, 1993), 294–322.

48. Ronald Radano picked up on this materiality when describing the transcription of slave spirituals as working at cross-purposes. As a group, he argues, these transcriptions "worked to discipline and constrain, inscribing white racialisms onto the textualized body of black song. Yet by conceptualizing difference as a realm beyond white access, so did they supply a reinvented slave music with formidable 'spiritual' power." Radano, "Denoting Difference," 508.

49. Henry Louis Gates Jr., *Figures in Black: Words, Signs and the 'Racial' Self* (New York: Oxford University Press, 1987), 177, 186.

50. For other takes on the subject of "po-mo-Bo" (post-modern Boas), see the articles by Matti Bunzl, Ira Bashkow, and Richard Handler in the special issue of *American Anthropologist*, vol. 106, no. 3 (September 2004).

51. Radano, "Denoting Difference," 508.

52. For an illuminating study of a more recent political deployment of this idea of "cultural property," see Richard Handler's "On Having a Culture: Nationalism and the Preservation of Quebec's *Patrimoine*," in *Objects and Others: Essays on Museums and Material Culture*, ed. George W. Stocking Jr., History of Anthropology Series 3 (Madison: University of Wisconsin Press, 1985), 192–217.

53. For a convenient source, see *Smithsonian Institution Bureau of American Ethnology, List of Publications of the Bureau of Ethnology, with Index to Authors and Titles* (Washington, DC: U.S. Government Printing Office, 1962).

54. Harris, *Uncle Remus*, 62. See, for example, Richard H. Brodhead's *Cultures of Letters: Scenes of Reading and Writing in Nineteenth-Century America* (Chicago: University of Chicago Press, 1993).

55. Joel Chandler Harris, "At Teague Poteet's," in *Mingo, and Other Sketches in Black and White* (Boston: James R. Osgood, 1884), 40. Future references will be cited in the text.

56. Boas, "Museums of Ethnology," 66.

57. The most thorough account of Harris's political position has been written by Wayne Mixon, "The Ultimate Irrelevance of Race: Joel Chandler Harris and Uncle Remus in Their Time," *Journal of Southern History* 56 (1990): 457–80. Sundquist picks up on Mixon's article in *To Wake the Nations*, especially 339–41. Another very nice review of the subject was recently published by Mark Schone, "Uncle Remus Is Dead, Long Live Uncle Remus," *Oxford American* (January–February 2003): 86–92.

58. Joel Chandler Harris, "Public Men on Public Questions," originally published in 1900 in *Saturday Record's;* reprinted in Julia Collier Harris, ed., *Joel Chandler Harris, Editor and Essayist: Miscellaneous Literary, Political and Social Writings* (Chapel Hill: University of North Carolina Press, 1931), 110.

59. Reprinted in Joel Chandler Harris, *The Complete Tales of Uncle Remus* (1955; Boston: Houghton Mifflin, 1983), 579, 580.

60. "The Negro as the South Sees Him," *Saturday Evening Post*, January 2, 1904, reprinted in Julia Collier Harris, *Joel Chandler Harris, Editor and Essayist*, 114–29, 129.

61. Most notably Sundquist.

62. For example, see Boas, "Mythology and Folk Tales of the North American Indian," (1914), reprinted in his *Race, Language and Culture*, 451–90, 479.

63. Julius Lester, *The Tales of Uncle Remus: The Adventures of Brer Rabbit* (New York: Dial, 1987), xx–xxi.

64. Franz Boas, in "William Wells Newell—Memorial Meeting," *Journal of American Folk-Lore* 20 (1907): 59–68, 63.

65. Antonio Gramsci, "Observations on Folklore," from *Prison Notebooks,* vol. 1; reprinted in Alan Dundes, ed., *International Folkloristics: Classic Contributions by the Founders of Folklore* (Boston: Roman and Littlefield, 1999), 131–36, 135.

CHAPTER THREE

1. *Epigraph.* Sarah Orne Jewett, *A Marsh Island* (Boston: Riverside Press, 1885), 186. Future references will be cited parenthetically.

2. Sarah Orne Jewett, *Deephaven,* in *Novels and Stories* (New York: Library of America, 1994), 1–141, 65; and *The Country of the Pointed Firs,* in *Novels and Stories,* 371–487, 485, 486.

3. On the significance of things as objects of ethnography in Jewett's writing, see chapter three of Bill Brown's *A Sense of Things: The Object Matter of American Literature* (Chicago: University of Chicago Press, 2003).

4. In other words, her books came to be collected in much the same way as the water-jug in *A Marsh Island.* Sandra Zagarell makes a similar point about Jewett's books as collectible objects in "Troubling Regionalism: Rural Life and the Cosmopolitan Eye in Jewett's *Deephaven,*" *American Literary History* 10, no. 4 (1998): 639–63. Zagarell notes that the marsh reeds printed on the cover of the original edition of *Deephaven* were the same as the ones the girls collected in the book, which suggests that there was a certain equivalence between going to Maine to get reeds and going to the bookstore to get Jewett.

5. A point made both by Richard H. Brodhead in *Cultures of Letters: Scenes of Reading and Writing in Nineteenth-Century America* (Chicago: University of Chicago Press, 1993), and more recently by Brown, *Sense of Things,* 215n21.

6. Hippolyte Taine, *History of English Literature*, rev. ed., trans. Henri Van Laun, 2 vols. (New York: Colonial Press, 1900), vol. 1, 1.

7. René Wellek, *A History of Modern Criticism: 1750–1950*, vol. 4 (New Haven, CT: Yale University Press, 1965), 55.

8. Evident in the three most influential evaluations of regionalism in the late 1980s and early 1990s: Eric Sundquist, "Realism and Regionalism," in *Columbia Literary History of the United States,* ed. Emory Elliott (New York: Columbia University Press, 1988), 501–24 ("anthropological dimension, 503); Amy Kaplan, "Nation, Region, Empire," in *The Columbia History of the American Novel,* ed. Emory Elliott (New York: Columbia University Press, 1991), 240–66 (compares "local-color fiction," to "anthropological fieldwork," 252); and Brodhead, *Cultures of Letters,* especially chapters 4 and 5 on "The Reading of Regions" and Sarah Orne Jewett respectively ("regional fiction is also a nineteenth-century ethnography," 121).

   As for the change in nomenclature away from "sections," Joel Chandler Harris, for example, frequently argued of the need for Southern fiction to over-come "sectionalism" and embrace what he called "localism." See Harris, *Editor and Essayist,* ed. Julia Collier Harris (Chapel Hill: University of North Carolina Press, 1931), 45, 186. Throughout this chapter I will use the terms "local color" and "regional" interchangeably in most instances, noting only here that the former term can imply a more definitive periodization. "Local color" was the most familiar appellation given during the period to the new, nonsectional literature (as by Hamlin Garland in *Crumbling Idols* [1894]), though it was being called "'regional' literature" at least as early as 1912 by scholars like Bliss Perry, *The American Mind* (1912; Port Washington, NY: Kennikat Press, 1968), 28. For a general discussion of some critical implications of the nomenclature, see June Howard, "Unraveling Regions, Unsettling Periods: Sarah Orne Jewett and American Literary History," *American Literature* 68 (1996): 365–84, especially 366n1.

9. Neil Harris, introduction to *The Land of Contrasts, 1880–1901,* ed. Neil Harris (New York: George Braziller, 1970), 1–28, 6.

10. This move clearly followed from auto-critiques from within anthropology, particularly volumes edited in 1986 by George Marcus and Michael Fischer, *Anthropology as Cultural Critique: An Experimental Moment in the Human Sciences* (Chicago: University of Chicago Press, 1986) and George Marcus and James Clifford, *Writing Culture: The Poetics and Politics of Ethnography* (Berkeley: University of California Press, 1986).

11. Brodhead, *Cultures of Letters,* 121; Kaplan, "Nation, Region, Empire," 252; Sundquist, "Realism and Regionalism," 503. For the critique of anthropology, one might turn to Renato Rosaldo, who rather too succinctly sums up and footnotes this story in the first ninety pages of *Culture and Truth: The Remaking of Social Analysis* (1989; Boston: Beacon Press, 1993); a more useful source is James Clifford, *The Predicament of Culture: Twentieth-Century Ethnography, Literature, and Art* (Cambridge, MA: Harvard University Press, 1988).

12. As in his 1914 essay, "Folktales of the North American Indians," where he writes that "the tales of each particular area have developed a peculiar literary style, which is an expression of the mode of life and of the form of thought of the people." Reprinted in Franz Boas, *Race, Language and Culture* (1940; Chicago: University of Chicago Press, 1982), 451–90, 479.

13. In addition to those already cited above, see for representative examples the volume edited by June Howard, *New Essays on* The Country of the Pointed Firs (New York: Cambridge University Press, 1994), and Walter Benn Michaels, "Local Colors," *Modern Language Notes* 113, no. 4 (1998): 734–56.

14. Hamlin Garland, *Crumbling Idols* (1894; Cambridge: Harvard University Press, 1960), 8. Barrett Wendell, a Harvard professor: "Partly, however, this prevalence of short stories seems nationally characteristic of American as distinguished from English men of letters," in *A Literary History of America* (New York: Scribner's, 1900), 516. Fred Lewis Pattee, a University of Pennsylvania professor: "The exploiting of new and strange regions, with their rough manners, their coarse humor, and their uncouth dialects, brought to the front the new, hard-fought, and hard-defended literary method called realism," in *A History of American Literature since 1870* (New York: D. Appleton-Century, 1915), 17. Bliss Perry: "Our task is to exhibit the essential Americanism of these spokesmen of ours," in *The American Mind* (1912; Port Washington, NY: Kennikat Press, 1968),

45. Arthur Hobson Quinn, *American Fiction: An Historical and Critical Survey* (New York: Appleton-Century-Crofts, 1936). Warner Berthoff: "It was by concentration on the local, the long-familiar, the particular, that each had achieved the formal authority which is the precondition of significance as well as of permanence," in "The Art of Jewett's Pointed Firs," *New England Quarterly* 32 (1959): 32.

15. See, for example, Josephine Donovan, *New England Local Color Literature: A Women's Tradition* (New York: Frederick Ungar, 1980).

16. Howard, ed., *New Essays on* The Country of the Pointed Firs. The "return" to nationalism has not gone uncontested; indeed, one of the best recent books on the subject is a feminist rejoinder from Judith Fetterley and Marjorie Pryse, *Writing Out of Place: Regionalism, Women, and American Literary Culture* (Urbana: University of Illinois Press, 2003).

17. Hans Kohn, *The Idea of Nationalism: A Study in Its Origins and Background* (New York: Macmillan, 1944), vii.

18. William Dean Howells, *Criticism and Fiction*, in *Selected Literary Criticism, Volume II: 1867–1897* (1891: Bloomington, IN: Indiana University Press, 1993), 298–354, 340.

19. George William Curtis, "Editor's Easy Chair," *Harper's Monthly* 42 (1871): 924.

20. Hamlin Garland, *Crumbling Idols,* 53. Future references will be cited parenthetically.

21. Hutcheson Macaulay Posnett, *Comparative Literature* (New York: D. Appleton and Company, 1892), 43.

22. Taine, *History of English Literature,* vol. 1, 1. Future references will be cited parenthetically. Translations without citation are my own. For the genealogy of Boasian anthropology, see in particular Matti Bunzl, "Franz Boas and the Humboldtian Tradition: From *Volksgeist* and *Nationalcharakter* to an Anthropological Concept of Culture," in Volksgeist *as Method and Ethic: Essays on Boasian Ethnography and the German Anthropological Tradition,* ed. George W. Stocking Jr., History of Anthropology Series 8 (Madison: University of Wisconsin Press, 1996) 17–78.

23. Hippolyte Taine, *Histoire de la littérature anglaise,* vol. 1 (Paris: Librairie de la Hachette, 1863), xxii. Future references will be cited parenthetically.

24. James's review of the English translation of *Histoire* was published in the *Atlantic Monthly* in 1872; reprinted in Henry James, *Literary Criticism,* vol. 2 (New York: Library of America, 1984), 841–48, 843.

25. Pascale Seys, *Hippolyte Taine et l'avènement du naturalisme: Un intellectuel sous le Second Empire* (Paris: Éditions L'Harmattan, 1999).

26. "Aujourd'hui, l'histoire comme la zoologie a trouvé son anatomie, et quelle que soit la branche historique à laquelle on s'attache, philologie, linguistique ou mythologie, c'est par cette voi qu'on travaille à lui faire produire de nouveaux fruits." Taine, *Histoire,* xii.

27. "What have we under the fair, glazed pages of a modern poem? A modern poet . . . in a black coat and gloves, welcomed by the ladies." Taine pushes the figure further by way of syllogism: "like Alfred de Musset, Victor Hugo, Lamartine or Heine" (2).

28. Johann Gottfried Herder, *Selected Early Works, 1764–1767*, ed. Ernest A. Menze and Karl Menges (University Park: Pennsylvania State University Press, 1991), 102.

29. Herder quoted in Richard Bauman and Charles L. Briggs, "Language Philosophy as Language Ideology: John Locke and Johann Gottfried Herder," in *Regimes of Language: Ideologies, Polities, and Identities*, ed. Paul V. Kroskrity (Santa Fe, NM: School of American Research Press, 2000), 174.

30. Washington Irving, *The Sketch Book of Geoffrey Crayon, Gent.* (1819–20; New York: Penguin, 1988), 17, my emphasis. Future references will be cited parenthetically.

31. Jeffrey Scraba discusses Irving's historical project at length in a dissertation chapter, "History Carried on by Other Means: Washington Irving," forthcoming at Rutgers University.

32. Washington Irving, *A History of New York* (1848; Boston: Twayne, 1984), 4.

33. Quoted by Harry H. Clark, "The Influence of Science on American Literature Criticism, 1860–1910, Including the Vogue of Taine, *Transactions of the Wisconsin Academy of Sciences, Arts and Letters* 44 (1955): 109–64, 114. See also Clark's "The Role of Science in the Thought of W. D. Howells," *Transactions of the Wisconsin Academy of Sciences, Arts and Letters* 42 (1953): 263–303.

34. William Dean Howells, "Editor's Study," *Harper's Monthly* (July 1886); reprinted in *Editor's Study*, ed. James W. Simpson (New York: Whitston, 1983), 32.

35. Howells quoting Posnett, in *Editor's Study*, ed. Simpson, 33.

36. Edward Eggleston, *The Circuit Rider: A Tale of the Heroic Age* (New York: J. B. Ford, 1874), vi–vii. See Everett Carter, *Howells and the Age of Realism* (Philadelphia: J. B. Lippincott, 1950). That "higher form of history" was clearly the same that would go on to produce the historicism behind the Boasians' concept of culture.

37. Fred Lewis Pattee, *A History of American Literature* (New York: Silver, Burdett, 1896); Moses Coit Tyler, *A History of American Literature, 1607–1765* (1878; Ithaca, NY: Cornell University Press, 1949), 523; Barrett Wendell, *A Literary History of America* (1900; New York: Scribner's, 1905), 9. Pattee, *History of American Literature*, 2–3.

38. See Michael Warner, "Professionalization and the Rewards of Literature," *Criticism* 27 (1985): 1–28; and Gerald Graff, *Professing Literature: An Institutional History* (Chicago: University of Chicago Press, 1987).

39. Wellek, *History of Modern Criticism*, 27. For the most extensive documentation of Taine's "vogue," see Harry H. Clark, "The Influence of Science on American Literary Criticism, 1860–1910, Including the Vogue of Taine," *Transactions of the Wisconsin Academy of Sciences, Arts and Letters* 44 (1955): 109–64. See also chapters on Taine and American realism in Everett Carter's classic, *Howells and the Age of Realism* (Philadelphia: J. B. Lippincott, 1950).

40. Appiah's is one of the few contemporary critiques of Taine: *In My Father's House: Africa in the Philosophy of Culture* (New York: Oxford University Press, 1992), 51.

41. "And all the more distinct as the differences between the climates become more pronounced." Hippolyte Taine, *Philosophie de l'art*, vol. 1 (1865; Paris: Librairie Hachette, 1893), 277.

42. Howells, "Editor's Study," *Harper's Monthly* (November 1891); reprinted in *Editor's Study,* ed. Simpson, 342.

43. For source material on Lamarck, see especially George Stocking Jr., "Lamarckianism in American Social Science, 1890–1915," in *Race, Culture, and Evolution: Essays in the History of Anthropology* (1968; Chicago: University of Chicago Press, 1982), 234–69.

44. Appiah notes Taine's racialism, but does nothing to understand it as a combination of social and biological traits. *In My Father's House,* 51.

45. Stocking, *Race, Culture, and Evolution,* 245.

46. Frederick Jackson Turner, "The Significance of the Frontier in American History," in *The Frontier in American History* (1893; Tucson: University of Arizona Press, 1986), 23.

47. Hamlin Garland, *Main-Travelled Roads* (1891; Lincoln: University of Nebraska Press, 1995), 86. Future quotes will be cited parenthetically.

48. "Tragedy" and "epic" are referred to five times in the space of four pages, making sure that readers do not miss the point. See pp. 76–79.

49. See especially Brodhead's chapter on Jewett in *Cultures of Letters.* Zagarell also notes the Arnoldian influence, but in my opinion very much misreads it, suggesting a path through Arnold's Hellenism to Jewett's latent racialism. As we will see, there are much more direct routes to understanding Jewett in terms of race—routes that have the additional merit of not obscuring her universalism. Zagarell, "*Country*'s Portrayal of Community and the Exclusion of Difference," in Howard, ed., *New Essays on* The Country of the Pointed Firs.

50. Sarah Orne Jewett, *The Story of the Normans, Told Chiefly in Relation to Their Conquest of England* (New York: Putnam's Sons, 1890); this language is ubiquitous throughout the volume.

51. Sarah Orne Jewett, *A Country Doctor,* in *Novels and Stories,* 143–370, 190. Future references will be cited parenthetically.

52. Stocking, *Race, Culture, and Evolution,* 240.

53. See Sarah Orne Jewett, *The Irish Stories of Sarah Orne Jewett,* ed. Jack Morgan and Louis A. Renza (Carbondale: Southern Illinois University Press, 1996).

54. One of the major contributions offered by Kaplan in "Nation, Region, Empire," 242, is that regionalism produces a "willed amnesia."

55. Sarah Orne Jewett, *The Tory Lover* (Boston: Riverside Press, 1901), 60. Future references will be cited parenthetically.

56. Wellek, *History of Modern Criticism,* 32.

57. ". . . avec les forces du dedans et du dehors, il y a l'oeuvre qu'elles ont déja faite ensemble, et cette oeuvre elle-même contribue à produire celle qui suit" (xxvii).

58. "New Figures in Literature and Art," *Atlantic Monthly* 76 (1895): 840.

59. Arthur Penn, *The Home Library* (New York: D. Appleton, 1883), 73, 64.

60. Edward Sapir, "Culture, Genuine and Spurious," *American Journal of Sociology* 29 (1924): 401–29; reprinted in *Selected Writings in Language, Culture, and Personality,* ed. David G. Mandelbaum (Berkeley: University of California Press, 1985), 308–31, 319, 320; W. H. Holmes, "On the Evolution of Ornament—An American Lesson,"

American Anthropologist 3 (1890): 137–46, reprinted in Frederica de Laguna, ed., *American Anthropology, 1888–1920* (Lincoln: University of Nebraska Press, 1960), 498–507, 500.

61. Franz Boas, "The Decorative Art of the North American Indians," reprinted in Boas, *Race, Language and Culture,* 546–63, 546.

62. These lines are actually Hamlin's, quoted by Boas in the text. Hamlin was analyzing art in the "Old World," and Boas's point was that the same thing applied to Native Americans.

63. Judith Fetterley, "'Not in the Least American': Nineteenth-Century Literary Regionalism," *College English* 56, no. 8 (1994): 877–88, 888. Also see the recent volume by Fetterley and Pryse, *Writing Out of Place.*

64. A point that both Bramen and Nancy Glazener make by pointing to, among others, the writing of Hamlin Garland in the *Arena.* Carrie Tirado Bramen, *The Uses of Variety: Modern Americanism and the Quest for National Distinctiveness* (Cambridge, MA: Harvard University Press, 2000), 152. Nancy Glazener, *Reading for Realism: The History of a U.S. Literary Institution, 1850–1910* (Durham, NC: Duke University Press, 1997). See also Stephanie Foote, *Regional Fictions: Culture and Identity in Nineteenth-Century American Literature* (Madison: University of Wisconsin Press, 2001).

65. Sandra Zagarell, "Troubling Regionalism: Rural Life and the Cosmopolitan Eye in Jewett's *Deephaven,*" *American Literary History* 10, no. 1 (1998): 639–63.

66. Laurie Shannon, "'The Country of Our Friendship': Jewett's Intimist Art," *American Literature* 71, no. 2 (1999): 227–62.

67. Brown, *A Sense of Things,* 124.

CHAPTER FOUR

1. William Dean Howells, *A Hazard of New Fortunes* (1890; New York: Meridian, 1994), 212, 174. Future references will be cited parenthetically.

2. William Dean Howells, "Dialect in Literature," originally in *Harper's Weekly* (June 8, 1895); reprinted in William Dean Howells, *Selected Literary Criticism,* vol. 2 (Bloomington: Indiana University Press, 1993), 219–23, 220.

3. I will elaborate on these two versions of reading regionalism—neither of which is as independent from the other as is implied here—in the next section. For now, let me simply mark their places by citing the ideological critique of Amy Kaplan, "Nation, Region, and Empire," in *Columbia History of the American Novel,* ed. Emory Elliott (New York: Columbia University Press, 1991), 240–65; and for the commodity version, Richard Brodhead, *Cultures of Letters: Scenes of Reading and Writing in Nineteenth-Century America* (Chicago: University of Chicago Press, 1993).

4. This chapter will not take up the topic of primitivism in detail; the point is merely that local color's *chicness,* in its exploitation of an aura of dislocation, anticipates the modernist relationship between anthropology and art in, say, the appearance of African masks in Picasso's famous painting of French prostitutes, *Les demoiselles d'Avignon* (1907). The "anthropological dimension" of local-

color fiction is, as discussed in the previous chapter, from Eric Sundquist, "Realism and Regionalism," in *Columbia Literary History of the United States*, ed. Emory Elliott (New York: Columbia University Press, 1988), 501–24, 503.

5. Roberto Mario Dainotto, "'All the Regions Do Smilingly Revolt': The Literature of Place and Region," *Critical Inquiry* 22 (1994): 489.

6. Dainotto, "'All the Regions Do Smilingly Revolt,'" 505.

7. The benchmark history of antimodernism is T. J. Jackson-Lear's *No Place of Grace: Antimodernism and the Transformation of American Culture, 1880–1920* (New York: Pantheon, 1981). For the purchase of that idea in the analysis of local-color fiction, see, subsequently, Kaplan, "Nation, Region, and Empire"; Sundquist, "Realism and Regionalism"; Brodhead, *Cultures of Letters;* and Elizabeth Ammons and Valerie Rohy, eds., introduction to *American Local Color Writing, 1880–1920* (New York: Penguin, 1998).

8. William Dean Howells, "Editor's Study," *Harper's Monthly* (September 1887); reprinted in *Editor's Study,* ed. Jane Simpson (Troy, NY: Whitson Publishing, 1983), 95–99, 97.

9. Kaplan, "Nation, Region, and Empire," 251.

10. William Dean Howells, *Criticism and Fiction* (1891), reprinted in *Selected Literary Criticism,* vol. 2 (Bloomington: Indiana University Press, 1993), 295–354, 340.

11. I am referring, of course, to *The Rise of Silas Lapham* (1885).

12. Henry James also combined the regional and the transnational when writing, admiringly, of Turgenev. Not only did his works "savour strongly of his native soil . . . and give one who has read them all a strange sense of having had a prolonged experience of Russia," but he also enjoyed "what is called a European reputation, and it is constantly spreading." Henry James, "Ivan Turgenev," originally in the *Atlantic Monthly,* 1884, reprinted in *Literary Criticism, Volume Two: European Writers, Prefaces to the New York Edition* (New York: Library of America, 1984), 968–1027, 976, 968.

13. Howells, *Criticism and Fiction,* 340.

14. "Thirty Years of Paris, A. Daudet," *North American Review* 147, no. 384 (1888): 595–96.

15. Brodhead, *Cultures of Letters,* 137.

16. Laurie Shannon, "'The Country of Our Friendship': Jewett's Intimist Art," *American Literature* 71, no. 2 (1999): 227–62.

17. Bill Brown, *A Sense of Things: The Object-Matter of American Literature* (Chicago: University of Chicago Press, 2003), see especially 110–11.

18. Nancy Glazener, *Reading for Realism: The History of a U.S. Literary Institution, 1850–1950* (Durham, NC: Duke University Press, 1997); Carrie Tirado Bramen, *The Uses of Variety: Modern Americanism and the Quest for National Distinctiveness* (Cambridge, MA: Harvard University Press, 2000). Foote's argument holds even though the volume as a whole is something of a disappointment for the way it brackets local color within the confines of the literary monthlies and the period 1870 to 1900, when the form has a much longer afterlife and was frequently published in newspapers, lesser magazines, and directly as books.

Stephanie Foote, *Regional Fictions: Culture and Identity in Nineteenth-Century American Literature* (Madison: University of Wisconsin Press, 2001), 15.

19. Gavin Jones, *Strange Talk: The Politics of Dialect Literature in Gilded Age America* (Berkeley: University of California Press, 1999), 98, 48.

20. Chris Bongie, "Resisting Memories: The Creole Identities of Lafcadio Hearn and Edouard Glissant," *SubStance* 84 (1997): 153–78.

21. The quote is from Amy Kaplan's reading of Howells in *The Social Construction of American Realism* (Chicago: University of Chicago Press, 1988), 25.

22. Brander Matthews, *Bookbindings Old and New* (New York: Macmillan, 1895), 238. Tellingly, the next cover that Matthews discusses is one by Daudet. The novel was number 661 in Harper's Franklin Square series, novels that were published with paper covers on a monthly basis, the subscription price being $5 a year. Appleton had a similar series, which is even closer to the publishing scheme of *Every Other Week*, the "Town and Country Library," which was bimonthly and printed on red-brown covers. They charged $10 per month, which gives some weight to what Fulkerson calls the "absurd sum of six dollars" that they would be charging for their magazine. The difference between these two series and *Every Other Week*, besides the price, would have been that they were publishing entire novels, whereas Fulkerson's plan is original for following the magazine format.

23. Matthews, *Bookbindings*, 247.

24. The quote is from Charles Dudley Warner, in Ibid., 237.

25. With the word *distinction*, Bourdieu suggested the way that cultural goods— museum paintings, etiquette, fine food—could be appropriated and deployed for the secondary purpose of signifying class affiliation. As such, all judgments of taste were relativized. See Pierre Bourdieu, *Distinction: A Social Critique of the Judgement of Taste*, trans. Richard Nice (Cambridge, MA: Harvard University Press, 1984).

26. See under "chic," in *Oxford English Dictionary*, 2nd ed.

27. Theodore Child, "Along the Parisian Boulevardes," *Harper's Monthly* 85 (1892): 855–872, 868.

28. Charles H. Moore, "The Modern Art of Painting in France," *Atlantic Monthly* 68 (1891): 805–16, 813.

29. That the gender identities of Beaton and Alma are blurred is a point made forcefully by Christopher Diller, who uses it to explain their ability to link high aesthetic and mass market tastes. Christopher Diller, "'Fiction in Color': Domesticity, Aestheticism, and the Visual Arts in the Criticism and Fiction of William Dean Howells," *Nineteenth-Century Literature* 55, no. 3 (2000): 369–98. Androgyny, itself, had been a sign of the aesthetic arts movement since the pre-Raphaelite moment of the Rosettis. See Kathy Psomiades, *Beauty's Body: Femininity and Representation in British Aestheticism* (Stanford, CA: Stanford University Press, 1997).

30. We never really know what the cover of the first issue looks like, in part because the narrator gives two versions of it—once here and once after it had just come out—as if the very question of the physical object produces an excess that can

never be fully brought under control. For the mock-up, it is on "ivory-white pebbled paper . . . prettily illustrated with a watercolor design irregularly washed over the greater part of its surface, quite across the page at top and narrowing from right to left as it descended" (120). As to content, there is a hint that it might be a "delicate little landscape," but that goes unconfirmed in the edition as it is published (121). There, we learn simply that the paper color was a "delicate gray tone" and the "decorative design . . . was printed in black and brick-red" (169). What we get instead of the design is the effect, which in both cases is, once again, said to be "decorative" and "chic" (174).

31. Rolf Söderberg, *French Book Illustration, 1880–1905* (Stockholm: Almqvst and Wiskell International, 1977), 33.

32. Alphonse Daudet, *Port of Tarascon,* trans. Henry James, *Harper's Monthly* 81 (1890): 2–25, 4.

33. Diana Strazdes, *The Illustrator's Moment* (Stockbridge, MA: The Old Corner House, 1978), 17.

34. "Holiday Books," *Atlantic Monthly* 67 (1891): 121–26, 125. The review refers to the Harper and Brothers 1891 edition of *Port Tarascon,* translated by Henry James.

35. On the "little magazines," see Larzer Ziff: "*The Chap-Book* began in May 1894. It was the best as well as the first of the self-consciously avant-garde magazines of the period that soon earned the name of "little magazine . . . ," in his *The American 1890s: Life and Times of a Lost Generation* (New York: Viking, 1966), 134.

36. Recently collected and provocatively edited by Edwin H. Cady, see Howells's *Pebbles, Monochromes and Other Modern Poems, 1891–1916* (Athens: Ohio University Press, 2000).

37. From Cady's notes to *Pebbles, Monochromes and Other Modern Poems, 1891–1916,* 175n12; xv.

38. Howells, introduction to *Pastels in Prose,* ed. and trans. Stuart Merrill (New York: Harper and Brothers, 1890), v–viii, vi, vii.

39. Matthews, *Bookbindings,* 248.

40. On the American art poster, see Joseph Goddu, *American Art Posters of the 1890s* (New York: Hirschl & Adler Galleries, 1990); Frederick R. Brandt, *Designed to Sell: Turn-of-the-Century American Posters in the Virginia Museum of Fine Arts* (Richmond: Virginia Museum of Fine Arts, 1994); Helen S. Hyman, *Design to Persuade: American Literary Advertising Posters of the 1890s* (New Haven, CT: Yale University Art Gallery, 1978); *Catalogue of the Metropolitan Museum of Art Poster Collection;* and Roberta Wong, *American Posters of the Nineties* (Lunenburg, VT: Stinehour Press, 1976). The search for a distinctive style led each of the magazines to highlight particular artists. It was, most famously in *Harper's* case, Edward Penfield (see Fig. 4.7); Joseph J. Gould Jr. and William L. Carqueville did *Lippincott's;* Louis J. Rhead did covers for both *Scribner's* and the *Century;* Maxfield Parrish for the *Century,* Will H. Bradley for the *Chap-Book.*

41. Lina Gertner Zatlin offers an extensive history of *Japonisme,* to which this chapter is much indebted, in *Beardsley, Japonisme, and the Perversion of the Victorian Ideal* (New York: Cambridge University Press, 1997). By 1890, *Japonisme* had a

three-decade-long history in France and Britain, starting in France with Edgar Degas, Edouard Manet, Vincent Van Gogh, Henri Toulouse-Lautrec, and Paul Gauguin, and carried to London largely by the American, James Whistler, who had spent extensive time in Paris. This style is picked up most influentially in illustrations by Aubrey Beardsley, by art nouveau in the later 1890s, and by art deco in Austria in the 1920s.

42. The estimate is from one of the more thorough histories of illustrations, Rowland Elzea, *The Golden Age of American Illustration, 1880–1914* (Wilmington, DE: The Wilmington Society of the Fine Arts, 1972), 8. See also Linda S. Ferber and Duncan Cameron, eds., A *Century of American Illustration* (New York: The Brooklyn Museum, 1972); Nancy Thomas, "The Character and Characters of Literature," *The American Personality: The Artist-Illustrator of Life in the United States, 1860–1930*, ed. Maurice Bloch (Los Angeles: Grumwald Center for the Graphic Arts, 1976).

43. Here I part ways with Diller's account of the aesthetics of *Every Other Week*, which according to him offers a "feminized visual emulation of canonical culture" (389). His own turn to Cézanne's controversial painting, *L'eternel féminin*, at the end of his essay would seem to suggest a more radical Howellsian aesthetic formulation.

44. Elzea, *Golden Age*, 16. See Selma Lanes, "The Brandywine Legacy," *Portfolio* 3, no. 3 (May-June 1981): 70 77; Anne Mayer, *Women Artists in the Howard Pyle Tradition* (Chadds Ford, PA: Brandywine River Museum, 1975); Anthea Callen, *Women Artists of the Arts and Crafts Movement, 1870–1914* (New York: Pantheon, 1979); Pat Likos, "The Ladies of the Red Rose," *Feminist Art Journal* 5, no. 3 (1976): 11–15; Clara Erskine Clement Waters, *Women in the Fine Arts* (Boston: Houghton Mifflin, 1904).

45. Kaplan, *Social Construction*, 21 ("exhorts"), 16 ("lack," "emerging"). Kaplan's reading of Howells's realism as an attempt to exert control over "reality" has been extremely influential; however, its assertions of Howells's discomfort with modernity are beginning to appear exaggerated. To take but one example of relevance to this chapter, Kaplan suggests that one of Howells's "most scathing reviews" attacks popular fiction, *Ben Hur* and *Trilby*, the circus, the burlesque, card-playing, and horse-racing—entertainment for the "unthinking multitude" (17). Beyond the fact that the article she cites never mentions either *Ben Hur* or *Trilby*, that Kaplan hears those two texts in this context suggests a deeper misunderstanding of Howells's relationship to mass culture. Although one can imagine him disliking *Ben Hur* (he does not, to my knowledge, review it), it's less easy to imagine him disliking *Trilby*, written by George Du Maurier, an author Howells otherwise respected, about a world, the Parisian expatriate bohemians, that clearly intrigued Howells. And Howells evidently liked the circus and vaudeville. On this, see Cady's discussion in Cady, ed., *Pebbles, Monochromes*, 178.

46. In Howells's novel, March considers Lindau's words to be "violent enough," while Mrs. March worries about how the "violence of Lindau's sentiments" affected her husband and children (168, 253). See Walter Benjamin, *Charles*

Baudelaire: A Lyric Poet of the Era of High Capitalism, trans. Harry Zohn (London: Verso/NLB, 1997).

47. William Dean Howells, "Sphinx" (1894), reprinted in Cady, ed., *Pebbles, Monochromes*, lines 3–4.

48. In another essay that reads *Hazard* for its aesthetics, Kermit Vanderbilt makes the opposite point that Howells's excoriating treatment of Beaton in the final section of the novel, in which the artist's profligacy reaches distasteful extremes, concurs with Howells's statements in his "Editor's Study" columns against Maupassant and others of the French aesthetic school who divorced style from morality. He explains March's interest in and *Every Other Week*'s dependence on Beaton's aesthetics in the first sections of the novel as examples of the "confusion" that must, in the end, be overcome with a more developed vision of "the ideal within the real." Kermit Vanderbilt, *The Achievement of William Dean Howells: A Reinterpretation* (Princeton, NJ: Princeton University Press, 1968), 163. This reading is just wrong. Howells writes admiringly of Maupassant in the "Editor's Study," saying that his stories are "masterly" and "illustrative of the French sense of art in all things." That said, he thinks that Jewett is better. "In the work of some of our own tellers of short stories, we have something cleverer in the same kind than that of the cleverest Frenchman going." "Editor's Study," February 1890; reprinted in *Editor's Study*, ed. Simpson, 238. The broader point I'm making, however, is more of a methodological one. What I'm interested in doing is marking the place where Maupassant, the French visual arts, and immorality become objects that Howells's realism trades on—and cannot do without; that place is in the commodification of the local and the short story in the international market for art.

49. Edwin H. Cady, *The Realist at War: The Mature Years (1885–1920) of William Dean Howells* (New York: Syracuse University Press, 1958), 94.

50. Matthews, *Bookbindings*, 237–38.

51. Charles Dudley Warner, "Editor's Study," *Harper's Monthly* 92 (1896): 959–64, 961, 962.

52. William Dean Howells, "Editor's Study," *Harper's Monthly* (September 1890); reprinted in *Editor's Study*, ed. Simpson, 276.

53. In Stephen Crane, *The Portable Stephen Crane*, ed. Joseph Katz (New York: Penguin, 1969), 3–74, 20.

54. Henry James, "The Real Thing," reprinted in *The Portable American Realism Reader*, ed. James Nagel and Tom Quirk (New York: Penguin, 1997), 233–54, 241, 247. Future references will be cited parenthetically.

55. Charlotte Adams, "Artists' Models in New York," *Century Illustrated Monthly* 25 (1883): 569–77, 575–76.

56. William Schulyer, "Kate Chopin," *Writer* 7 (August 1894): 115–17.

57. Per Seyersted, *Kate Chopin: A Critical Biography* (Baton Rouge: Louisiana State Press, 1969). Seyersted provides a complete bibliography in his biography of Chopin; on his comparison of her to Maupassant, see especially 125–30.

58. Henry James, *The Wings of the Dove* (1902; New York: Penguin, 1986), 279.

59. Kate Chopin, "At the 'Cadian Ball," in *Complete Novels and Stories* (New York: Library of America, 2002), 302–11, 302. Future references will be cited parenthetically.

60. Daniel S. Rankin, *Kate Chopin and Her Creole Stories* (Philadelphia: University of Pennsylvania Press, 1932); noted by Seyersted, 188.

61. Kate Chopin, "The Storm," in *Complete Novels and Stories*, 926–31, 927. Future references will be cited parenthetically.

62. Christine Stansell, *American Moderns: Bohemian New York and the Creation of a New Century* (New York: Henry Holt, 2000), 17.

CHAPTER FIVE

1. *Epigraph.* "The Negro Digs Up His Past," in *The New Negro,* ed. Alain Locke (1925; New York: Atheneum, 1992), 231–38, 237.

2. W. E. B. Du Bois, *The Quest of the Silver Fleece, A Novel* (1911; College Park, MD: McGrath Publishing, 1969), 125. Future references will be cited parenthetically.

3. For examples, see George Hutchinson, *The Harlem Renaissance in Black and White* (Cambridge, MA The Belknap Press of Harvard University Press, 1995); Vernon J. Williams Jr., *Rethinking Race: Franz Boas and His Contemporaries* (Lexington: University Press of Kentucky, 1996); Mark Helbling, *The Harlem Renaissance: The One and the Many* (Westport, CT: Greenwood Press, 1999). Lee Baker's assessment in *From Savage to Negro: Anthropology and the Construction of Race, 1896-1954* (Berkeley: University of California Press, 1998) is finely nuanced, but he stills describes the relationship between Boas and Du Bois as a "lifelong friendship," which seems unsupported given their extremely limited correspondence (125). With the exception of one passing reference, Boas is not mentioned in either of David Levering Lewis's biographies of Du Bois: *W. E. B. Du Bois: Biography of a Race. 1868-1919* (New York: Henry Holt, 1993) and *W. E. B. Du Bois: The Fight for Equality and the American Century, 1919-1965* (New York: Henry Holt, 2000). Julia Liss's assessment of the divergence between Boas's and Du Bois's politics comes close to suggesting that the personal relationship between the two has been overstated; but then, I would go on to say that, in at least one respect, their intellectual relationship has not been stated strongly enough. See her "Diasporic Identities: The Science and Politics of Race in the Work of Franz Boas and W. E. B. Du Bois, 1894–1919," *Cultural Anthropology* 13 (1998): 127–66.

4. See, for example, Anthony Appiah, *In My Father's House: Africa in the Philosophy of Culture* (New York: Oxford University Press, 1992); Adolph Reed, "Du Bois's 'Double Consciousness': Race and Gender in Progressive Era American Thought," *Studies in American Political Development* 6 (1992): 93–139; Thomas Holt, "The Political Uses of Alienation: Du Bois on Politics, Race, and Culture," *American Quarterly* 42 (1990): 301–23; and Ross Posnock, *Color and Culture: Black Writers and the Making of the Modern Intellectual* (Cambridge, MA: Harvard University Press, 1998). It should be noted that the interest in Du Bois far exceeds academia, as is most poignantly demonstrated in the marvelous collection of essays by

prominent African Americans edited by Gerald Early, *Lure and Loathing: Essays on Race, Identity, and the Ambivalence of Assimilation* (New York: Penguin, 1993).

5. Williams *Rethinking Race.*

6. "Commencement Address at Atlanta University May 31, 1906," reprinted in Franz Boas, *Race and Democratic Society* (New York: J. J. Augustin, 1945), 61–69, 61, 66. Future references will be cited parenthetically in the text.

7. Franz Boas, *Anthropology and Modern Life* (New York: W. W. Norton, 1930), 59.

8. W. E. B. Du Bois, *The Souls of Black Folk,* reprinted in *Writings* (New York: Library of America, 1986), 357–548, 365. Future references will be cited parenthetically. Du Bois made slight revisions throughout the piece for *Souls;* in the line just cited, for example, the phrase "and his latent genius" did not appear in the original. This particular addition only strengthens the case for reading culture as the process of becoming civilized, the trajectory leading toward excellence.

9. At one point Du Bois mocks the self-critical Negro voices who would suggest that they "Be content to be servants, and nothing more; what need of higher culture for half men?" In the next paragraph, he reworks the theme by arguing that what is needed is "the training of deft hands, quick eyes and ears, and above all the broader, deeper, higher culture of gifted minds" (*Souls,* 369, 370).

10. "Cultural Equality," reprinted in Eric J. Sundquist, ed., *The Oxford W. E. B. Du Bois Reader* (New York: Oxford University Press, 1996), 394–400, 394.

11. George Stocking's point about the changes Boas made in his own use of the terms culture and civilization is relevant here: that when Boas revised some of his earliest manuscripts in putting together *The Mind of Primitive Man* (1911), he made some very simple yet telling changes in his use of these words that suggest he would no longer use culture to refer to the staged development of civilization. *Race, Culture, and Evolution: Essays in the History of Anthropology* (1968; Chicago: University of Chicago Press, 1982). See the chapter "Franz Boas and the Culture Concept," and especially 202–3.

12. Du Bois, "Cultural Equality," 397.

13. W. E. B. Du Bois, *The Autobiography of W. E. B. Du Bois: A Soliloquy on Viewing My Life from the Last Decade of Its First Century* (n.p.: International Publishers, 1968), 236, 349, 358, 363, 388, 392.

14. Du Bois, *Autobiography,* 392. Once again, "human culture" echoes the Arnoldian position: "culture, then, is a study . . . of harmonious perfection . . . which consists in becoming something rather than in having something." Matthew Arnold, *Culture and Anarchy* (1869; New Haven, CT: Yale University Press, 1994), 33.

15. E. B. Tylor, *Primitive Culture,* 2 vols. (London: J. Murray, 1871), vol. 1, 1.

16. Stocking, "Matthew Arnold, E. B. Tylor and the Uses of Invention," in *Race, Culture, and Evolution,* 69–90. See especially 89–90.

17. Arnold, *Culture and Anarchy,* 33. Arnold, of course, did not have the American Negro in mind when he suggested this harmony, but the idea is readily adaptable to Du Bois's use.

18. The terms are suggested in the dedication of *The Quest of the Silver Fleece,* and elsewhere.

19. Du Bois, "The Conservation of Races," in *Writings,* 819–26, 820. Future references will be cited parenthetically.

20. W. E. B. Du Bois, *Dark Princess, A Romance* (1928; Jackson, MS: Banner Books, 1995), 24.

21. W. E. B. Du Bois, *Dusk of Dawn: An Essay toward an Autobiography of a Race Concept* (1940; New Brunswick, NJ: Transaction Publishers, 1995), 173, 179–80.

22. See, in particular, Susan Hegeman's *Patterns for America: Modernism and the Concept of Culture* (Princeton, NJ: Princeton University Press, 1999), and Marc Manganaro, *Culture, 1922: The Emergence of a Concept* (Princeton, NJ: Princeton University Press, 2002).

23. T. S. Eliot, *Notes towards the Definition of Culture* (London: Faber and Faber, 1948), 26. Kroeber and Kluckhohn comment on Eliot that "Anthropologists are not likely to be very happy with [his] emphasis on an élite and his reconciliation of the humanistic and social science views." Alfred L. Kroeber and Clyde Kluckhohn, eds., *Culture: A Critical Review of Concepts and Definitions* (New York: Vintage, 1952), 63. Although, predictably, Du Bois does not appear in their volume, one can assume that their reception of him would be similarly gruff. There is, of course, an Arnoldian strain that runs throughout the social sciences, even among Boasian anthropologists.

24. The dynamic between culture and history remains a central one to theories of culture. The most important work informing my own account of it here has come from Marshall Sahlins. See, in particular, *Islands of History* (Chicago: University of Chicago Press, 1985). For a critique of Sahlins, see Adam Kuper, *Culture: The Anthropologist's Account* (Cambridge, MA: Harvard University Press, 1999).

25. In addition to "Franz Boas and the Culture Concept," cited above, see also "The Basic Assumptions of Boasian Anthropology," his introduction to *The Franz Boas Reader: The Shaping American Anthropology, 1883–1911* (Chicago: University of Chicago Press, 1974), 1–20. More recently, Regna Darnell has argued for the centrality of the Boasian culture paradigm to American anthropology in two volumes, *And Along Came Boas: Continuity and Revolution in Americanist Anthropology* (Philadelphia: John Benjamins, 1998), and *Invisible Genealogies: A History of Americanist Anthropology* (Lincoln: University of Nebraska Press, 2001).

26. Although in most respects a highly convincing study of the parallels between Boasian anthropology and the narrative strategies of American realism, Michael Elliott's *The Culture Concept: Writing and Difference in the Age of Realism* (Minneapolis: University of Minnesota Press, 2002) falls into the trap of recapitulating this version of Boas's culture concept as a "synchronic, static entity" (22).

27. This other Boasian line is beginning to come to the attention of cultural theorists. See the recent special edition of *American Anthropologist,* 106, no. 3 (September 2004), especially articles by Ira Bashkow, "A Neo-Boasian Conception of Cultural Boundaries"; Matti Bunzl, "Boas, Foucault, and the "Native Anthropologist": Notes toward a Neo-Boasian Anthropology"; and Richard Handler, "Afterword: Mysteries

of Culture." Also see Michael Silverstein, "Boasian Cosmographic Anthropology and the Sociocentric Component of the Mind," in *Significant Others*, ed. Richard Handler, History of Anthropology Series 10 (Madison: University of Wisconsin Press, 2005), 131–157; and Herbert S. Lewis, "Boas, Darwin, Science, and Anthropology," *Current Anthropology* 42, no. 3 (June 2001), 381–406.

28. Much of the argument that follows is keenly indebted to Bunzl's "*Völker-psychologie* and German-Jewish Emancipation," *Worldly Provincialism: German Anthropology in the Age of Empire*, ed. Matti Bunzl and H. Glenn Penny (Ann Arbor: University of Michigan Press, 2003), 47–85.

29. A number of recent titles explore the cultural pluralism of the early twentieth century; notably, they do so without very much reference to Boas. See Posnock, *Color and Culture;* Carrie Tirado Bramen, *The Uses of Variety: Modern Americanism and the Quest for National Distinctiveness* (Cambridge, MA: Harvard University Press, 2000); and Louis Menand, *The Metaphysical Club* (New York: Farrar, Straus and Giroux, 2001).

30. The phrase is from the title of Anthony Appiah, "The Uncompleted Argument: Du Bois and the Illusion of Race," in *"Race," Writing and Difference*, ed. Henry Louis Gates Jr. (Chicago: University of Chicago Press, 1986), 21–37. The article is taken from the second chapter of *In My Father's House.*

As already suggested, not everyone agrees on what Du Bois meant by race. While I think that Appiah is essentially correct, it is true that he does not do enough to adequately contextualize Du Bois's argument. Adolph Reed, for one, has pointed out that Du Bois was following a classical Lamarckian line on this point, arguing for the hereditary transmission of social traits. In locating Du Bois's universalistic tendencies, Priscilla Wald has insisted on the provisional nature of Du Bois's racial category. See her *Constituting Americans: Cultural Anxiety and Narrative Form* (Durham, NC: Duke University Press, 1995).

As we shall see, Appiah is essential in taking the Africa of Du Bois's Pan-Africanism seriously, noting that the diversity of the African context forces Du Bois to essentialize race. In light of Appiah, it will not do to accept, for example, Paul Gilroy's argument that criticism of Du Bois is too restricted by race, or that it can be opened up by taking Du Bois's transnationalism into account. See *The Black Atlantic: Modernity and Double Consciousness* (Cambridge, MA: Harvard University Press, 1992). Gilroy's argument is not, in the final analysis, an argument against strict racialism (against "roots" and for "routes"). Rather, it substitutes for race a "diaspora multiplicity," a concept developed by "paying more careful attention to the inner asymmetry and differentiation of black cultures" (122, 120). But to do so, Gilroy must do the opposite himself: "to attempt to specify some of the similarities to be found in diverse black experiences in the modern West" (120). Gilroy locates the primary influence of similarity in racial terror: in slavery, colonialism, and the subsequent subordination of people of color to white civilization. However, he chooses not to note that the differences between this "terror" (if that is the right word) in the locales where Du Bois would have known it best—in New England, Berlin, Georgia, and Ghana—are extreme. This point is the one Appiah handles very well: Du Bois surmounts these extremes by essentializing race, by giving primacy to "roots" over "routes." By looking at Du Bois's notion of culture, we can take both Gilroy and Appiah's arguments one step further (beyond an African diaspora or a voluntaristic association of oppressed, colored people) to see how Du Bois melded races into the ideal of a universal culture.

31. See Stocking, *Race, Culture, and Evolution,* 231; Walter Benn Michaels takes up Stocking to argue that "although admirers of Boas's antiracism . . . often identify that antiracism with his presumed pluralism, it is, in fact, the racists Boas meant to oppose whose conception of culture was more purely pluralist. Boas himself was a universalist. *"Our America: Nativism, Modernism, and Pluralism* (Durham, NC: Duke University Press, 1995), 173n99.

32. See Hegeman's *Patterns for America,* 47–51.

33. Boas, "Commencement Address at Atlanta University May 31, 1906," reprinted with title "The Negro's Past," in *Race and Democratic Society,* 61–69, 62, 63, 64, 65.

34. Boas, *Race and Democratic Society,* 55, 56, 57.

35. Michaels has developed the argument that the culture concept is little more than a supplement to race in a number of articles and books, starting with "Race into Culture: A Critical Genealogy of Cultural Identity," *Critical Inquiry* 18 (1992): 655–85.

36. Virchow and Bastian's impact on Boasian work is the topic of numerous essays in George W. Stocking Jr., ed., Volksgeist *as Method and Ethic: Essays on Boasian Ethnography and the German Anthropological Tradition* (Madison: University of Wisconsin Press, 1996).

37. See Bunzl, "*Völkerpsychologie* and German-Jewish Emancipation," 52–60.

38. Quoted in ibid., 82.

39. Boas, "Mythology and Folk-Tales of the North American Indians," *Journal of American Folk-Lore* 27 (1914); reprinted in Franz Boas, *Race, Language and Culture* (1940; Chicago: University of Chicago Press, 1982), 451–90, 456.

40. Quoted in Lewis, *W. E. B. Du Bois: Biography of a Race, 1868–1919,* 440.

41. W. E. B. Du Bois, ed., *Morals and Manners among Negro Americans,* The Atlanta University Publications, No. 18 (Atlanta: Atlanta University Press, 1913).

42. W. E. B. Du Bois, "The Talented Tenth," from *The Negro Problem: A Series of Articles by Representative Negroes of To-day* (New York, 1903); reprinted in *Writings,* 842–61.

43. For the best analysis of Du Bois's early training and intellectual history to date, see Shamoon Zamir's meticulously researched and documented *Dark Voices: W. E. B. Du Bois and American Thought, 1888–1903* (Chicago: University of Chicago Press, 1995). Especially relevant with regard to distinguishing between history and historicism is chapter three, "Local Knowledge in the Shadow of Liberty," 68–109. Zamir's text focuses on Du Bois's relation to institutional sociology and history.

44. Priscilla Wald also provides an extended reading of "history" in the *Souls of Black Folk.* While her approach is very different from mine, our readings are not necessarily contradictory. Wald's interest is in Du Bois's deployment of history as a

narrative genre, which she sees Du Bois mixing with other genres—autobiography, fiction, music—in order to produce an experimental, modernist text. See her *Constituting Americans: Cultural Anxiety and Narrative Form* (Durham, NC: Duke University Press, 1995). This reading provides a very nice description of the aesthetics of *Souls;* my own interest is in gauging Du Bois's institutional engagement with the field of history.

45. See Zamir, *Dark Voices,* 119–33.

46. Ibid., 136; Du Bois, *Souls,* 365.

47. Du Bois, "The Study of Negro Problems," reprinted in Philip S. Foner, ed., *W. E. B. Du Bois Speaks: Speeches and Addresses, 1890-1919* (New York: Pathfinder, 1970): 102–23, 108–9. Future references will be cited parenthetically.

48. Du Bois, "Study," 105. W. E. B. Du Bois, *The Philadelphia Negro: A Social Study* (1899; Philadelphia: University of Pennsylvania Press, 1996), 19.

49. Du Bois, *Dusk of Dawn,* 117.

50. For more on this argument, see Michael Rogin, *Ronald Reagan The Movie, and Other Episodes in Political Demonology* (Berkeley: University of California Press, 1987), especially 190–235; the first section of Walter Benn Michaels's "Race into Culture"; and Lawrence W. Levine, *Black Culture and Black Consciousness: Afro-American Folk Thought from Slavery to Freedom* (New York: Oxford University Press, 1977): "Indeed, one of the first results of emancipation in a number of areas of black life and culture was the intensification of black separatism" in such moves as secession from white churches and establishment of Negro churches throughout the South, migration to northern cities, racial polarization which created the "black belt" in the South, and racial separation in schools (144). More recently, see the arguments made by historians of whiteness: David Roediger, *The Wages of Whiteness: Race and the Making of the American Working Class* (New York: Verso, 1991); Ian Haney-Lopez, *White by Law: The Legal Construction of Race* (New York: New York University Press, 1996); and Matthew Frye Jacobson, *Whiteness of a Different Color: European Immigrants and the Alchemy of Race* (Cambridge, MA: Harvard University Press, 1998).

51. Du Bois, "Study," 114.

52. N. S. Shaler, "The Future of the Negro in the Southern States," *Popular Science Monthly* 57 (1900): 147–56.

53. W. S. Scarborough, "The Negro and Higher Education," *The Forum* 33 (1902): 349–55.

54. *Race Traits and Tendencies of the American Negro* (1896; New York: AMS Press, 1973), 328, 329. Hoffman, it will be remembered, was a statistician for the Prudential Insurance Company and based his findings on surveys he had made for them.

55. There are, to be sure, exceptions to be found to this trend, foremost among them being George W. Williams's *History of the Negro Race in America from 1619 to 1880 . . . together with a preliminary consideration of the unity of the Human Family, an Historical Sketch of Africa, and an Account of the Negro Governments of Sierra Leone and Liberia,* which, as the subtitle suggests, does make the link to Africa (New

York: n.p., 1883). Du Bois cites this text as early as 1897 in a footnote to "The Study of the Negro Problem." It should be noted, however, that Williams is far from adopting the tone or doing the work called for by Du Bois in "The Study of the Negro Problem." Williams adopts an ethnological stance dating from much earlier in the century when he works to confirm the Negro as part of the "Human Family" based on the authority of the Bible; he views the "Negro type" as being "the result of degradation"—that is of idolatry and geographical isolation from God's word—"nothing more than the lowest strata of the African race"; and considers Africa itself not as a source of inspiration but as the most "promising mission-field in the world" (109, 114).

56. Lavinia H. Egan, "The Future of the Negro in Fiction," *The Dial* 18 (1895): 70; Annie Weston Whitney, "Negro American Dialects," *The Independent* 53 (1901): 1979–81, 1979; Thomas Nelson Page, "The Old Time Negro," *Scribner's* 36 (1904): 522–32, 522.

57. In this regard, see especially Zamir.

58. William Stanley Braithwaite, "The Negro in American Literature," in Locke, ed., *The New Negro,* 29–44, 40.

59. My thanks to Corinna Segal for her translation of this verse.

On Du Bois's use of the term "folk," Arnold Rampersad notes the work of Bernard Bell in tracing it back to Herder, but argues that Du Bois's commitment to the term was more political than cultural and that, as such, he meant by it something more like "nation"—thus the roots of black nationalism. See Arnold Rampersad, *The Art and Imagination of W. E. B. Du Bois* (Cambridge, MA: Harvard University Press, 1976), 74–75, and Bernard W. Bell, *The Folk Roots of Contemporary Afro-American Poetry* (Detroit: Broadside Press, 1974), 16–31. My problem with this argument is that it assumes a conservative politics in the deployment of the folk, whereas Herder and later cultural pluralists endowed "folk culture" with political agency (of the type Rampersad reserves for "nation"). In this respect, we might consider the contemporary work of Eric Sundquist in *To Wake the Nations* (Cambridge, MA: The Belknap Press of Harvard University Press, 1993), who finds in Du Bois's use of the Sorrow Songs the beginnings of African American cultural politics.

I obviously agree with Rampersad that it is important to unpack the fact of Du Bois's ambivalence to the folk—especially folk art. However, I think that Rampersad is wrong in trying to turn attention away from this ambivalence by imagining Du Bois means something different from what he says. In this vein, we might note that by the 1960s "folk" had come to have significant political, anticapitalist inflections for Du Bois. In his *Autobiography,* Du Bois uses "folk" in relation to two groups of people: the communist masses he met during his trips to the Soviet Union and China (as in "the folk [in USSR] were better dressed and food more plentiful" 32, and also on pages 26, 80), and his fellow black Americans ("few of my folk," 64; "colored folk," 136). Already in *Souls,* the term folk must be recognized as having clear ties to the discourse of anti-industrialism (cf. Lears, *No Place of Grace*). What Du Bois does, however, is privilege the black

talented-tenth with this romantically positive, subcultural designation. "Gifted
with second sight," ostracized from white American civilization, yet inescapably
part of it, the American Negro (even the talented-tenth one) becomes "folk"
(*Souls,* 364).

60. When Du Bois wrote to Clark Wissler, an anthropologist sympathetic to Boas-
ian innovations, asking for the best anthropological information on Africa in
1907, Wissler wrote back that there was not much. W. E. B. Du Bois, *The
Correspondence of W. E. B. Du Bois, vol. 1, 1877–1934,* ed. Herbert Aptheker
(Amherst, MA: University of Massachusetts Press, 1973), 115. See also Williams,
Rethinking Race, 78.

61. In working to elucidate Du Bois's contribution to an "African-American cultural
poetics," Eric Sundquist makes productive use of the fact that these bars were not
identified, thus demanding "a familiarity with a cultural language that most whites
did not have and that an increasing number of middle-class blacks renounced as
an unhealthy reminder of slavery" (*To Wake the Nations,* 470). The claim sounds
somewhat dubious when one considers that, however imperfectly, the musical bars do make the songs more accessible to an audience unfamiliar with the
tunes than they might otherwise have been. Moreover, scripted like other music, they do not so much "rearticulate a trope of silence," as Sundquist argues,
but mark artistic life "within the Veil" as a familiar cultural form, like other music
(359).

62. Ross Posnock, "How It Feels to Be a Problem: Du Bois, Fanon, and the
'Impossible Life' of the Black Intellectual," *Critical Inquiry* 23 (1997): 323–49,
324. The argument is extended in *Color and Culture: Black Writers and the Making
of the Modern Intellectual.*

63. Carrie Tirado Bramen follows the same intellectual trajectory as Posnock back to
James, but attends, instead, to how pluralism and universalism came to define
each other. See *The Uses of Variety,* 71.

64. For another example of Miss Smith's pluralism, see also "What I don't understand, I don't judge" (67).

65. Du Bois's own position on Spencer is less straightforward than might be suggested by this passage from the novel, for much of his early career was spent in
an attempt to wed Spencer's "vast generalizations" to "actual scientific accomplishment" (*Dusk of Dawn,* 51). For a discussion that plots Du Bois's desire to balance Spencer with the hard science of his undergraduate professors at Harvard,
particularly William James, see Zamir, *Dark Voices,* especially 56–60. Zamir
insists upon Du Bois's rejection of Spencer in favor of a more empirical social
science (in American sociology, not Frank Giddings but Albion Small) when he
was doing his social scientific work in the late 1890s and early 1900s (69). But, as
is typical with Du Bois, his position was continually being worked out and modified. As we shall see in *Quest,* Du Bois's heroine follows a similar route to Du
Bois, working to wed the universal idealism that Spencer represents with the
material realities of the manufacture of Southern cotton.

66. Rampersad, *Art and Imagination,* 120.

67. Theodore Roosevelt, *Theodore Roosevelt, An Autobiography* (1913; New York: Da Capo Press, 1941), 395–96.

68. Euripides, *Medea,* in *Medea and Other Plays* (New York: Penguin, 1993), 41.

69. For recent work on these three figures, see Bramen and Menand. On their relationship, or lack thereof, with Du Bois, see the second volume Lewis's biography of Du Bois.

70. Du Bois, *Dusk of Dawn,* 270.

AFTERWORD

1. Alfred L. Kroeber and Clyde Kluckhohn, *Culture: A Critical Review of Concepts and Definitions* (New York: Vintage, 1952), 11.

2. Kroeber and Kluckhohn, *Culture,* 67.

3. Ibid., 65.

4. See my discussion in the introduction, especially around note 5. For two of the most convincing arguments that such a consensus on culture should be reached, see Walter Benn Michaels's, "Race into Culture: A Critical Genealogy of Cultural Identity," *Critical Inquiry* 18 (1992): 655–85; and Michel-Rolph Trouillot, "Adieu, Culture: A New Duty Arises," in *Anthropology beyond Culture,* ed. Richard G. Fox and Barbara J. King (New York: Berg, 2002), 37–60.

5. For recent accounts, see especially Robert Brightman, "Forget Culture: Replacement, Transcendence, Relexification," *Cultural Anthropology* 10 (1995): 509–46; and Ira Bashkow, "A Neo-Boasian Conception of Cultural Boundaries," *American Anthropologist* 106, no. 3 (2004).

6. Alain Locke, ed., *The New Negro: Voices of the Harlem Renaissance* (1925; New York: Atheneum, 1992), 12.

7. Alain Locke, "The Concept of Race as Applied to Social Culture" (1924), reprinted in Jeffrey C. Stewart, ed., *The Critical Temper of Alain Locke: A Selection of His Essays on Art and Culture* (New York: Garland, 1983), 423–31, 429. In the article, he quotes from Lowie's first book, *Culture and Ethnology* (1917), the argument that "there is obviously no direct proportional between culture and race" (425). He also cites Wissler and Sapir in the article.

8. Locke, "The Concept of Race," 425; Locke, ed., *The New Negro,* 11.

9. Locke, ed., *The New Negro,* 14.

10. Alain Locke and Bernhard J. Stern, *When Peoples Meet: A Study in Race and Culture Contacts,* rev. ed. (New York: Hinds, Hayden and Eldredge, 1946), 4. Locke has been credited with having written most of the notes.

11. Quoted in Locke and Stern, *When Peoples Meet,* 12–13.

12. Quoted in ibid., 22.

13. Locke and Stern, *When Peoples Meet,* 6.

14. As, for example, his claim in an article for the magazine *Opportunity,* "Who and What is 'Negro'?" (1942; reprinted in Stewart, *Critical Temper,* 309–18): "Neither national nor racial cultural elements are so distinctive as to be mutually exclusive. It is the general composite character of culture which is disregarded by such over-simplifications" (311).

15. Franz Boas, "The Decorative Art of the North American Indians," *Popular Science Monthly* (1903), reprinted in *Race, Language, Culture* (1940; Chicago: University of Chicago Press, 1982), 546–63, 563.

16. It makes little sense because the political problem is not the culture concept. As proven historically, there is no inherent politics to stands on culture and identity: social evolutionists were often taking clearly progressive social positions, for they, at least, granted that nonwhite races were part of humanity; Boas and Locke, for all their relativism, were assimilationists; cultural pluralism, especially in the populist mode developed by Horace Kallen and rejected by W. E. B. Du Bois, remained racist and discriminatory.

INDEX